SO-CFL-593

PP
1750

THE PLAZA
COOKBOOK

F. KREDEL

THE PLAZA COOKBOOK

BY
EVE BROWN

PRENTICE-HALL, INC.
ENGLEWOOD CLIFFS, NEW JERSEY

ALSO BY EVE BROWN
Champagne Cholly
The Plaza: Its Life and Times

The Plaza Cookbook by Eve Brown
Design by Janet Anderson
Photography by Jerry Sarapochiello

Copyright © 1972 by Eve Brown
All rights reserved. No part of this book may be
reproduced in any form or by any means, except for
the inclusion of brief quotations in a review, without
permission in writing from the publisher.
Printed in the United States of America T
Prentice–Hall International, Inc., London
Prentice–Hall of Australia, Pty. Ltd., North Sydney
Prentice–Hall of Canada, Ltd., Toronto
Prentice–Hall of India Private Ltd., New Delhi
Prentice–Hall of Japan, Inc., Tokyo

LIBRARY OF CONGRESS CATALOGING IN PUBLICATION DATA
BROWN, EVE, DATE
THE PLAZA COOKBOOK
1. COOKERY. 2. THE PLAZA, NEW YORK. I. TITLE.
TX715.B849146   641.5   72-1867
ISBN 0-13-684555-x

DEDICATION   *To Arthur D. Dooley, former*
Vice President and Managing Director of the Plaza,
but even more important to me,
good boss, good friend and good sport

CONTENTS

CONTENTS

FOREWORD

It was a glamorous occasion-October 1, 1907, the formal opening of the Plaza, New York's newest, most prestigious hotel, overlooking from the south the long green stretches of Central Park. The opening elicited columns of space in the press of the nation, with accounts of the architectural beauty of the hotel, its exquisite furnishings, the elegance of its decor, the great, handsome public dining rooms and the magnificent gold and white ballroom, already engaged for a banquet a few weeks later in honor of the Lord Bishop of London.

No small part of the accounts concerned the great chefs in the enormous white-tiled kitchen, headed by the greatest of them all, Eugene Laperruque, who had been chef to the Rothschilds, the leading banking family of Europe, and who had but recently retired as executive chef of the great Delmonico's restaurant, over which he reigned first at its famed old 14th Street site, and later when it moved to 26th Street.

The Plaza's first manager, Fred Sterry, who was determined to secure the best of everything for his fine hotel, succeeded in bringing Laperruque out of retirement to head the Plaza's kitchen, and not one, but two Laperruques held forth there. His sous chef was Laperruque's nephew Charles, who had been trained in his father's hotel in Le Havre.

From the very first day-a day which saw the elite of New York on view at festive breakfasts, luncheons, dinners, and supper parties-the fame of Plaza cuisine spread.

Many of the Plaza's most noted dishes, popular to this day, were originated by the elder Laperruque; subsequent chefs contributed their original recipes, notably Laperruque's successor, Albert Leopold Lattard. It was Chef Lattard who started the custom of naming dishes he created after celebrity guests. His best-known creation, still a great specialty at the hotel, is Crab Meat Remick, named for William H. Remick, president of the New York Stock Exchange from 1919 to 1923.

Of all the chefs who followed Laperruque and Lattard over the years Chef André René came closest to equalling their culinary genius. The youngest chef ever employed by the Plaza, André has the distinction of having won the greatest number of culinary awards for one so young, including the highest of all, the Medal of the French Government presented by the Société Culinaire Philanthropique. In 1964 he was one of two American chefs selected by the United States Department of Agriculture to represent our country at the annual International Hotel and Catering exhibit in London.

The task of selecting the over 350 special recipes in this book, out of the thousands and thousands which for more than sixty years have passed through the Plaza kitchen—to great banquets, charity dinners and luncheons, wedding receptions, and other special and festive events—was a difficult task, and is was only through former Chef André's great patience and detailed assistance that I was able to bring this book to fruition. André has been succeeded by his able sous chef, Joseph Trombetti, to whom I owe thanks for editorial assistance.

To Beda Havelka, former Director of Food and Beverage for the Plaza, with whom I had many hours of consultation, I also extend my heartfelt thanks. My thanks, too, to my former secretary Rita Irwin, who assisted in research; to Rosemary Wayfrock, secretary to Mr. Dooley; to Janice Devine, for many documentary facts concerning the great chefs of Europe and elsewhere; to Henry Krupka of the D'Arlene Studios, and most particularly to Grace Manney, who assisted in the editorial compilation of the recipes.

A very special thanks to Mr. Paul Sonnabend, President of Sonesta Hotels and President of the Plaza Hotel, and also to Mr. Jack Craver, Vice President and General Manager of the Plaza, for all of their encouragement and cooperation in the preparation of this book.

THE PLAZA
COOKBOOK

CHAPTER ONE

AUTOCRATS OF THE KITCHEN

On a sunlit patio in California, guests at Sunday brunch murmured delighted approval as they sampled the crab flakes, golden brown on top and nested in big, polished clam shells.

Their hostess, handsome in white slacks and turquoise blouse and looking as though she had never been near a hot stove, smiled happily.

"It's the easiest thing when you know how," she said. "I got tired of the scrambled eggs and bacon bit and suddenly I remembered Crab Remick."

"Crab Remick," one woman exclaimed. "Of course, we always have it when we go to New York . . . at the Plaza."

"It might amuse you to know that's where I first tasted it, too," her hostess went on. "At the Plaza, twenty-five years ago, my dear. And the chef, bless his heart, let me have the recipe."

Everywhere in the United States women are turning out meals with imagination, experimenting with sauces and seasonings, discovering the subtle use of wines in cooking, the difference between a pancake and a crêpe, the secret of a perfect soufflé.

How did the American housewife, almost overnight, become a gourmet cook? What motivates today's bright young brides to experiment with exotic dishes their grandmothers never heard of and wouldn't have dreamed of trying to prepare?

Of course, the upsurge of fine home cookery has been helped along by modern technology—the mixers, blenders, magic stoves,

1

the battery of temperature controls, and so on—as well as the
newspapers, magazines, radio, television cook-and-tell
shows and a dazzling array of cookbooks, all of which find their
way into millions of American homes. But it is essentially the
great chefs who have been responsible for the fine recipes that
hostesses the country over proudly prepare for their guests.
It is a host of shadowy figures stretching back over the years—
figures in white with towering white caps, *toques blanches,*
the crown of the master chef; they are the ones who have
gradually and unconsciously sophisticated the tastes of Americans and the efforts of the home cook.

At one time the masterpieces of a great chef were the
exclusive property of the rich and titled, and his life was dedicated
to pleasing the palates of kings, popes, scions of great houses
and vast fortunes.

It was in the papal household of Leo X that the name Carême,
in a long line of celebrated chefs, was born nearly four centuries
ago. There a gifted cook known simply as "Jean" concocted
for His Holiness a Lenten soup that contained no meat but was
so delicious that the Pope, as a reward, bestowed the name
Carême, meaning Lent, upon his proud chef.

The fame of a multitude of Carêmes reached its zenith in the
person of Antoine, who was born in Paris. Fleeing nobility during
the Revolution had left a scattering of chefs who of necessity
began opening public restaurants and producing gourmet dishes
for anyone who had the price. Marie Antoinette's disastrous
advice, "Let them eat cake," proved ironically prophetic, for now
"they"—the political leaders, the newly rich and powerful and
a rising upper-middle class—did, indeed, enjoy the creations
of the great patissiers.

Antoine Carême served his apprenticeship in a Paris restaurant as
a gangling 15-year-old. From the first he had a passion for
pastries and for creating cakes of turreted castles and cathedrals
ornamented in fantasias of spun sugar, creams and frostings.

The reigning houses of Europe must have agreed with Carême,
for he was invited to practice his art by no less a personage than

Czar Alexander of Russia. Carême prided himself on going where he pleased, when he pleased, and often declined royal summonses, including that of George IV of England. It was more important to him to set down his confectionery secrets, his experiences and his opinions. They made culinary history.

The most lustrous of all authorities on elegant eating, Brillat-Savarin, came by his genius for gastronomy naturally. One of of his classics of *haute cuisine* was named for his mother, Claudine Aurore Recamier: *L'Orreiler de la Belle Aurore* (The Pillow of the Beautiful Aurora). It was a pâté of superlative delicacy, a blend of saddle of hare, duck, chicken, partridges, veal tenderloin, pork fillet and seasonings.

Brillat-Savarin's belief that everyone should eat well was tempered by his distinction between what the man of modest means might have (a farm turkey stuffed with chestnuts, for instance, and fat pigeons "suitably cooked," or that rather plebeian but mouth-watering combination of sauerkraut *garni* with sausages and crowned with smoked bacon). But for the well-heeled diner he recommended fowl "made spherical with Perigord truffles, Strasbourg pâté molded into 'a bastion,' carp from the Rhine garnished with truffles, quail on toast, pike in crabfish sauce, roast pheasant with a *Saucel-Aience* plus a hundred early asparagus of about half an inch in diameter." This was a main course!

When friends came to his country house in Belley in late fall, he served them a fillet of beef stuffed with black truffles, pistachio nuts, mushrooms, olives and bits of bacon marinated in white wine and herbs, the whole grilled on the spit and covered with "excellent fresh butter."

Brillat-Savarin traveled widely and in 1794 visited America. He said nothing about our cooking, which tended to be quite primitive in most places. But he is reported to have visited the "public ordinary" opened that year by Jean Baptiste Gilbert Papyplat, a French refugee who must have startled Bostonians with his Perigord truffles, cheese fondue and subtle soups. The great gourmet gave his blessing to the eating place, and to its proprietor, christened the "Prince of Soups."

3

After hunting wild turkey in Connecticut and playing his Stradivarius violin in a New York concert hall, Brillat-Savarin returned to Europe, prophesying that before long famous chefs would bring their skills across the Atlantic, invading new hotels that were springing up and introducing French cookery to America. But even he could hardly have dreamed of the impact French cuisine would have in the late 19th century when newly minted millionaires became overnight gourmets and everyone struggled with menus in French.

Brillat-Savarin published his notable works anonymously during his lifetime, but even then his epigrams were quoted wherever gastronomy was discussed. One of his pet beliefs was: "Dessert without cheese is like a pretty girl with only one eye." Another, destined to become a classic: "Tell me what you eat and I will tell you what you are."

Another French émigré, Albignac, brought salads to London in the 1790's, and made himself a tidy fortune. Dining at a fashionable tavern one night, he got into conversation with several young men-about-town who asked whether he would mix them a salad "for which your nation excels." Albignac obliged and found himself an overnight success in the fine houses of Grosvenor Square. He hired a servant to accompany him, carrying a mahogany case equipped with a wide range of vinegars and oils, truffles, anchovies, ketchups and hard-boiled eggs. The French salad-maker became so popular that he went into business, manufacturing "salad cases" to order and furnishing them completely.

There is a little house in a little town in France to which gourmets from everywhere come to spend an afternoon or a day. Auberge du Muses is the only museum devoted to the career and achievements of a chef—Auguste Escoffier. It is in the town of Villeneuve-Loubet, tucked into the French Alpes Maritimes, where Escoffier was born. He left that town as a thin, intense boy of 12, to serve his kitchen apprenticeship.

Escoffier is still the magic name in the world of *haute cuisine*. The eighty-eight-year lifetime of this remarkable man spanned the arrival of the automobile, radio, television, the airplane. Yet the verities of his genius remain unchanged, still the gospel for

the chefs who today preside over the kitchens of the world's
fine hotels and restaurants.

It was a long way from Villeneuve to the luxury liner *Imperator*
and to the personage of Emperor William II of Germany. Summoned into the royal presence from the kitchen where he was
turning out succulent dishes, Escoffier was given a new title.
Said William: "I am the Emperor of Germany, but you are the
Emperor of Chefs."

The beaming new "emperor" was even then creating the sixty-
three garnishes and sauces for steak; the thirty-two different
ways to serve peaches as a desert; and a marvelous recipe for
pheasant stuffing, combining mushrooms, truffles and pâté de
foie gras, which he said was found among ancient manuscripts
in Alcintara, a Spanish monastery. The manuscripts dated back
to Napoleon's wars, and Escoffier noted that "it was almost the only
benefit that unhappy campaign has brought us."

A disciple of Escoffier, and indeed one of his protégés, was
Joseph Donon, once described as "the richest private chef in the
world," quite a distinction when it is realized that executive chefs
at prestigious hotels such as the Plaza are reputed to earn
upwards of $40,000 annually.

The years just around the turn of the century saw rich Americans
fancying themselves gastronomes and vying with each other
to lure famous chefs into their kitchens. Donon was one. In
1912 he brought his talents across the ocean from the kitchens
of the Savoy in London, where he had worked with Escoffier.
The invitation to emigrate came from Henry Clay Frick as a
result of one meal prepared entirely by Donon for the rich
industrialist and art collector. From the Frick household Donon
went to one of society's grande dames, Mrs. Hamilton McK.
Twombley, who was born a Vanderbilt and was rich enough to
pay her private chef upwards of $25,000 and $30,000 a year.
The food and wines served at her table added to her fame as a
hostess, and to Donon's as a chef.

Now retired and living near Newport, R.I., Donon continues to
take an active part in the affairs of Les Amis d'Escoffier, a select

group of gentlemen with exquisite tastes in food and wine, whose annual dinners are always an adventure in eating. Donon was there to help honor the master when Les Dames des Amis d'Escoffier, tired of being banned from the all-male feasts of Les Amis, staged a great gourmet dinner of their own in Boston's Ritz Carlton Hotel.

No one knows what financial rewards Fred Sterry, first manager of the Plaza, offered the legendary Eugene Laperruque to come out of retirement for the hotel's opening in October, 1907. The temperamental Frenchman had his loyal following from his days as chef at Delmonico's and the old Hoffman House. It was the talk of the town that he had been lured away from Delmonico's by the Rothschilds at a salary of $300 a month! The faithful were to find their favorite dishes and many more when fashionable New York clamored for choice tables at Gotham's newest luxury hotel. The lustre Laperruque brought to the Plaza cuisine was never allowed to be dimmed by succeeding chefs.

"Sauces are the very soul of digestion," maintained another famed Plaza chef, Pierre LaFarge, proving his point by the rich mint sauce that adorned lamb roasted to a deep pink. Domestic cooking in the average American home in those years preceding World War I had barely begun to emerge from dull mediocrity. The epicurean meals served at the Plaza were still beyond the imagination of most housewives, although women's magazines were beginning to print recipes and urge women to try such subtle touches as a blend of lemon juice and butter, spiked with garlic, topped with parsley, to make something special of their plain broiled fish.

Today's woman, proclaiming her liberation in a loud, sometimes shrill voice, would have found one Plaza chef particularly infuriating. He was Albert Lattard, and very clearly he stated: "It is superior intelligence that rules men . . . chefs as well as all others."

But it is nevertheless a fact that the kitchens of fine hotels and restaurants remain a man's world. The master chef has usually spent a lifetime perfecting his art. Often he has started in Europe at the age of 10 or 12, working his way up through long and difficult hours to the great day when his perfect omelette wins the approving nod of the head chef or he is allowed to try his hand at inventing a new dish.

"I myself discovered fifty new ways of preparing oysters in a week," said Chef Lattard, who believed that every time a scientific invention changed the world, an equally great discovery was made in the kitchen. "A few years ago, guinea hens were never used, fruit salads unheard of," he said.

That was more than half a century ago. He would have been pleased, perhaps surprised, at the salad revolution that has swept the United States in recent years. And the supermarket spectacle of women selecting choice Rock Cornish game hens or plump guinea fowl would have convinced him that American tastes were indeed becoming more sophisticated.

In the Lattard era, however, chefs concentrated on the appetites of the male. For instance, it was a president of the New York stock exchange, William Remick, who was honored by Chef Lattard with the first serving of Crab Remick. And Colonel Edward Bradley–whose horses won many Kentucky Derbies and who, when at home on his Blue Grass farm, Idle Hours, always breakfasted on the front porch with his favorite horse, Blue Larkspur–claimed he would travel across the continent for the Lattard creation Cream of Chicken Soup, Plaza, still a perennial favorite.

One exception was the elaborate dish M. Lattard created at the Plaza for that temperamental diva, Madame Melba. That lady was miffed when she discovered that the Plaza menu featured a dish named for her manager. She even hid the menu, hoping he would not see his name in such a star role. M. Lattard caught on at once and served her a creation he christened in her honor, Eggs Melba.

"It was easy," he explained later. "All it needed was an artichoke bottom, a hash of broiled mushrooms and the poached eggs over it . . . then all topped by a sauce Hollandaise with foie gras. Simple, but very good."

Simple, indeed! But that "simplicity" is part of a great chef's special talent. In Lattard's case, he combined these talents with

7

such gifts as sculpture, painting and an educated taste for opera. His bust of Chef Laperruque won honors at the National Academy of Design. Meantime he was charming a Plaza prize patron, John "Bet-a-Million" Gates, with a Bisque Semiramis concocted of soft clams and named, of course, "for a grand and very beautiful opera."

While Lattard sauces were, and still are, the pride of the Plaza, the chef insisted that certain meats, such as prime beef and lamb, be allowed their natural flavors.

"Preserve their taste and richness," he advised, "by cooking into them all the vapor, the juices that the dullard lets escape."

A proud family heritage was that of Humbert Gatti, who came from two generations of renowned cooks and was named executive chef of the Plaza in the posh post-war year of 1950. He had some welcome advice for the burgeoning female innovators in ranch house and apartment kitchens across the country:

"Sauces . . . by all means," he said. "But remember that the excellence of a dish is not dependent upon its being complicated. Better a simple dish, properly prepared, than an elaborate affair all garnishing and no flavor. Quality must always take precedence over quantity, and care of preparation over variety."

This is also the credo of André René, youngest executive chef in the Plaza's history. He achieved that honor before his fortieth birthday and has won countless accolades in the succeeding years, including the singular award by the Association of Master Chefs of France, United States Delegation, as "Chef of the Year" of 1968. The life-size sterling silver chef's cap, *Toque Blanche*, was one of the hotel's prize exhibits during that year until the award passed to the next deserving winner.

Recently one of the Plaza's more literate gourmet guests remarked that Antoine Carême's definition of the perfect chef was the best description he knew of the gastronomic young genius who presides over the great Plaza kitchens:

"He will be a cook above all–able, alert, productive. He will be cut out for active command and be animated by an invincible ardour for work. He will be a man of parts, an enthusiast, vigilant to minuteness–he will see all and know all."

Any of his *sous* chefs who have watched André taste a sauce and slowly, firmly nod his head, or stop a waiter with a loaded tray to whisk off an offending lettuce leaf, knows that André does "see all and know all." He is a true disciple of Escoffier and Brillat-Savarin.

The nervous bride, wondering how to manage to have everything come out simultaneously and hoping her dinner for six will not be a disaster, ought to be allowed one grand tour of the Plaza kitchens. The equipment would be her envy and the timing her despair.

The Plaza has an acre of kitchen space! Huge gas ranges dominate the scene, and great copper pots, shined to a fare-thee-well, hang in splendor. The copper pots are there not for decoration but because they retain heat best for top-of-the-stove cooking. Gas is used for cooking because delicate degrees of temperature are best controlled by the knowing hand of the cook.

During the massive blackout of 1965 electrical power failed up and down the East Coast. But in the Plaza kitchens the gas stoves went on working, and in the candlelit Edwardian Room, hungry and grateful diners waited out the darkened city with rare roast beef, hot rolls, soufflés . . . the whole roster of the Plaza menu except for frozen desserts.

Eggs at the Plaza come farm-fresh from New Jersey. Chef André prefers the brown for poaching and baking and for such sauces as Hollandaise, because they are firmer. He chooses white eggs for soft boiling, omelettes and general use.

It would be a challenge to try to count the different versions of chicken emerging from the Plaza kitchen to tempt appetites in the hotel's five high-ceilinged restaurants and countless private banquet and dining rooms. The chef keeps careful watch over the special refrigerator where they are stored along with wild duck, English quail and snipe, game hens, turkeys and squabs. Temperatures there are quite different from the huge "meat ager" where aging cuts of beef and lamb are hung, each with its stamp and date tag, and the vast walk-in refrigerators for seafood, the coolers for vegetables and–kept under lock and key in a strongbox, like crown jewels–the fresh Beluga caviar worth $70 per pound and up.

Procuring exotic foods from far away has become simpler with fast overland trucks, refrigerating techniques and jet planes to bring rare stone crab from Bimini, sole from England, brook trout from Scotland and the Rocky Mountains, pompano from Florida. Even as early as 1890, *Harper's Weekly* was boasting that "the limitations of season have ceased to be any bars to the demands of the appetite."

At posh palaces such as the Plaza in the early 1900's, patrons could feast on strawberries in December, pecan-fed turkey on the Fourth of July and even, for a brief period, kangaroo steak! The latter did not meet with any enthusiasm from the Plaza chef, but he tried it out at the urging of an important guest. Kangaroo later vanished from the menu, and in the first palmy years of the Plaza, no one asked for such delicacies of an earlier day as roast bear, cold buffalo tongue or filet of prairie chicken.

Dining out has become greatly simplified since the turn of the century. Nobody wants the six-course lunch and the ten-course dinner of the early 1900's. Yet in a way the executive chef finds his task more exacting than when one elaborate dish followed another in a seemingly endless parade. The three or four courses he does offer must be as near perfection as possible, for he is tempting appetites undulled by a surfeit of food, and the public he caters to has developed a palate sophisticated by travel. Americans, always a mobile people, no longer need to be rich in order to range the far corners of the world. The couple from Kansas, scanning a Plaza menu, may have eaten curry in the East Indies and developed a taste for *Cordon Bleu* cuisine in a five-star restaurant in France.

So a top international chef, such as the Plaza's André, must be a perfectionist even as Laperruque was over half a century ago. In contrast to that old master, however, André did not begin as a bay apprentice with his heart set on the *toque blanche*. Son of a French automobile mechanic, André had finished high school and served a stint in the French Army when the Germans occupied his country. He fled to Switzerland, where a happy accident brought the young man, eager for some sort of career, to the attention of a chef in Basel.

André worked long hours for almost no pay, studied far into the night and finally won his laurels by proving that he could turn out an uncurdled Hollandaise, a spicy curry and a perfect Béarnaise . . . all prerequisites to becoming chief saucier or sauce-maker. This he achieved in the record time of three years. His ambitions and dreams were fixed across the Atlantic, where he first landed a job in the Hotel New Yorker in 1951, graduating shortly to the lofty pinnacle of the Plaza and an impressive series of honors and awards, which crowd the walls of his office and overflow into his home.

11

CHAPTER TWO

FOOD AND COMFORT FOR THE STRANGER

"If the history of Greece is in its temples, that of the United States is in its hotels," wrote Gene Fowler, biographer of the famous and chronicler of the American scene.

Since its very beginning, the American hotel has been a mirror of its times, reflecting the mood of the country during periods of affluence and depression, war and peace, political upheaval and changing life styles. Often it has been the arbiter of social customs and fashions, and most important, of our eating habits.

Americans have always been a people on the move, and ever since the *Mayflower* dropped anchor there was a need for places where food and lodging could be found. Smoky little inns, taverns and ordinaries followed the colonists as they rode along crude trails and later as they jogged over the post roads in stage coaches, carriages and farm wagons.

Often the weary travelers found sleeping accommodations on the floor, as close as possible to the banked-down fire on the hearth. The "victuals" were whatever the proprietor had on hand. Sugar was such a rare commodity that the "loaf" was often kept in a locked cupboard. Nutmeg was in demand for seasoning, and many people carried their own in a tiny enameled box. The first fork arrived on the American continent with Massachusetts Governor Winthrop in 1633. He kept it in a velvet-lined case, knowing that when he stopped for a wayside meal the only utensil for spearing the meat and vegetables would be a knife.

Breakfast at these early inns was usually a wooden or leather tankard of ale or cider. Pewter came later, and so did coffee. A bowl of cornmeal and milk boiled in molasses and known as

13

"suppawn" was another morning eye-opener. Midday and evening meals were likely to feature a stew of venison, "y-mynced" or "skerned," and kept bubbling on the open hearth that served as cookstove and oven.

The proud survivals of colonial days are the Indian combination of lima beans and corn, still called succotash, and turkey stuffed with chestnuts. Wild turkeys were so plentiful that they were exported to France, where they were stuffed with truffles and regarded as a great delicacy.

The burgeoning town of New York developed its own special food fad in the late 17th and early 18th centuries, when country inns along the East River served "turtle feasts" to coachloads of gay young people on a day's outing. The same turtle soup that George Washington fancied at Fraunces Tavern (where it is still served in the colonial dining room) was the first course of these "feasts," followed by turtle stews and steaks.

Another and even madder food fad that swept the nation in the 1800's was oysters. Oyster parlors sprang up in downtown New York. Oyster suppers became the "in" thing at Rectors, which was as proud of its theatrical clientele as of the "yachting table" reserved for sundry Vanderbilts, Goulds and Astors. It was the first restaurant with a revolving door, which proved such a curiosity that for a while a parade of people went around and around and back out on the street again.

An "oyster express" was set up just before the arrival of the railroad. The oysters were packed in damp straw and loaded on light carts, which were drawn by relays of horses over the mountains from Baltimore to Pittsburgh, where they proceeded by riverboat down the Ohio to Cincinnati, to be kept alive in barrels of salt water sprinkled with cornmeal. All this for the gourmet tastes of rich Germans who were making "The Queen City" famous for beer and ale. Chefs in hotel restaurants from New York to the farthermost points the oyster could reach were busy inventing new ways to serve the succulent bivalve.

Proprietors of the very earliest inns welcomed the wealth of seafood in New York waters. Eleven Fish, as the Dutch called shad because it arrived on the 11th of March, was always regarded as a delicacy. Dutch cooks took lessons from the Indians and cooked their shad on a birchbark plank. Up in Connecticut one innkeeper reported that he could not hire a cook unless he promised that the cook's personal diet should have shad no more than once a week and salmon no oftener than twice in that period!

Coffee houses, which are enjoying such a vogue in the 1970's, with the Plaza's elegant "After-Eight" menu in the Palm Court setting a high standard, were an important part of the business and social life of our first cities. Merchants from around the world met at Brown's Coffee House in New York for oysters, ales, wines and "segars" in addition to coffee. Political gossip was traded, the onerous Stamp Act discussed and later, such ventures as Fulton's steamboat, the building of the Erie canal, the launching of transatlantic ships were all planned over a chop, a turtle steak or what they called "made dishes" such as Fricassee of Chicken, À la Mode of Beef or Pork and Beans.

While the early caravansaries are an integral part of our heritage, it was not until the hotel as we know it today made its appearance, that the mores of everyday American life began to be affected by what went on in the lobbies, ballrooms and especially the kitchens and restaurants of the famous-name establishments.

A single photograph of a hotel luncheon in the popular magazine *Harper's Bazar* in 1899 changed the look of dinner tables all over the country as women studied the formal place settings, the flower centerpiece and the silver candelabra, the tallest of which stood by the place of the hostess. By this time women also knew that it was perfectly correct to invite their female friends to luncheon at a hotel. Hadn't Mrs. Stuyvesant Fish done just that with her revolutionary luncheon party at the Waldorf?

As women read magazines and cookbooks and society pages, they became eager to learn, ready to experiment. They were middle-class America at the turn of the century, when the rich were very rich, the poor very poor, but in ever increasing numbers this in-between group was surging upward and outward in what seemed to them the best of all possible worlds.

15

Although the influence of hotels reached fruition in the waning Victorian era and blossomed in Edwardian days, it does go back to the old Tremont House in Boston.

The title "Father of the American Hotel" goes to Isaiah Rogers, who as a 28-year-old architect designed the Tremont House. His claim to fame, and the Tremont's, is that this was the first structure planned and built from the ground up *as a hotel*. It boasted such innovations as a separate lobby where guests might register and have their luggage carried to their rooms, private parlors, eight indoor privies and eight bathing rooms.

It was at the Tremont that French cuisine made the first tentative inroads, competing on the menu with boiled cod, corned beef, boiled ham and roast goose. Guests were invited to try Pâté aux Huitres, Gigiers de Volaille en Caisson, Ameurettes de Mouton à la Tartare, Poisson Noir au Gratin and Castelettes de Mouton Arnees . . . even if they hadn't the faintest idea what they were about to be served!

The classic Greek Revival design of the Tremont House, which opened in October 1829, set the pace for hotel architecture in the United States for the next half century. Isaiah Rogers' first accolade was to be summoned by John Jacob Astor to supervise the building of the elegant Astor House, which opened near New York's City Hall Park in 1836. Here the venturesome female who traveled alone, or the wife who wanted a quiet meal away from the menfolk, found a Ladies Ordinary offering mock turtle soup, Bifticks and Pommes de Terre, Charlotte Russe, Curaçao sherbet, nutmeg melon or fritters with vanilla sauce.

The Astor also gets the credit—some might say the blame—for that dubious American innovation, the quick lunch. Its famed Rotunda was jammed at noon with gentlemen in high silk hats, which they did not remove as they perched on stools at two immense circular counters for bean porridge, soft clams and roast beef sliced by a skilled carver. Those who came to the Rotunda came to eat, not to talk. There were even messenger boys who carried bowls of soup to hurried men who "must satisfy their hunger in their offices." Thus began the gastronomic indignity of the take-out office lunch encased in cellophane, aluminum foil and plastic which daily challenges the digestions of millions of Americans.

The old St. Nicholas was the first hotel to cost over one million dollars. When it opened on Prince Street in New York in 1856, its rosewood fittings, gold-embroidered draperies and bridal suite hung in "the purest white satin" were an obvious bid for feminine favor. This was the decade that came to be known as the "Feminine Fifties." Yet only a few years later, the lady columnist of *Demarest's* magazine declared indignantly that "it is a rather curious fact that in a republic alone, of all forms of government, no place of honor, trust or respectability has been permitted to women." And in the year 1907, when the glamorous new Plaza welcomed a growing clientele of fashionable women, one redoubtable crusader named Mrs. Harriet Blatch sued the Hoffman House because the management refused to serve her, unescorted, on the roof garden. Mrs. Blatch lost the case; the court ruled that management of hotels could refuse service to unescorted ladies in public rooms, provided they "served them elsewhere." With true Women's Lib spirit, however, Mrs. Blatch did not wish to eat "elsewhere"; she wished to dine on the roof garden. Chef Eugene Laperruque, then reigning at the Plaza, must have been amused at the story of the indignant female guest, for it was he who made famous the Hoffman House cuisine and planned the bird-and-bottle suppers where glamorous musical-comedy stars were greeted with hit songs from their Broadway shows and, as often as not, found costly trinkets in the elaborate folds of their napkins. Then, as during his whole career, Laperruque wrote directions in French to his staff, explaining the basics of certain sauces and the meaning of culinary phrases. His staff had to be fluent in his native tongue, which he rightly regarded as the official language of gastronomy.

Hotels grew steadily more magnificent as the 19th century came to a close. The Fifth Avenue Hotel in New York introduced "Mr. Edison's incandescents" to replace its gaslight and to illuminate such visiting dignitaries as the Prince of Wales and the Emperor of Brazil. For the entourage of the Chinese Embassy, it is claimed by some that the chef created a concoction known the world over as Chop Suey, but other food researchers claim this distinction for the Palace Hotel in San Francisco. Nobody

17

argues, however, that both chow mein and chop suey are strictly American versions of Oriental cuisine. Chow mein holds its own at the Plaza today, a delectable blend of crisp vegetables and tender meat or shrimp.

The coming of the railroad saw hotels established at a comfortable distance from the station. Such was New York's Grand Union, only a walk away from Grand Central Station and stressing economy for travelers, with rooms "one dollar and upwards a day." Meantime, a quiet, imposing hotel called the Buckingham rose in 1876. New York was marching steadily uptown, as it has from its beginnings, and the Buckingham was "way up" at 50th Street and 5th Avenue, then being described by a publicist not known for understatement as "one of the most magnificent streets in civilization." The Buckingham had a charming breakfast room where the continental breakfast of rolls and coffee was introduced and immediately became popular with guests, especially women who were beginning to shy away from the steaks, eggs, chops and chicken with which Americans were wont to start their day. Saks Fifth Avenue now stands on the site of the Buckingham.

Another hotel experiment was that of A. T. Stewart, merchant prince, who was concerned about the morals of young working women and so built a huge hotel for them on New York's Park Avenue. Unfortunately the young ladies did not share his belief that they were better off in their rooms by nine o'clock, protected from the male of the species and strictly chaperoned. The young ladies stayed away from Mr. Stewart's hotel and it changed its role, its name—from the Women's Hotel to the Park Avenue—and its prices from six dollars a week, meals included, to the going rate of city hostelries. Furthermore, it enlisted the inspired kitchen services of Edward Schlecher, whom it referred to as a *Cordon Bleu* professor, and who had previously delighted the fastidious clientele of the Grand Union in Saratoga. A "dining verandah" was introduced, and candlelit dinners for two, with soft music by a Hungarian band, became a popular summer pastime.

But the railroads did more than encourage the growth of hotels. Their coming also brought a gentleman named Fred Harvey to the fore. He traveled a great deal and found that he was nearly always hungry and nearly always failed to find anything fit to eat when he jumped off the train at a stopover station. Thus the Harvey Houses came into being, with the demure and pretty Harvey girls serving piping hot meals for seventy-five cents. From the time the first Harvey House opened in Topeka, Kansas, in 1876, until railroads introduced their own dining cars, Harvey quality and service were dependables for the traveling public. The Harvey girls were all between 18 and 30 years of age, and practically all of them acquired husbands in record time from among the ranks of men who patronized the Harvey restaurants. Pure food and pretty girls paid off. And gentlemen without jackets were not permitted in the Harvey dining rooms.

Major cities in the United States rapidly followed the East in the style of their grand hotels and the skills of the chefs they often lured from New York, Boston and Philadelphia. Denver's aristocratic Brown Palace Hotel was one of the glories of the West in the 1890's, with seventeen-course "collations" challenging even the lusty appetites of mining and ranching moguls. Champagne accompanied foie gras, caviar, venison, trout from the Rocky Mountain streams. Higher in the mountains stood a unique and charming little hotel called, with reason, Hotel de Paris. It was run by Louis du Puy, nicknamed "French Louis." The fame of the hotel's cuisine attracted the great and near-great to the mountain town of Georgetown for the crisp salads, hot rolls and breads, imported cheeses, frozen Champagne punch. Such personages as Jay Gould and Russell Sage, railroad magnate Sidney Dillon and others came there by private railway car and ordered du Puy's famed stuffed ptarmigan, fresh French peas and venison steak. When the silver boom ended and the 1897 panic set in, M. du Puy's lovely little establishment closed its doors.

The skills of the French chef and the nuances of French cuisine spread across the continent as fast as did the express trains and boom times of gold and copper strikes. San Francisco's Palace Hotel was perhaps the most glamorous establishment west of the Mississippi. Its entrepreneur, William Chapman Ralston, committed suicide during the financial panic that was a dreary prelude to the opening of the hotel. But the Palace rallied, and by mid-1875 it had begun a glittering career of supper parties for the millionaires of Nob Hill and such affairs as the 1876 "Millionaire's Banquet," with the menus engraved on silver from the fabulous Comstock Lode. The Palace chef invented an omelette using the succulent little oysters of the West Coast. But later food historians claim this creation really dated to Placerville, California, during the Gold Rush, when a miner's court condemned an erring miner to be hanged. His plea for mercy was based upon his promise that, if allowed to go free, he would create a new inexpensive dish for the men, during those pioneer days when most food was imported and sold at staggeringly high prices. With a combination of eggs, then valued at $2 apiece and a can of oysters, nearly unheard of, he put together an omelette that soon became known up and down the mining country as "Hangtown Fry."

The lore of the American hotel is endless, and its record for refining the food tastes of Americans is a splendid one. By the turn of the century, fashions in food were becoming sophisticated, cookbooks were a best-selling item and many women even enrolled in "cookery" schools. The stage was set for an auspicious event to take place in the year 1907–the opening of the Plaza, New York's beautiful new "Hotel on the Park."

CHAPTER THREE

ENTRENCHED ELEGANCE

The history of the Plaza is a social history of New York that spans two thirds of a century in a cavalcade of changing fads and fancies and fashions in living. For sixty-five years it has managed in some subtle way to retain the special ambiance of the graceful Edwardian era in which it was born, yet keep pace with the swift-changing way of life during the vigorous, tumultuous mid-20th century.

It is something of a minor miracle of the 1970's that this oasis of opulence and elegance has stood foursquare and stalwart while the city around it shot skyward in faceless office buildings of poured concrete, glass and steel and as one after another the stately mansions of the past and the eminent hotels of a bygone era gave way to luxury shops and towering apartments.

Conceived in beauty and born in luxury, the Plaza Hotel came into being in the serene world of 1907. Yellowed and flaking newspapers of those days attest to the excitement attending the opening, on October 1, of the luxurious new hotel rising in French Renaissance splendor at the southern gateway to Central Park at Fifth Avenue, the richest street in America.

The press informed readers of the cost of the eighteen-story structure, the then staggering price of $12,000,000. Articles gave long descriptions of the marvels of the most expensive hotel ever built: the marble foyers with mosaic-inlaid floors; the gleaming crystal chandeliers throughout; the beautifully appointed rooms with sculptured ceilings, boiserie, paneled walls and marble-mantled fireplaces; the huge Tiffany dome aloft in the Palm Court, whose multicolored, leaded glass cast fascinating diadems

21

of lights on the guests; the handsome restaurants; and, of course, the great kitchen, walled entirely in gleaming white tile, equipped with the latest culinary appurtenances and stocked with epicurean delights to serve its guests.

Titillating as all this was, the public was more excited by printed lists of the financial and social greats who were to inhabit the new hotel.

Up to that time it was practically unheard of for persons of consequence and wealth to live in a hotel. New York, circa 1907, was a city of homes and home life. There are still some old-timers around who can recall a Park Avenue without a single shop, a Madison Avenue vista of town houses with projecting stoops and bellying with Victorian bays and bulges; a Fifth Avenue mansion-lined with the ornate homes of the newly rich, appropriately named "Millionaire's Row," and the brownstones of the West Side, a model of middle-class respectability.

Hotels were for travelers and were patronized only by those in search of immediate provender or a likely place to lay their heads. It was but natural, then, that the stories listing the magical names of those who had leased apartments and were actually going to live in a hotel intrigued the public and lured crowds to the curbs on opening day to catch a glimpse of the socially anointed guests arriving to take up their residence or attend the many special luncheon and dinner parties planned for the gala opening.

Alfred Gwynne Vanderbilt, who was to lose his life only eight years later in the tragic sinking of the *Lusitania*, was one of those magical ones, a son of Cornelius Vanderbilt, said to be the richest man in America at the time. The elder Vanderbilt and his grande-dame wife lived in a great French-château-like structure, which occupied the entire length of Fifth Avenue between 57th and 58th streets, now the site of Bergdorf-Goodman; the apartment of the younger Vanderbilts was just catercorner to the mansion. Interestingly enough, the names of Mr. and Mrs. Alfred Gwynne Vanderbilt were the first on the hotel's virgin register.

Another magical name was that of George J. Gould, son of the legendary Jay Gould who had amassed millions in railroads and in

Wall Street manipulations. Stories of young Gould's wooing and winning of the beauteous actress Edith Kingdon were as familiar to the reading public as a later-day Frank Sinatra–Mia Farrow romance, a Richard Burton–Elizabeth Taylor marriage. The Plaza was also to be the town residence for the Goulds whose country home was a fantastic, feudal-like Georgian estate fittingly named "Georgian Court," at Lakewood, N.J., with its own golf course, playhouse, tanbark ring, indoor and outdoor swimming pools; whose yacht, the *Atlantis*, was one of the largest ocean-going yachts afloat.

There were the Harrimans, Mr. and Mrs. Oliver Harriman, representing a family of untold railroad millions, who had a country house at White Plains, N.Y. They had signed a long lease on an apartment long before the hotel opened. Another of the palatial Plaza apartments became the "town residence" of Mr. and Mrs. Cornelius K. G. Billings, whose "country home" was in what is now crowded Washington Heights. Where it stood, high on a bluff overlooking the Hudson, the magnificent medieval museum, The Cloisters, now attracts visitors from all over the world.

Far ahead of her time was Clara Bell Walsh, a statuesque blonde from Kentucky, who arrived with her tycoon husband Julius Walsh on October 1, 1907, and lived at the Plaza for half a century–until her death in August, 1967. An expert horsewoman, a blue-ribbon winner at countless international horse shows, she brought her own saddle horses and a matched pair for her carriage. Clara Bell did not restrict her friends to the Social Register. Long before anyone had heard of Brotherhood Week and integration marches, Mrs. Walsh counted among her close friends the Negro dancer Bill (Bojangles) Robinson. He often came to her suite, a rendezvous for three worlds–the turf, the theatre and society–where the furnishings remained unchanged for fifty years and the trademark was laughter, music and good talk. Ed Wynn, Jimmy Savo, Amos 'n Andy, Vincent Lopez, Mary Martin–they were all there to share her hospitality when the doors of her suite opened daily at 5 P.M., the only requirement being that those who came be interesting.

John "Bet-a-Million" Gates–who, it was said, would bet on anything, even which of two raindrops would reach the sill first–

had leased an apartment reported to cost $35,000 a year, $10,000 more than the Vanderbilts were paying. The Harrimans and the Goulds, the public was informed, were paying $25,000 annually, while the quarters of Mr. Billings were of so mean an order that they rented for a mere $20,000 a year.

"Essentially the home of millionaires" was the way one newspaper described the Plaza in 1907, and the roster of names then and in succeeding years would seem to give substance to the statement: the John Wanamakers; the Benjamin Dukes of tobacco fame; the Philip D. Armours, already reaping millions from the abattoirs of Chicago; Mr. and Mrs. Theodore Havemeyer; Countess Boni di Castellane; George Gould's sister Anna and his brother Jay; Mr. and Mrs. Ogden Mills, the "jeweled" name of the Pierre Cartiers, whose child was the first baby born at the Plaza.

Overnight the hotel became the vogue. Society embraced it, and it soon was the rendezvous for the greats of the operatic and theatrical world, dealers in art, tycoons in high finance. On any given day, one could see such noted Edwardian glamor girls as Lillian Russell, accompanied by her flamboyant escort "Diamond" Jim Brady; Maxine Elliot, for whom a Broadway theatre was subsequently named; Billie Burke, the delicate China-doll beauty who married Flo Ziegfeld of "Ziegfeld Follies" fame; Ethel Barrymore and her brother Lionel; musical comedy's Fritzie Scheff; Anna Held, who reportedly bathed only in milk to retain her beauty; Lily Langtry, "The Jersey Lily" to whom kings had lost their hearts; Mrs. Patrick Campbell, the first woman to smoke in public, who had the temerity to light a cigarette in the Palm Court, thereby unleashing nationwide critical editorials and sermons from the pulpit; authoress Elinor Glyn, whose "shocking" novel *It*, was banned in Boston, assuring its immediate success.

The Plaza's epicurean cuisine became as famous as its tenants, and accounts of dinner parties in the various restaurants, then and long into later years, filled the columns of the society pages when New York boasted fourteen newspapers, all of which had an impressive "society section" reporting in detail the social activities of the rich and the regal. Hostesses of another era, old conservatives and wealthy newcomers alike, loved the mention and never balked at giving out the names of their guests. And

24

"by those present" was the reputation of the Plaza further enhanced.

It was, indeed, the various restaurants where wealth and fashion were on view every day and night that gave lustre to the very name of the Plaza. The lofty, chandeliered Rose Room, later to be transformed into the Persian Room, was the nightly scene of formal dinner parties, where that sporting figure, Reginald C. Vanderbilt, father of today's Gloria Vanderbilt Cooper, and his first wife liked to dine on pheasant, served *en plumage*, and where his sister, Gladys Vanderbilt, could be seen dining with her fiancé, Count Lazslo Szechenyi, who was quartered at the Plaza while awaiting their marriage.

In the mahogany-paneled Edwardian Room at a table beside windows draped in ruby-colored velvet, lunched such proper Edwardians as E. Berry Wall, "The King of the Dudes," who is credited with having introduced the tuxedo to the American sartorial scene. Chicken livers sautéed with mushrooms was a favorite dish of the Duchess of Marlborough, née Consuelo Vanderbilt. In later years in the room, one could look up from Eggs Benedict to catch the eye of Charles Boyer or Bette Davis or Jack Benny, the latter looking carefully around lest his image be impaired, before leaving a large tip for the waiter; or Mrs. Rose Kennedy, faithful Plaza habitué; or a future President, relaxing from political cares as he lunched with Pat and Julie and Tricia; or Barbra Streisand being interviewed at a corner table while devouring a Steak Tartar.

Today the stately Edwardian Room has been renamed the Green Tulip, decorated to suggest a garden of living trees and flowers, with tables on two levels, surrounded by a promenade.

For the collegiate set, the old Plaza Grill was an island of enchantment, at its gayest during the tea-dance craze of the Twenties. Constance Bennett was the belle of New York and the idol of the Ivy Leaguers, who fluttered about her on the dance floor as they constantly cut in; maids and matrons sighed over Rudolph Valentino executing the graceful tango with an ecstatic debutante, and Mae Murray, her Kewpie Doll lips pursed, waltzed dreamily with a gay young blade to the tune of "The Merry

Widow." Scott Fitzgerald and his Zelda tea-danced like crazy to "The Japanese Sandman," and when evening cast its shadow on the Avenue, dunked gaily in the fountain in the Square, to the musical accompaniment of police whistles.

The Plaza was part of their enchanted world. Fitzgerald characters out of *The Great Gatsby*, or *The Beautiful and the Damned*, wandered in and out of the Plaza as often as Fitzgerald did. Ernest Hemingway, trying to lure him down to Key West to cover a Cuban revolution, wrote that if he really felt blue enough, he should get himself heavily insured "and I'll see you can get killed . . . take out your liver and give it to Princeton, and cut out your heart and give it to the Plaza Hotel."

A whole world of coeds and young adults wept when the Grill was closed during Prohibition, but young marrieds beamed when years later the room was transformed into the Rendez-Vous, a stunning dinner and supper-dance room endowed with Continental charm reflecting the grandeur of Czarist Russia. An understandable transition, since its mentor-manager was White-Russian Serge Obolensky, then publicity director for the Plaza, who discarded his princely title for the Colonel honors he won as a paratrooper in World War II.

As the Fifties gave way to the Sixties, the Plaza, always in tune with the times, turned the Rendez-Vous into "Plaza 9," a nightclub with entertainment in tune with the times: a satirical Julius Monk revue, a renaissance of jazz, the presentation of an off-Broadway play.

The great baronial Oak Room, paneled in the finest of oak, was a male sanctuary until Prohibition; later it was reserved "for men only" during weekday luncheon hours, permitting the distaff side after 3 P.M. Inevitably it fell prey to Women's Lib. The ladies– some called them by another name–demanded to be admitted at all times. Admitted they were; accepted they were not.

The Oak Room has long been the after-theatre, after-the-opera meeting place for such notables of the entertainment world as Helen Hayes, Judith Anderson, Bea Lillie, George Jessel, Richard Rodgers, Morton Downey, Roddy McDowall, Rosalind Russell.

26

On any Monday night during the opera season, Lucius Beebe would stroll in after the performance, top-hatted and opera-cloaked. But the Oak Room's most famous habitué was George M. Cohan, who daily would take his place at the northeast banquette, which soon became known as "The Cohan Corner." An average afternoon would see fifteen to twenty friends gathered around, drinking and exchanging quips and shoptalk with the Grand Old Man of the stage. Today the softly lighted alcove bears a plaque in memory of the beloved Cohan, whose songs lifted the spirits of thousands from World War I to the last years when he held court there.

The lofty, chandeliered Rose Room, closed during Prohibition, became the Persian Room following repeal of the 18th Amendment. The Persian Room still sets fashions in entertainment, just as it did when the dancing DeMarcos at its April, 1934, opening restored ballroom dancing to public favor after the frenetic craze of the Charleston. Hildegarde, the chanteuse whose long white gloves became her trademark, first gave long-stemmed roses to guests. And there, too, Burl Ives had everyone joining him and his guitar in "The Blue Tail Fly"; Ethel Merman belted it out with "There's No Business Like Show Business"; Eartha Kitt tossed yards of sables across a chair and silenced the crowded room with her songs. Two dance bands, top entertainers, plus the undeniable ambiance of the room itself have kept the Persian Room as popular as in its Rose Room days half a century ago, and today it is an acknowledged showcase for show-biz entertainers.

The famed Palm Court, with its great marble pillars, huge gleaming pedestaled hurricane lights, its four-season caryatids in archway formation (copies of famous originals made by Donato Donati, a pupil of Michelangelo) remains virtually the same as it was in the beginning, except for the great Tiffany dome that was removed during Conrad Hilton's regime, to be replaced by a lowered ceiling shedding more modern light. Nobody raises an eyebrow if you order tea in the afternoon instead of a cocktail, for tea at the Plaza has been a New York tradition since the opening, and almost as many people sip their oolong there as stop for a cocktail in the Oak Bar. It is no unusual sight to observe a three-generation group on any mid-afternoon, as a dowager who

was married at the Plaza relives memories of her youth with
her children and grandchildren.

A Continental mood descends upon the Palm Court in the
evening as lights are lowered, huge brandy glasses floating
romantically lighted gardenias appear on the marble-topped
tables, and soft music beguiles but does not distract the guests.
This becomes "The Palm Court After Eight," where after-dinner
coffee and Continental pastries round out a dinner party, an
evening at the theatre or just a neighborly stroll. Waitresses in
Victorian uniforms proffer coffees from around the world and
trays of pastries so eye-appealing and palate-whetting as to cause
the most rigid dieter to throw caution to the winds.

In 1965, when the Savoy-Plaza was demolished, to the anguished
cry of an outraged public and resulting in the formation of the
New York Landmarks Commission to preserve the city's fine,
historic structures, "Trader Vic's" restaurant was moved from its
location there to its new home at the Plaza. The pleasures of
Polynesian feasting amid a South Sea Island decor–which includes
the huge outrigger canoe used in filming *Mutiny on the Bounty*–
became another part of the Plaza.

Something new was added in 1969: The Oyster Bar at the Plaza,
specializing in every kind of seafood from oysters to sea
urchins. Its decor, accented by murals suggestive of the Victorian
period as it merged with the Edwardian, is in the best tradition
of the Plaza. Here guests can see the oysters shucked in the open,
and can order such specialties as bouillabaisse, Quiche of King
Crab* and Mussels Marinière*, as well as the customary clam
chowders and oyster stews.

Day after day the Plaza is a hotel of habit. Sunday breakfast
at the Plaza is a ritual. The windows of the erstwhile Edwardian
Room–now the Green Tulip–looking out on Fifth Avenue and
59th Street, where the hansom cabs are unique in New York, are
preferred positions, and breakfast, as Lucius Beebe wrote, "is
no nonsense of fruit juice and collie fodder out of a patent
package . . . it runs to grilled beef bones, kidney liver, vast soufflé
omelets, hot cakes." Similarly another ritual at the Plaza is Sunday

* See Index for recipe.

luncheon at the Oak Room. Although the menu fare bristles with good things such as Broiled Sole, Béarnaise, Breast of Chicken Supreme*, and Chicken Pot Pie Maison*, old Sunday patrons invariably order the famous Creamed Finnan Haddie à la Kitchen*, a Plaza specialty from the very beginning.

The passing scene was always vividly alive at the Plaza. Through wars and depressions, rising taxes, declining manners, from the opulence of a prosperous and singularly untroubled decade in history to the frenzy of the jet age, it has served as a lively indicator of our social history.

It has been the address of diplomats, artists, society and visiting royalty. Mrs. Oliver H. P. Belmont, leading a suffragette parade up Fifth Avenue, halted at the Pulitzer Fountain and dropped into the Palm Court for a refreshing cup of tea. Khrushchev was booed at the Plaza; General Eisenhower was cheered; Thomas Masaryk, first president of the Czechoslovakian Republic, after conferring in Washington with President Woodrow Wilson, was to see the first flag of the newly created Republic of Czechoslovakia fly from the Plaza flagpole on October 30, 1918; a King awaited the arrival of an Emperor in the Plaza lobby, as young King Hassan II of Morocco, in his long white robe, affectionately greeted the venerable Emperor Haile Selassie, come to visit him in his suite; Frank Lloyd Wright, who scorned almost all architecture but his own, allowed as how the Plaza was a lovely place, and lived there while he was planning the great Guggenheim Museum on Fifth Avenue. Coincidentally, much of the art displayed there was once housed at the Plaza, in the apartment occupied by the Guggenheims for years. Christian Dior decorated a suite that was named for him; the King of Siam and his beautiful Queen received in the Terrace Room, where an incredible sight was that of many former subjects and Thai students in this country proceeding on hands and knees to pay homage to them; Svetlana Alliluyeva, Stalin's daughter, presided at probably one of the largest press conferences ever held at the Plaza, following her escape to this country; author Ferenc Molnar, who lived at the hotel during the Second World War, declared, "After two decades of wandering . . . any time I come home to this mighty edifice I have a sense of quiet security and steadiness." One of the greatest private art collections of the world for years "lived" at the Plaza, when the late Chester Dale, hailed as one of the world's great collectors of French Impressionist and Post-Impressionist paintings, resided there. The majority of these art treasures now hang in the National Art Gallery in Washington; a smaller group was left to the Metropolitan Museum of Art.

President Betancourt of Venezuela shared a birthday party with the first president of the United States on February 22, 1963; Andrei Gromyko and the Russian delegation to the United Nations chose the Plaza as their headquarters before moving to a Park Avenue mansion. Admittedly it was stretching tolerance a bit when the internationally known portrait painter, Princess Parlaghy, who had done the portraits of Andrew Carnegie, Theodore Roosevelt and Henry Clay Frick, arrived with a blanket-wrapped lion cub in her arms. She rented a separate room to house her pet and ordered the finest meats from room service for Goldfleck, the beastie.

But nothing quite prepared the Plaza for the arrival of the Beatles on their first visit to the United States in 1964. In its innocence, the reservations department did not recognize the names of the four "businessmen" from London who cabled for rooms—Lennon, McCartney, Harrison and Starr. The press knew, however, and they reacted with a barrage of telephone calls. The sedate Plaza knew it was really in for it. Like a general going into battle, the Plaza mapped out a campaign worthy of military strategy to cope with the stay. When the most famous quartet in the world arrived, the Plaza was ready. Hysterical teen-agers were somehow kept at bay; service areas alerted so that regular guests would not be neglected; security measures enlarged and tightened. And as it had from the very beginning, in all emergencies, in all surprises, the Plaza emerged from the bedlam unscathed and only slightly bruised.

It is significant that in more than six decades of a vastly changing world, the Plaza has had but three owners. The New York Realty Company—whose Board of Directors include such notables as John "Bet-a-Million" Gates; Ben Beineke, a German immigrant who amassed millions and whose descendants control, among other projects, the Sperry-Hutchinson Green Stamps thing; international financier Harry St. F. Black; Vincent Starrett;

Casimir Stralem–were the builders and first owners of the Plaza. It stands on the site of an earlier, smaller Plaza, which in turn occupied land originally a skating pond, where Mrs. William Astor and her "400" indulged in winter sports.

Henry Hardenbergh, one of the leading architects of his day, who also designed the famed Willard Hotel in Washington, was the architect who executed a blueprint dream of an eighteen-story Renaissance structure done in the graceful style of an oversized French château. Fred Sterry, its first manager, with his great sense of perfection in all phases of operation, set the fine tone that has been maintained in traditional good taste and service right up to the present by vice-president and general manager, Arthur Dooley.

Conrad Hilton bought the hotel in 1943; ten years later he sold it to another prominent hotel man, the late A. M. Sonnabend. By the terms of the sale he was given a lease that extended to 1960, when it was taken over by the Hotel Corporation of America, as it was then known (it now has a new corporate name, Sonesta Corporation). Many honors and accolades have been bestowed upon the Plaza since the old *New York World*, reporting the opening of New York's newest luxury hotel on October 2, 1907, headlined its story: "The Greatest Hotel in the World."

Six decades later the Plaza was again described as the world's outstanding hostelry by *Esquire* magazine, in a six-page illustrated feature of the 1967 Christmas issue titled "The Three Greatest Hotels in the World." The Gritti Palace in Venice placed second, with the Mauna Kea Hotel in Hawaii, built by Laurance Rockefeller, ranking third. Travel Editor Richard Joseph, who had roved the world in search of his choice, wrote that the Plaza was selected for the No. 1 distinction "because it remains an island of continental elegance . . . retains the leisured pace of the turn of the Century in the midst of the Frenzied Sixties . . . because it has maintained its opulence and elegance . . . and kept up its rare standard of service."

The noble Plaza again qualified for special distinction when it was officially designated a New York Landmark by the New York Landmark Commission on December 17, 1969.

A bulwark of tradition, a place of nostalgia for generations of
New Yorkers, a legend in its time, the Plaza has managed to span
a fantastic arc in our history with superb skill, still a symbol
of elegance and good taste in a world gone vulgar and confused.

CHAPTER FOUR

WHAT'S IN A NAME?

The day Lemuel Benedict got up with a hangover proved a lucky day for gastronomy. The year was 1894, the place was the fashionable old Waldorf on New York's Fifth Avenue. To Lemuel, a young man-about-town, it was a real "morning-after." He entered the dining room and surveyed the menu gloomily. Then he brightened.

"I will have," he told the waiter, "a hooker of Hollandaise sauce, two poached eggs, buttered toast and crisp bacon . . . the eggs on top of the toast, then the bacon, then the Hollandaise."

This unorthodox concoction cheered him immensely and also impressed the maître d'hôtel, who forthwith named the dish Eggs Benedict.

Since then it has been improved upon, and the Plaza prides itself on serving as good Eggs Benedict as can be had anywhere. Instead of bacon, there is a thin slice of broiled ham; instead of ordinary toast, two halves of browned English muffins.

People with and without hangovers have been ordering Eggs Benedict ever since, and skilled home cooks have mastered the secret of the perfectly poached eggs and the perfectly blended Hollandaise along with the muffin toasted to the perfectly right state of crisp-outside-tender-inside doneness.

Proper poaching of eggs is a fine art. Several Plaza guests had pet ways of eating them. Poached Eggs Doolittle, named for the redoubtable Jimmy who executed World War II's daring raid over Tokyo, is an unusual combination, served on a base of deviled eggplant with Sauce Italienne. Poached Eggs Walsh, named for that vivacious long-time Plaza tenant Clara Bell Walsh, combines the eggs with deviled tongue and Sauce Remick, served au gratin.

One Plaza chef, the famed Lattard, even named a dish for himself. Roast Beef Salad Lattard is a taste-tempting mixture of diced beef, watercress, olives and potatoes with a dressing spiced by a dash of Worcestershire, chile, mustard with oil and vinegar. The chic wife of the influential publisher of *Vogue* magazine, "Chessy" Patcévitch, became so devoted to the Plaza's version of lamb curry that it appeared on the menu as Curry of Lamb, Chessy.

Sea Bass Duveen was so christened for the wife of Sir Joseph Duveen, one of the great art connoisseurs of all time. The Duveens, who lived at the Plaza, were appreciators of fine food as well as fine paintings. And they found American seafood unsurpassed in quality, especially as served by the experts of the Plaza, who hand-pick the best of the catch at Fulton Fish Market and have a near-monopoly on the stone crab and lobster flown in on order, the choice clams and oysters, the delicate fresh-water salmon.

The same Benedict who gave his name to a truly international dish also fancied himself a gourmet and loved to tell tales of the Broadway lobster palaces of the early 1900's and of Sunday luncheons when he entertained in his own Manhattan town house such food fanciers as Caruso and the bosomy Schumann-Heink. But his favorite story was of Joseph, renowned private chef in the ménage of W. K. Vanderbilt, who claimed that before he cooked terrapin he put them in a cheerful state of mind by reading them the morning newspaper! Joseph might have hesitated to treat his terrapin to today's headlines.

Nights on the town were not the problem of a certain British nobleman. What he wanted was to keep on gambling at lunchtime and still not go hungry. So he had his favorite meat encased between two slices of bread. This was not really a new idea, since women had been using the same device in one form or another ever since the first bread was baked in primitive outdoor ovens. "Journey Bread" was taken on trips to provide quick, easy nourishment. But it took the Earl of Sandwich to give the world a new food name. Generations of mothers, packing school lunches,

owe the Earl a debt of gratitude. And where would the modern
American city be, from noon until 2 P.M., without the millions
of sandwiches that satisfy millions of rush-hour appetites. The
familiar lunchtime lingo of the short-order lunch counter–
"B. T., Mayo, to travel" (bacon, tomato and mayonnaise)–is a
far cry from the gaming table in the Earl's manor house. And
it is a far cry, too, from the beautifully structured edifices of crisp
toast, garnished and pinned together with frilled toothpicks,
that go by the name of sandwich at the Plaza.

One world-famous dish became the darling of ladies' committees,
meetings and garden club groups because it was so easy to make
in quantity, to keep respectably warm and to serve quickly.
This dish, Chicken à la King, saturated the banquet circuit,
appeared usually in patty shells at every other club luncheon
and became the despair of every politician or lecturer who toured
the United States.

Yet Chicken à la King was not named for a king at all. Nobody
seems quite sure how it did get its name or where it was first
served. Some believe the first Chicken à la King was really
named Chicken à la Keene in honor of the socialite-sportsman J.
R. Keene, who suggested the concoction to the chef at Claridge's
in London in 1881. Another holds out for his son as the creator.
Foxhall Keene (for whom his father named a thoroughbred which
won the Grand Prix in Paris) is credited with making the first
Chicken à la Keene in Delmonico's restaurant in New York. Then
up pops Chef George Greenawald, of the old Brighton Beach
Hotel near Coney Island. He had been experimenting in his
kitchen and he rather fancied the result: a rich sauce made of
cream, shredded green pepper, mushrooms, onion juice and a dash
of paprika. The hotel's owner, E. Clark King, was in the breeze-
swept dining room with his wife when a waiter approached and
asked them to sample the chef's new creation. They were so
pleased that they asked for a second helping. The next day the
menu had a new feature, Chicken à la King.

Plaza chefs have always had a way with Chicken à la King, a
special fillip of flavor which is their secret and which keeps this
classic of Victorian days a popular menu feature.

35

Because Charles Delmonico, restaurateur par excellence, got mad at a sea captain, one of America's favorite dishes and one in which Plaza chefs take special pride, is known as Lobster Newburgh.

The sea-going gourmet, Ben Wenberg, entered the famous New York café on Madison Street in downtown New York, fresh from Paris and brimming with enthusiasm over a new way to prepare lobster. At Captain Wenberg's request, Mr. Delmonico had wheeled to his table a chafing dish warmed by a spirit lamp, a freshly boiled lobster, butter, cream and various other ingredients. He stood by while the captain stirred up a delectable-looking combination of lobster and creamy sauce. Then he sampled it, gave it his smiling approval and ordered it added to the menu as Lobster Wenberg. Not long after that the two friends had a falling out, and Mr. Delmonico, in a fit of pique, reversed the spelling and gave to the world the new culinary delight, Lobster Newberg, now spelled Newburgh.

Baked Alaska was a great fad in the early 1900's, and the hostess who could produce this miracle of "baked" ice cream was envied. Why didn't the ice cream melt in the oven? Who had dreamed up this fantasy? The idea of encasing ice cream in a meringue coating is supposed to have originated with Thomas Jefferson. At any rate there are reports of a dessert served in the White House in 1802 in which "ice cream, very good" was in a "crust wholly dried, crumbled into thin flakes."

More amusing is the legend that Baked Alaska was originated by a scientist, Ben Thompson, who left the United States for England and became Count Mumford. He claims to have been experimenting with the resistance of beaten egg whites to heat when the idea occurred to him of covering ice cream with a meringue and testing his theory by browning the dessert in the oven. Because it was cold inside, hot outside, it was known as Alaska-Florida. By the time it reached New York's fine restaurants, it was the darling of the dessert menu and was listed as Baked Alaska.

Thomas Jefferson, who fancied gourmet cooking and also raised his own vegetables so that he might have the newest and most tender of spring peas, the tiniest of new potatoes and the like, amused himself by giving his steward, Etienne Lemaire, a recipe for Pannequaiques. Pronounced phonetically, of course, it comes out pancakes, and Jefferson liked his thin and small in the French fashion of crêpes.

Almost every woman in diet-conscious America is Melba toast conscious. It is far more popular now than when it was originated at an English country house by no less a personage than Escoffier himself. He was visiting the famed Ritz family on a summer day in 1897. Mme Ritz, presiding over the tea urn in the garden, wondered why toast could never be produced as crisp and thin as she would like. Escoffier and M. Ritz got into a discussion and decided the toast could be sliced through and retoasted. Escoffier did just that. He experimented and emerged with a plate of thin, crisp, curling wafers. He christened the new dish "Toast Marie," in honor of his hostess. Later, when Nellie Melba was staying at the Carlton in London, she confessed that she was trying desperately to lose a few pounds. The chef promptly produced Toast Marie and rechristened it Toast Melba.

Welsh Rarebit is pronounced *rabbit* and, according to experts in the history of cooking, that is the way it should be spelled, for it originated in Wales and was intended to distract the guests of a Welsh nobleman from realizing that the kitchen had run out of game. The ingenious chef invented this rich cheese dish and gave it a rabbit's name!

Welsh Rabbit became a real food fad in the United States when the chafing dish became popular. It was the "in" thing to make when a young woman and her escort arrived home after the theatre or a ball at an hour when no servants were around. The chafing dish and the easy recipe allowed her to turn cook in the drawing room without disturbing a curl or a ruffle.

Food fads have always intrigued (or harassed, as was sometimes the case) the American people. Salisbury steak, still popular in both restaurants and homes, was originally intended by its inventor, Dr. J. H. Salisbury, as a remedy for colitis, pernicious anemia, bronchitis, gout, even tuberculosis!

Oysters Rockefeller is a dish inadvertently named for old John D. A gentleman who dined often at the famed Antoine's in New Orleans says the concoction of oysters so delicately seasoned and oven-browned in their shells was really invented by M. Antoine Alciatore, but got its name when a guest tasted it and exclaimed, "This is wonderful–as rich as Rockefeller."

No cocktail party is complete without potato chips. They go with picnics, too, and beer and casual drinks at bars. Yet until the 1890's they were unknown. Some time in that gilded era, when Saratoga Springs was the mecca for those seeking the beneficial waters and the excitement of the gambling houses and race track, Moon's Lake House was a rendezvous for gourmets and gamblers alike and boasted a regal cuisine. George Crum, who presided over the kitchen, tried to please a diner who complained that the French fried potatoes were too thick and too soft. He sliced a batch tissue thin, popped them into boiling fat and *voilà*– Saratoga chips were born.

It is difficult to believe that with uncounted generations of fine French cooks, a classic such as vichyssoise should have originated in New York City. Yet Chef Louis Diat did serve it at the Ritz Carlton in 1910 and did explain that it was a refined version of a peasant leek and potato soup his mother served back home. Diat experimented with flavor and texture and served this gourmet soup for the first time to steel magnate Charles Schwab. In the Ritz Carlton version it was hot, but before long it had evolved into the chilled summer soup that has delighted Americans ever since.

In an excess of patriotism and at a time when Vichy was not a name to be proud of, the Plaza's French chef changed the name of this classic soup to DeGaulloise. It appeared that way on the menu until the end of World War II and Le Grand Charles' triumphant return to Paris. Some older Plaza guests smiled reminiscently, recalling the fervor of World War I when sauerkraut became victory cabbage!

Another spectacular creation, Crêpes Suzette, has not only survived the years but is a triumphant success in the American kitchen. The gifted chef and restaurateur Charpentier made Crêpes

Suzette almost a trademark of his cuisine, but its originator is believed to be Escoffier. It is said that the master, noting Edward VII, then Prince of Wales, dining one night at the Carlton in London with a lovely lady, brought in a dessert he had just created . . . paper-thin pancakes in a chafing dish, flamed with brandy as they were served. The Prince was charmed and asked the name of the new dish. Escoffier said it had no name as yet, and His Royal Highness, with a smile, suggested it be named Suzette for his companion. The mysterious Suzette's identity is lost to history, but she lives on in flaming brandied splendor as a pet dessert for special occasions.

Chicken Marengo, one of the few dishes ever named for a battle, has graduated to many standard cookbooks. Plaza chefs have always known how to give it a special fillip, perhaps with a sprinkle of marjoram, perhaps with a single slice of tomato. That is their secret. But at any rate, it is an easy casserole dish to prepare ahead of time, as was done on the battlefield at Marengo where Napoleon scored a great victory and celebrated by having his favorite chicken, shrimp, mushroom, carrot and celery dish served up as a concoction for breakfast.

On one historic occasion a handsome maître d'hôtel named Paul Boiardi invaded the chef's domain, the sacrosanct Plaza kitchen, with spectacular results. Paul had been attending the wants of Plaza tenants Mr. and Mrs. John Hartford in the Persian Room. He watched with concern one night as Mr. Hartford scanned the elaborate menu. Then he heard him murmur to his wife that what he really would like was a dish of good spaghetti. Paul offered to make it, explaining that he had a superb recipe, originated by his brother Hector, who had opened a small restaurant in Cleveland. Paul was as good as his word, and the spaghetti was even better. Before the end of the meal, Mr. Hartford had heard the story of the Brothers Boiardi and how they dreamed of some day producing their fine Italian specialties in quantity and selling them to supermarkets.

The Hartfords were none other than the A & P family, whose vast chain of food stores had grown from the small shop started by George Huntington Hartford on Vesey Street in New York. Paul Boiardi could scarcely have chosen a more likely "fan" for

39

his bowl of spaghetti, or a more sympathetic listener to the tale of two ambitious brothers from Italy. Mr. Hartford saw to it that their products were introduced into the A & P chain. They, in turn, labeled their brand name phonetically, and Chef Boy-Ar-Dee became a byword in supermarkets and a $6 million success story.

CHAPTER FIVE

EAT, DRINK AND BE MERRY

It is difficult for hostesses today in the large cities where the leading hotels are looked upon as the natural arenas in which to give dinners, dances, luncheons, banquets, benefit balls, coming-out parties, wedding receptions or whatever occasion of a gala nature to realize that seventy years ago ladies and gentlemen seldom entertained in public–in hotels, that is.

By 1900 New York, with the largest hotel population of any city in the world, was continuing to build hotels with lavish new features and innovations. The structure of fashionable life was undergoing a drastic change as the ranks of society were augmented by a never-ending army of rich and successful merchants, miners, bankers, railroaders and magnates in oil, copper and steel who, after migrating to New York, created a need for more and more hotels in which people like unto themselves might live lavishly and entertain handsomely.

A distinctive feature of the new hotels springing up in high-structured luxury was their large ballrooms and other function rooms. Feminine society took the stylish new caravansaries to their gem-bedecked bosoms and tentatively spread their hostess wings, but not until the opening of the Plaza in 1907 did society of the Edwardian era embrace, en masse, the custom of giving large dinners and dances in a hotel. As the century progressed, town houses slowly but surely began making way for apartment living in smaller quarters. Dowagers dismantled their ballrooms and music rooms and scrapped their little gilded chairs. Their daughters and granddaughters were now coming out in hotel ballrooms; wedding receptions followed the trend; it was much jollier to give a dinner party in a hotel than at home. And as society went, so went the rest of the feminine populace.

Few of the new luxury hotels built in the early 1900's could match the Plaza in the number of function rooms or in the grandeur of its first ballroom, ringed by a balcony on all sides, one section of which could be hydraulically lowered to create a stage for the private theatricals, musical mornings, and the tableaux vivants that had become the vogue.

In this ballroom the George J. Goulds gave a ball in January, 1909, to introduce their daughter Marjorie, an event of such magnificence that it still ranks as one of the most lavish debutante parties in the history of the Plaza, a setting to this day of the town's outstanding coming-out parties. Over 5,000 orchids were used in the decor, and guests as they arrived passed through a long line of liveried footmen. Favors for the men were gold pocket knives, cigar cutters and key rings; for the ladies there were, among other things, gold-bangled bracelets in dainty gold boxes, stamped with Miss Gould's monograms and the date of the party.

A new ballroom in the new wing, added to the Plaza in 1921, replaced the first but matched it in beauty and elegance. It was christened in great social style with the coming-out party given by Mr. and Mrs. Payne Whitney for their daughter Joan, who in later years, as Mrs. Charles S. Payson, was to be the angel of the New York Mets baseball team.

From the very beginning the Plaza did things in style. And from the very beginning the comings and goings and social activities of Plaza guests have been the stuff of which news and romance were made.

The first great public function was a dinner on October 15, 1907, two weeks after the opening, given by The Pilgrims in America for the Rt. Rev. Arthur Foley Winnington Ingram, Lord Bishop of London. Four hundred people sat down to table in the Grand Ballroom, with President Nicholas Murray Butler of Columbia University proposing the toast, and Chauncey M. Depew adding sparkling wit to the occasion.

Fifty years later at a ball commemorating the golden anniversary of the Plaza, the guests were served a dinner that duplicated as nearly as possible the one prepared for the Pilgrims' dinner. Following is the menu for that first banquet, in the original French, and also in English translation:

PILGRIMS' DINNER

French menu	English translation
Buffet à la Russe et Hors d'Oeuvres Variés	Buffet with Hot and Cold Hors d'Oeuvres
Huîtres au Raifort	Oysters with Horseradish Sauce
Aspic de Homard en Bellevue	Lobster Aspic, Bellevue
Feuilles Farciés	Stuffed Grape Leaves
Tortue Verte Oloroso	Green Turtle Soup
Crème à la DuBarry	Cream of Cauliflower Soup
Radis Olives Amandes Salées	Radishes Olives Salted Almonds
Filet de Bar Raye à l'Amiral	Striped Bass, Admiral
Suprème de Poulet, à la Plaza	Suprème of Chicken, Plaza
Pommes de Terre Surprises	Potatoes Surprise
Bouquets de Chouxfleur	Little Bouquets of Cauliflower
Terrapin à la Baltimore	Terrapin, Baltimore
Pluvier Rôti sur Canapé	Roast Plover on Canapés
Salade Rachel	Salad Rachel (Artichokes on Romaine)
Sorbet à la Fine Champagne	Sherbet with Brandy
Glacé Moscovite	Ice Cream Bombe
Petits Fours	Petits Fours
Bonbons Fruits Café	Bonbons Fruits Coffee

Probably the most elaborate private dinner given at the Plaza, and possibly anywhere else, was in January, 1909. The host was Frederick Townsend Martin, brother of the Bradley Martin who had to flee the country because of public outcry over an outrageously extravagant costume ball he had given at the old Waldorf Astoria. Frederick Martin, like his brother, was a great party-thrower. When he learned that Lady Paget—a leading London hostess whose dinners for King Edward VII and Queen Alexandra had set a high mark for such functions in Europe—was coming to visit New York, he brought all his entertainment skill to play to arrange a party in her honor that would outdo anything Her Ladyship had given. The result was as spectacular a culinary feast as had ever been given in an age when the spectacular and the extravagant were the rule rather than the exception.

The fifty guests even ate the centerpiece, not because there were not enough Noisettes d'Agneau de lait to go around, or because they were shy on Bouchee d'Epinards, but because the enormous circular table in the Grand Ballroom (100 feet in circumference) was overflowing with the choicest fruits that could be brought to 59th Street and Fifth Avenue. Guests approached the ballroom under arches of azaleas, japonica and smilax. Dominating the table was a tall cherry tree in full bloom, its blossoming branches the result of a four-day forcing process. Two massive crystal chandeliers shed softened light on an enormous cornucopia spilling apples from the Hood River ranch in Oregon; peaches from the groves of South Africa; bananas from the West Indies; Malaga grapes from Spain; Indian River pineapple from Florida; tangerines, kumquats and grapefruit from the Halifax River in Florida; pears from Southern California; and huge strawberries, specially cultivated, from South Carolina.

When the guests had had their fill of an elaborate menu plus the fruit they were invited to eat, with wines accompanying each course, they had another surprise in store. Harry T. Burleigh, a Negro who had appeared before King Edward VII, was present to sing and was heartily applauded by such as Mrs. Cornelius Vanderbilt, Mr. and Mrs. John R. Drexel, Mr. and Mrs. George J. Gould, Mrs. William K. Vanderbilt, Mrs. Lewis Cass Ledyard, Mr. and Mrs. James Speyer, Mr. and Mrs. Arthur Iselin, Foxhall Keene and the other bon tons who made up the half-hundred guests.

Nearly sixty years later–in December, 1966–Author Truman Capote's exotic Black and White Masked Ball was one of the most fantastic events ever held at the Plaza. The guests were an international "Who's Who" of notables from all over the world. Most were New Yorkers, but others had arrived in relays from Paris, Rome, Washington, London, San Francisco, Hollywood: diplomats, politicans, scientists, painters, writers, composers, actors, producers, financial tycoons, dress designers and, of course, society. They made up the more than 500 guests asked to come attired in black or white, and to wear masks. The advance publicity fired public curiosity–particularly the printed names of the "greats" who were to attend. As the guests arrived they had to push their way through a mob of rubberneckers jamming the lobbies of the hotel.

The New York Times, on the day following, headlined the ball "The Most Exquisite of Spectator Sports." That it was. Further describing "The Ball of the Century," the *Times* quoted Capote as declaring, "I wanted it at the Plaza, because I think it is the only beautiful ballroom left in the United States."

No attempt was made to decorate the beautiful gold and white room. The guests, in their exotic masks, provided the most colorful decor. As for the supper menu, it was probably the simplest ever served in the Grand Ballroom, where great culinary feasts are an everyday affair:

CHICKEN HASH, PLAZA,* *well flavored with sherry*

SCRAMBLED EGGS, COUNTRY STYLE,
BACON

SPAGHETTI AU BEURRE,
SAUCE BOLOGNAISE

ASSORTMENT OF FRENCH ROLLS AND BREAD

SMALL DANISH PASTRIES*

DEMI TASSE

MILK

But, as they say, Champagne flowed.

45

The Plaza Ballroom was also the setting for the historic wedding reception of President Nixon's daughter Julie and President Eisenhower's grandson, David Eisenhower, on December 22, 1968. Five hundred guests were seated at round tables covered with pink tablecloths, crisscrossed with wide bands of apple-green satin; the centerpiece was a wreath of Christmas holly surrounding a big fat pink candle.

The buffet was served from a number of elegantly arranged crescent tables. The menu of hot foods consisted of:

STANDING ROAST OF BEEF, *served on tiny tartines (carved by the chef himself)*

CASSEROLE OF SEA-FOOD À L'AMÉRICAIN

PILAFF OF RICE

QUICHE LORRAINE*

SWEDISH MEATBALLS IN CURRY SAUCE*

OYSTERS PROVENÇALE*

TINY FRANKFURTERS ON PICKS

CRABMEAT REMICK*

And there was a cold buffet:
CORNETS OF PROSCIUTTO HAM WITH MELON BALLS

CELERY STUFFED WITH ROQUEFORT

CROUSTADE OF FOIE GRAS*

CORNETS OF NOVA SCOTIA SALMON

DEVILED EGGS

TINY BISMARCK HERRING ON RYE

ROULADE OF DANISH HAM WITH CREAM CHEESE*
PUMPERNICKEL

DAINTY FINGER SANDWICHES

SELECTION OF PETITS FOURS   DEMI TASSE

46

At a side table towered the wedding cake, a six-tier, five-foot creation by Plaza pastry chefs Joseph Lancianti and Joseph Tarantino.
It weighed 500 pounds, and each tier was decorated with sugar
roses, lilies and lilies of the valley, alternating with hearts and bells.
Between the fifth and sixth tiers was a set of columns entwined
with pale green vines and white rosebuds made of spun sugar.

Between the layers was a lemon filling, and the top layer was
decorated not with the customary candied bride and groom, but
a tiny bouquet of fresh bouvardia in a small rose.

At the request of feminine members of the press, Chef André
reduced the recipe to make two nine-inch layers, two to three
inches high. Prospective brides who want to duplicate the wedding
cake of a President's daughter will find the recipe on page 298.

In 1964 Britain celebrated the 400th anniversary of Shakespeare's
birthday, and all England went Elizabethan. A highlight event
for London was partying in the Elizabethan Room of the Gore
Hotel, which had been transformed into a veritable museum
of Elizabethan life and customs during coronation week for
Queen Elizabeth II. The hotel has since become one of the
landmarks of the city.

The Elizabethan Room of the Gore Hotel came to the Plaza in the
spring of 1964, when the British Travel Bureau gave the first
of a series of Shakespeare parties in this country. In Elizabethan
days, feasting began with the boar's head. Wenches, as the
waitresses were called, would come into the great dining halls
singing and each bearing a feast food. And so they came into
Plaza 9, dressed in 16th-century service costumes, carrying a
boar's head, a peacock, "lamb in a coffin," and other Elizabethan
fare, prepared from authentic recipes supplied to Chef André,
and served buffet with lute music and appropriate ceremony.

This mighty fare was washed down with draughts of mead, one
of the oldest drinks in the world, made from honey and spices.
The ancient Goths considered it an aphrodisiac, and it was
the custom for brides and grooms to sip it for a month after
marriage—hence the word "honeymoon."

47

THE MENU

Stuffed Boar's Head

Royal Sturgeon

Salamugundi Salad

Good King Henry

Lamb in a Coffin

Champ

Syllabub

Artichoke Pye

This menu is hardly one the average housewife could prepare; certainly not stuffed boar's head. But here are some recipes for the adventurous hostess wishing to give a Shakespearean buffet at home.

 ## GOOD KING HENRY

2 pounds fresh spinach, OR *2 packages (10 ounces each) frozen spinach*

2 tablespoons butter

⅛ teaspoon each ground nutmeg and cloves

Small clove garlic

1 teaspoon salt

Freshly ground black pepper

Makes 6 servings

Wash spinach, drain well. Melt butter in large pan, add spices, garlic crushed with salt, and spinach. Stir spinach in butter, cover and cook over moderate heat about 5 minutes. Stir, then cook quickly, uncovered, for about 3 minutes more. Taste for seasoning, add freshly ground black pepper and more spices if wished. Serve piping hot. Good King Henry can also be served chilled, in which case olive oil may be substituted for butter; drain off liquid before serving.

SALAMUGUNDI SALAD

2½ pound roasted chicken

4 lemons, peeled

5 large dill pickles

2 cups sorrel

2 cups fresh spinach

1⅓ cups grated fresh horseradish

1 cup raw cranberries, chopped

4 hard-cooked egg yolks, chopped

4 ounces anchovies

Makes 10 servings

Remove chicken meat from bones and cut into julienne strips. Cut lemons, pickles, sorrel and spinach into julienne strips. Combine all ingredients except anchovies. Toss lightly to mix. Add ½ cup salad dressing (recipe follows). Toss. Add another ½ cup dressing, tossing well. Place anchovies on top of salad. Serve with extra dressing.

SALAD DRESSING

2 teaspoons English mustard

¼ cup water

Juice of 6 lemons

1 teaspoon salt

¼ teaspoon pepper

1½ cups olive oil

Makes 2 cups

Combine mustard and water; mix well. Stir in lemon juice and seasonings. Gradually beat in the oil.

"LAMB IN A COFFIN"

Saddle of lamb

Chopped veal

Chopped pistachio nuts

Bread crumbs

Mixed spices

Salt and pepper

*Large quantity of Short Pastry**

Skin should be preserved on the saddle of lamb. Make a stuffing of the veal, pistachio nuts, bread crumbs, mixed spices, salt and pepper. Stuff lamb and roast slowly until nearly done, allow to cool. Encase in short pastry, à la Wellington. Bake until pastry is nicely browned (at medium heat) and allow to cool, then cut in thick slices.

CHAMP

1½ pounds potatoes, peeled

Boiling water, salted

1 cup frozen green peas

¾ cup milk

2 tablespoons butter OR *margarine*

½ teaspoon salt

⅛ teaspoon black pepper

1 small onion, minced

½ cup dairy sour cream

Makes 6 servings

Cook potatoes in boiling, salted water until tender; drain. Meanwhile, cook peas in milk until tender; drain, and add hot milk to potatoes along with the butter and seasonings. Mash potatoes, beating until light and fluffy. Stir in peas and remaining ingredients.

One of the most novel functions at the Plaza was the Bullwinkle Picnic in the Grand Ballroom—a picnic minus the ants. The entire meal, except for the dessert, was served à la box luncheon, in cartons wheeled into the ballroom on stainless steel wagons. Each guest received a box, the top of which was imprinted with the contents, which were as follows:

SMOKED LOIN OF PORK*

DEVILED DISJOINTED CHICKEN*

PORK SAUSAGES

ROAST DUCK

ASSORTED COLD CUTS, *including Pâté Maison**

HARD-BOILED EGG

WHOLE TOMATO

ELBOW MACARONI SALAD

GRUYÈRE CHEESE

ASSORTED FRESH FRUITS

ONE SEEDED BUTTERED ROLL

SMALL SALT AND PEPPER SHAKERS

Dessert, served by the waiters, was vanilla ice cream in the shape of Bullwinkle's horns, topped with Brandied Strawberries Jubilee*. In tune with the al fresco nature of the party, a Good Humor Man made the rounds with his own particular commodity.

At cocktail hour preceding dinner, the hors d'oeuvres were Moose-Burgers Flambé, Hot Moose Dogs and Bull Shrimp. Libations were poured from two large kegs of beer, and Martinis were served from barrels set up in the foyer.

It was all in honor of the first anniversary of Bullwinkle the Moose, the TV brainchild of Jay Ward Productions.

51

Chef André invented a new kind of committee meeting in
cooperation with the committee for the Feather Ball, to benefit
JOB (Just One Break) for the handicapped. It was in reality a
"tasting party" in his kitchen, with the ladies meeting to select
the menu for the elaborate buffet to be served at the Ball in
the Grand Ballroom. After sampling this and that and the other,
the group settled upon the following menu:

HOT   SCALLOPED CHICKEN BREASTS, WITH ALMONDS*
       ORANGE AND LEMON MARMALADE

       CURRY OF LAMB, CHESSY* (named for one of the committee)
       SESAME NOODLES, CHUTNEY, SHREDDED FRESH COCONUT

       HOT GLAZED AND DECORATED CORNED BEEF*
       KUMQUATS, DRIED APRICOTS, PRUNES

       HOT POPOVERS AND ORANGE SODA BISCUITS

COLD   STRIPED BASS EN GELÉE*
       SQUEEZED CUCUMBER, IN SAVORY CABBAGE,
       SAUCE VERTE

       INDIVIDUAL HEARTS OF BIBB LETTUCE WITH WATERCRESS
       LEMON DRESSING MIMOSA

       SALAD PARISIENNE

       LARGE BOARDS OF BRIE, GOURMANDISE, GRUYÈRE, GRAPPE
       CHEESE, THIN RYE BREAD, THIN BLACK PUMPERNICKEL,
       FRENCH BREAD

       ASSORTED FRESH FRUITS

       BOMBE GLACÉ ANDRÉ*

       CHEESE CAKES

       FRESH CANDIED STRAWBERRIES ON STEMS IN PAPER HOLDERS

       CHOCOLATE MINTS   DEMI TASSE

On the occasion of the first state visit of His Majesty Hassan II of Morocco to this country in 1963, he was accompanied by an entourage that required an entire floor at the Plaza, sixty rooms in all. The majority of his retinue took their meals in a separate dining room set up on the floor, and because of the special dietary habits of the Moroccans, a part of the Plaza kitchen was set aside for the cooks the party brought with them, who would prepare their native cuisine. Special attention was given to their wants; orders of goat's milk, goat's cheese, figs, and so on were purchased, and the Plaza food-handlers, catering department and room service were briefed for the specific needs of the Moroccans.

Morocco's national dish is cous-cous, a hearty, tasty concoction of meat, vegetables and seminola meal. It is not simple or quick to prepare as the native cooks do, but a relatively simple version, as prepared in the Plaza kitchen, can be found on page 192.

Poultry is a popular ingredient for Moroccan tajine.
They also like to do shad cooked with stuffed dates. Kabob is another popular native dish.

The King, of course, was the honored guest at a number of private and official functions, where Continental cuisine was served. The menu for a reception and luncheon in the Persian Room follows:

BOULA BOULA GRATINÉ*

MOUSSE OF TURBOT,*
SAUCE CARDINALE

        GOURMANDISE CHEESE

CHÂTEAUBRIAND,*
SAUCE BÉARNAISE   NORWEGIAN FLAT BREAD

WHITE ASPARAGUS   FROZEN SOUFFLÉ FRAMBOISE*
                 SAUCE FRAMBOISE*

ANNA POTATOS À CRU*

        MIGNARDISES

KENTUCKY BIBB LETTUCE

        DEMI TASSE

The highlight of a reception in the Grand Ballroom, given by the
Permanent Mission of Morocco to the United States for some
400 guests, was the five whole roasted baby lambs, carved at
the table. This was part of an elaborate buffet, which consisted of:

HOT   EMINCÉE OF FILLET OF BEEF STROGANOFF

         EMINCÉE OF CHICKEN MEXICAINE

         WHOLE ROASTED BABY LAMB

         CURRY OF LAMB, CHUTNEY, PILAFF OF RICE*

COLD   WHOLE TURKEYS

         SLICED BEEF TONGUE

         VEGETABLE SALAD IN ASPIC

         STRINGBEAN SALAD

         WHOLE KENNEBEC SALMON EN BELLEVUE

         ASSORTED TARTINES–ROLLS

         TRAYS OF ASSORTED CHEESES

         CRACKERS, FRENCH BREAD

         FRENCH AND VIENNESE PASTRIES*

         MACÉDOINE OF FRESH FRUIT

The Lion in Winter had a fabulous supper party in the Plaza's
Grand Ballroom. Five hundred guests, arriving after the premiere
of the movie, gasped as they found themselves transported into
another age. The entire ballroom had been transformed into a
setting reflecting the period of the prize-winning movie. Mrs.
Joseph E. Levine, wife of the producer, had labored for days to
create a great medieval hall, using the actual sets from the

picture. All the furniture–most of it especially made, some of it found in English antique galleries–had been shipped over from England. Guests entered the ballroom via a simulated moat, and dined at great oak tables unadorned of tablecloths but polished to a gleam. Each table held a whole round large French bread and crocks of butter.

THE MENU

DARNE OF KENNEBEC SALMON ON LETTUCE BED
SAUCE VERTE

DOUBLE-CUT SIRLOIN STEAKS, *presented on flaming chariots*

WHOLE LARGE MUSHROOMS WITH STEMS

HALF ACORN SQUASH IN SHELL*

WHOLE HEART OF BIBB LETTUCE
OIL AND LEMON DRESSING WITH CHOPPED CHIVES

WHOLE CHEDDAR FOR EACH TABLE,
presented on board with cheese knife

CHRISTMAS PLUM PUDDING* *(one for each table), decorated with Christmas holly and one red candle*

GOLDEN RHUM SAUCE   DEMI TASSE

In dramatic contrast was a luncheon in the Grand Ballroom given in honor of Her Royal Highness Princess Alexandra and her husband, the Hon. Angus Ogilvy. They were in New York in October, 1967, on behalf of the British Chamber of Commerce. The simple menu:

HEARTS OF ARTICHOKE, VINAIGRETTE

ROAST LAMB   FRUITS IN SEASON

GREEN BEANS, NIÇOISE   ASSORTED CHEESES

POTATOES, BOULANGÈRE   COFFEE

Cocktail parties in profusion keep the Plaza catering department about as busy as with any other type of function–a press conference; a cocktail party to introduce a new book, launch a new fashion, follow a fashion show by Dior, honor a prospective bride and groom, honor a visiting celebrity; an office party, a farewell party–just name it and the Plaza can whip it up pronto.

There is no denying that the cocktail party has become a way of life in America–and at the Plaza they can prepare almost any type of native party, from the Italian with its antipasto to the Russian zakuskis, the French hors d'oeuvres, the Scandinavian smorgasbord. For the really big party there is usually a huge buffet table laden down with the prize products of the kitchen: from whole hams, turkeys and roast beef, down to the last sardine or deviled egg.

Early in 1964, months prior to the opening of the New York World's Fair, the Plaza, in conjunction with the New York Convention Bureau and Pan American Airways, was inspired to invite over 200 travel agents from all over the world to a special preview of the World's Fair. The group–representing such countries as India, Morocco, England, France, Japan, Italy, Spain, Portugal, Holland–were quartered at the Plaza. Among the many functions given for them was a cocktail party in the Terrace Room, where Chef André's culinary excellence came into full play.

Some 250 guests sampled such delicacies as the following:

COLD   CANAPÉS BISMARCK

          CORNETS OF PROSCIUTTO, À LA ANDRÉ

          SPLIT JUMBO SHRIMPS

          GENOA SALAMI

          STUFFED CORNETS OF NOVA SCOTIA SALMON

          LAKE STURGEON

          PÂTÉ DE FOIE GRAS STRASBOURG

HOT   BARQUETTES OF MAINE LOBSTER*

MILLEFEUILLES AU ROQUEFORT

SCAMPI FRA DIAVOLO*

OYSTERS PROVENÇALE*

CRABMEAT REMICK*

GLAZED CORNED BEEF*

MINIATURE QUICHE LORRAINE*

TINY HOT PIROJKIS*

MEAT BALLS IN CURRY SAUCE

PIGS IN A BLANKET

Probably the most publicized nontenant of the Plaza is Eloise, the incorrigible child whose portrait by Hilary Knight is as well known to a generation of mothers and a second generation of children as Lewis Carroll's Alice. Created by Kay Thompson, Eloise is the fictitious little hoyden whose sophisticated mother boards her in a Plaza suite with her English nanny while she skips from Palm Beach to Paris to Palm Springs to Acapulco. Eloise was into everything–crossing up elevator operators, calling Room Service to send up a raisin and seven spoons, cavorting with Weenie (the dog who looks like a cat), hunting for Skipperdee the turtle, and declaring "half the time I'm lost, but mostly I am on the first floor, because that's where the catering is."

A special Eloise Room was set up by the Plaza. Small fry from all over the country visit when Mummy and Daddy bring them to New York, and could order from a special Eloise Menu that featured:

KIDDIE KAR KOCKTAIL *(jumbo juice)*

SIRLOIN SUZIE-Q *(sizzling, special chopped sirloin hamburger)*

57

TURKEY-IN-THE-STRAW *(turkey hash à la Plaza)*

EGGS ELOISE *(a dainty omelette for tiny tots)*

TEENY WEENIES *(two delectable junior frankfurters)*

MARY-HAD-A-LITTLE-LAMB-CHOP *(you know what)*

SKIPPERDEE SANDWICH *(peanut butter and jelly)*

SMASHED POTATOES, FUNNY FRENCH FRIES, POPEYED BAKED POTATOES

PUNCH AND JUDY PEAS, SPACE SHIP SUCCOTASH, JACK & THE BEAN-STALK, JULIENNE

SUPERSONIC SHERBERT

RICE PUDDING MARY JANE*

A-TISKET-A-TASKET

TOOTY FRUITY

COPY CAT CAKE

MILK, MILK, MILK!

Needless to say, the young fry loved it and literally ate it up. And needless to say, the printed menus disappeared so fast that management had to keep ordering more.

The room is still there, the menu has grown up, and something new was added–an enchanting Eloise Ice Cream Parlor, all pink and white, with typical ice-cream parlor chairs and little marble-topped tables; a lovely niche situated in a cozy corner of the 58th Street lobby. A very likely spot to find Eloise and her friends.

HORS D'OEUVRES

ASPARAGUS VINAIGRETTE

BLINIS WITH CAVIAR AND SOUR CREAM

BARQUETTES OF CLAM

BARQUETTES OF MAINE LOBSTER

BHELPURIS

CHEESE ROUNDS

BRANDIED ROQUEFORT BALLS

CELERY STUFFED WITH RED CAVIAR

CELERY STUFFED WITH ROQUEFORT

CHAMPIGNONS A LA GRECQUE

MARINATED HERRING

MUSHROOMS IN SOUR CREAM

CLAM AND CHEESE APPETIZERS

DEVILS ON HORSEBACK

KEFTEDES

OYSTERS REMICK

PATE MAISON

CORNETS OF HAM WITH MELON

SAMOSAS

DEVILED EGGS

MUSHROOMS STUFFED WITH CLAMS

RUMAKI

PETITES QUICHES LORRAINE

SHRIMP REMOULADE

PLAZA PIZZA

OEUFS A LA ROYALE

ROULADE OF HAM AND CHEESE

PLAZA MARINATED HERRING

PIROJKI

FILLINGS FOR FINGER SANDWICHES

TERRINE FOIE GRAS

ENDIVE WITH HAM AND CHEESE

LEGUMES VARIES

ASPARAGUS VINAIGRETTE

2 pounds fresh asparagus

½ cup red wine vinegar

½ teaspoon mustard

1 clove garlic, crushed

1 teaspoon salt

⅛ teaspoon seasoned pepper

¾ cup olive oil

2 canned pimientos, diced

3 tablespoons finely chopped parsley

Makes 6 servings

Thoroughly wash the asparagus and snap off tough ends. Cook in boiling water until just tender, about 10 minutes. Drain and chill.

Combine the remaining ingredients and chill.

Serve the asparagus on individual plates with some of dressing spooned over. Serve remaining dressing separately to be added to taste.

Leeks prepared in the same way are different and delicious. E.B.

BLINIS WITH CAVIAR AND SOUR CREAM

¾ cup buckwheat flour

½ cup white flour

½ package active dry yeast

2 tablespoons warm water

1½ cups milk, heated

2 whole eggs

2 teaspoons sugar

½ teaspoon salt

4 teaspoons butter, melted

2 egg whites

Makes about 2½ dozen small cakes

Combine and sift the two flours. Measure ½ cup into a bowl.

Dissolve the yeast in the warm water, stir into ½ cup warm milk. Add this mixture to the flour in the bowl, and blend to a smooth creamy batter. Cover and let rise in a warm place for about 2 hours.

Beat the whole eggs with the sugar, salt and butter. Stir into the "sponge" (risen yeast mixture). Alternately beat in the remaining milk and the remaining flour. (Add the milk last as you may not need to use all of it.)

Whip the egg whites until stiff but still moist. Fold into the batter until all traces of egg white disappear.

Using 1 tablespoon batter for each cake, bake on a lightly greased hot griddle.

Serve at once with ice-cold caviar, melted butter and dairy sour cream.

BARQUETTES OF CLAM

1 can (8 ounces) Doxsee minced clams	Mix clams, seasonings and cream in a saucepan. Stir over low heat until hot.
½ teaspoon black pepper	Blend together egg yolk, cornstarch and Sherry, adding water if necessary to make a smooth paste. Stir this mixture into clams.
Salt to taste	
1 cup heavy cream	Continue to stir over low heat until mixture thickens.
1 egg yolk	Fill barquettes with mixture. Sprinkle with buttered crumbs or grated Parmesan cheese.
2 teaspoons cornstarch	
2-3 tablespoons Sherry	Brown under broiler and serve hot.
Barquettes (tiny boat-shaped pastry shells), baked	
Makes 3-4 dozen depending on size barquettes used	

BARQUETTES OF MAINE LOBSTER

2 tablespoons butter	Heat the butter in a small saucepan. Stir in shallot and parsley. Simmer for a minute or two.
1 shallot, minced	
1 tablespoon minced parsley	Add the lobster meat (shredded or chopped into very small pieces) and the wine. Simmer for a minute or two.
Meat of 1 cooked Maine lobster, shredded or chopped	
½ cup white wine	Season to taste with salt and pepper. Stir in the cornstarch dissolved in 2 tablespoons water.
Salt and pepper	Stir over low heat until slightly thickened and heated through.
1 teaspoon cornstarch	Fill barquettes with lobster mixture and sprinkle with buttered crumbs. Brown lightly under broiler and serve hot.
Barquettes (tiny boat-shaped pastry shells), baked	
Buttered crumbs	
Makes 3-4 dozen depending on size barquettes used	

BHELPURIS

½ cup all-purpose flour

½ cup rice flour

1 teaspoon salt

½ teaspoon black pepper

½ cup cold water (about)

Peanut oil for deep frying

Combine the dry ingredients and stir in water until dough forms a compact ball. If necessary, add more water a tablespoon at a time until dough reaches workable state.

Knead the dough on a floured board as you would bread dough. After 5 minutes or so the dough should be very elastic.

Pat the dough into a ball, wrap and let rest 30 minutes.

On a floured board roll out half the dough into a paper-thin sheet. Cut in 2-inch rounds.

Keep the cut rounds moist under a damp towel while you shape and reroll the scraps.

Repeat with remaining half of dough.

Deep fry the rounds in hot fat (375°) 2 minutes or until a deep golden brown.

Remove from fat with a slotted spoon and drain on paper towels.

Makes about 7-8 dozen chips

Serve with chutney, finely chopped onion and chopped fresh coriander.

CHEESE ROUNDS

½ cup soft butter

1 cup grated sharp Cheddar cheese

1 cup all-purpose flour

¼ teaspoon salt

Pinch of cayenne pepper

Pinch of crushed fresh garlic OR *instant garlic*

Cream butter and cheese together until smooth. Stir in flour and seasonings. Mix until thoroughly blended.

Shape the mixture into small balls and place on an ungreased cookie sheet.

Bake in a moderate oven, 375°, about 12 minutes.

Makes about 2 dozen

BRANDIED ROQUEFORT BALLS

2 cups crumbled Roquefort cheese

¼ cup sweet butter

¼ teaspoon dry mustard

3 tablespoons Brandy

Chopped walnuts

Makes about 2 dozen

Cream the cheese and butter together until smooth. Blend in mustard and Brandy. Chill.

Shape the chilled cheese mixture into balls and roll in chopped nuts.

CELERY STUFFED WITH RED CAVIAR

Celery

1 cake (3 ounces) cream cheese

1–2 tablespoons heavy cream

1 small jar red caviar

1 teaspoon lemon juice

Minced chives

Makes about 1 dozen pieces

Cut celery in 2-inch pieces. Crisp in ice water.

Soften cream cheese and thin slightly with heavy cream. Stir in chilled caviar and lemon juice.

Stuff into dried celery pieces and sprinkle with minced chives.

CELERY STUFFED WITH ROQUEFORT

Celery

¼ pound Roquefort cheese

½ teaspoon coarsely ground black pepper

1 teaspoon grated onion

3-4 tablespoons dairy sour cream

Makes about 1 dozen pieces

Cut celery in 2-inch pieces. Crisp in ice water.

Mash cheese and blend with remaining ingredients.

Stuff dried celery pieces with mixture. Sprinkle with paprika and serve chilled.

CHAMPIGNONS A LA GRECQUE

Pulp and juice of 2 large lemons

1½ cups dry white wine

½ cup olive oil

3 tablespoons vinegar

1 teaspoon whole peppercorns

Salt and pepper

1 pound small fresh mushrooms†

†Cauliflowerets, tiny whole artichokes or frozen artichoke hearts, zucchini rounds–almost any vegetable will lend itself to this treatment.

Makes 6-8 servings

Combine all ingredients except mushrooms and bring to a boil. Reduce heat and simmer 5 minutes.

Add mushrooms a few at a time and cook until just tender (about 3 to 4 minutes).

Skim out cooked mushrooms and repeat until all the mushrooms are cooked.

Put the cooked mushrooms into a bowl or jar and add the hot liquid remaining in saucepan.

Refrigerate 2 or 3 days, the longer the better. Serve cold.

Three or four tender young vegetables prepared this way can combine to make a salad that is more than special. E.B.

MARINATED HERRING

½ cup olive oil

12–14 small fresh herring, cleaned

1 cup dry white wine

1 cup vinegar

2 onions, thinly sliced

1 small carrot, thinly sliced

1 tablespoon chopped parsley

1 bay leaf

½ teaspoon cracked black pepper

Makes 6 servings

Pour the oil into saucepan large enough to hold the herring without bending them. Lay the herring in the oil.

Combine the remaining ingredients and simmer for 15 minutes. Pour this mixture over the herring and let stand about 2 hours.

Place the saucepan over low heat and again simmer very gently for about 12 minutes. Do not stir or move the fish about; they should remain whole. Cool.

Serve the herring cold with the marinade strained over. Garnish with lemon slices and onion rings.

A delightful and simple dish on a hot summer day. And good to know about when you have a fisherman in the family. E.B.

MUSHROOMS IN SOUR CREAM

1½ pounds fresh mushrooms

⅓ cup sweet butter

½ teaspoon oregano

Dash of nutmeg

2 tablespoons lemon juice

2 cups dairy sour cream

Makes 6–8 servings

Rinse the mushrooms, trim and slice. Sauté in hot butter.

Cover the pan, reduce heat and cook 10 minutes. Stir in seasonings.

When ready to serve, stir in sour cream and heat gently. Do not allow to reach boiling point.

Serve on thin, crisp, dry toast.

I cut mushrooms for this dish lengthwise, cap and stem together, making them look like little umbrellas. E.B.

CLAM AND CHEESE APPETIZERS

1 cup shredded sharp cheese

1 can (8 ounces) Doxsee minced clams, drained

1 tablespoon minced chives

Dash of Tabasco

4 slices toast, crusts removed

Makes 12 or 16 appetizers

Mix the cheese, minced clams, chives and Tabasco. Spread on toast.

Broil quickly to heat through and slightly melt cheese.

Cut each slice toast into 3 or 4 fingers.

A tangy salt-sea flavor that goes down well with a cold drink. E.B.

DEVILS ON HORSEBACK

Shucked oysters

White wine

Finely minced garlic

Freshly ground black pepper

Bacon

Drain the oysters and let them marinate in white wine flavored with minced garlic and black pepper.

Soak the oysters for about 40 minutes, then drain well. Wrap each oyster in a strip of bacon. Broil until bacon is crisp. Serve hot.

KEFTEDES

2 pounds ground beef

2 eggs, beaten

½ cup soft white bread crumbs

1 large onion, finely chopped

2 tablespoons minced parsley

¼ teaspoon cinnamon

¼ teaspoon allspice

Salt and pepper

Dry bread crumbs

Makes about 3 dozen

Thoroughly mix all ingredients and chill 1 hour.

Shape mixture into tiny balls (about 1 generous tablespoon mixture per ball) and roll in fine dry crumbs. Chill 1 hour.

Pan fry in hot oil, shortening or butter until golden brown. Serve hot.

I add a tablespoon of finely chopped fresh mint to bring back memories of the Greek islands. E.B.

OYSTERS REMICK

3 dozen medium oysters

Rock salt

2 cups mayonnaise

½ cup chili sauce

½ teaspoon dry English mustard

½ teaspoon paprika

Pinch celery salt

Dash of Tabasco sauce

Dash of Worcestershire sauce

Dash of tarragon vinegar

6 slices bacon, cut in 1-inch pieces

Makes 36 servings

Place each oyster with a little oyster liquor in a small scrubbed clam shell or a small scallop shell. Set the shells in a pan filled with heated rock salt.

Roast the oysters in a hot oven, 400°, for about 3 to 4 minutes.

Thoroughly combine the remaining ingredients, except bacon, to make a sauce. Spoon sauce over the hot oysters and top each with a piece of bacon.

Place shells under broiler until sauce browns and bacon crisps.

Crabmeat (Crabmeat Remick*) and clams are delicious prepared in the same way and served as hors d'oeuvres. E.B.

PATE MAISON

¾ pound pork liver

1¼ pounds boned pork shoulder,
cut up

2 shallots

1 clove garlic

2½ slices white bread,
crusts removed

¼ cup milk

1 teaspoon Marie spice

⅛ teaspoon ground allspice

1 teaspoon salt

¼ teaspoon freshly ground
black pepper

2 tablespoons Cognac

⅓ cup dry white wine

6-8 slices salt pork cut paper thin

Makes 1 quart molded pâté

Poach the pork liver in boiling water for a minute or two. Drain, cool and cut in pieces. Prepared in this way, it will be easier to handle for grinding.

Put the liver, pork, shallots and garlic through the medium blade of a meat grinder.

Tear up the bread and soak it in the milk. Add to the meat mixture and mix until bread completely disappears.

Mix in the seasonings, Cognac and wine.

Line a 1-quart pâté mold with the thin slices of salt pork. If they are big enough, let them lap over the edges of the mold.

Spoon the pâté mixture into the mold and fold the overlapping pieces of salt pork back over the top.

Cover top with a piece of heavy aluminum foil, pressing it down around the edges.

Bake in slow-moderate oven, 325°, for about 2 hours and 40 minutes. Let stand until slightly cool before turning out.

CORNETS OF HAM WITH MELON

1 large ripe Persian melon

Juice of 1 lemon

Black pepper

24 slices prosciutto OR
Westphalian ham

Makes 24 cornets

Peel and seed the melon. Cut into 24 fingers. Squeeze lemon juice over the melon fingers and sprinkle generously with black pepper.

Roll each finger in a slice of ham and serve as soon as possible.

SAMOSAS
East Indian Filled Pastries

PASTRY

3 cups flour

1 teaspoon salt

3 tablespoons clarified butter*

¾ cup cold water (approx.)

Lamb filling (recipe follows)

Oil for deep frying

Mix the flour, salt and butter. Rub the mixture together until it resembles coarsely ground cornmeal.

Add the water, mix quickly and gather the dough into a ball. If the dough is too stiff, or too crumbly, add 1 tablespoon water at a time until the dough ball is flexible and holds together.

Let the dough rest on a floured board for 10 minutes, then knead as you would bread. (After 10 minutes or so the dough should be smooth and very easy to handle.)

Gather the dough into a ball, brush with oil and place in a bowl. Cover with a damp towel until ready to use.

To make the pastry, pinch off a small piece of dough (keep the unused dough covered at all times) and roll it between the palms into a ball about 1-inch in diameter.

Flatten the ball on a floured board and roll it into a circle about 4 inches in diameter.

Use a small knife to cut the circle in half. Moisten the straight cut with water and shape each half circle into a small cone.

Fill the cones with 1 or 2 teaspoons filling (recipe follows), moisten the top edges and press together to close.

Deep fry the pastries to a golden brown in hot oil, 375° on deep-frying thermometer.

Drain on paper towels layered in a shallow pan. Keep warm in a slow oven, 200°, until ready to serve.

Makes enough pastry and filling for 5 or 6 dozen filled cones

Serve warm on a heated platter with a side bowl of chopped chutney.

LAMB FILLING

½ teaspoon saffron

3 tablespoons hot water

¼ cup salad oil

1 tablespoon peeled minced
fresh ginger root

1 large clove garlic, minced

1 cup finely chopped onion

1 teaspoon salt

1 pound lean ground lamb

Generous pinch of red pepper
(or more to taste)

1 teaspoon garam masala
(ground spice mixture)

Soak saffron in water. Heat the oil in a heavy skillet. Stir in ginger, garlic and onion. Fry until onions are golden, about 5 minutes. Sprinkle in salt.

Add the lamb, seasonings and saffron in water. Cook 10 minutes. Reduce heat to low and cook about 15 minutes more, stirring once or twice.

When the lamb mixture has lost most of its moisture and becomes an almost solid cake in the pan, remove from heat. Cool before using.

DEVILED EGGS

6 hard-cooked eggs

1 tablespoon soft butter

2 tablespoons mayonnaise

1 teaspoon minced parsley

1 teaspoon minced pimiento

1 teaspoon minced shallot

½ teaspoon dry English mustard

2-3 drops Tabasco

Salt and pepper

Makes 12 halves

Cut shelled hard-cooked eggs in halves. Remove yolks and put whites aside for filling.

Mash yolks, then mix with butter and mayonnaise until smooth.

Add remaining ingredients and blend well. If necessary, beat in an additional spoonful or two of mayonnaise for a fluffier filling. Correct seasoning.

Refill whites with yolk mixture put through a pastry tube.

MUSHROOMS STUFFED WITH CLAMS

2 3-ounce cakes cream cheese

1 can (8 ounces) Doxsee minced clams

1 teaspoon minced onion

1 egg yolk, beaten

½ teaspoon salt

⅛ teaspoon pepper

Dash of cayenne

40 large mushrooms caps

½ cup fine bread crumbs

Butter

Toast

Makes 10 servings

Mix the cheese with clams, onion, egg yolk and seasonings. Blend until smooth and creamy.

Pile cheese-clam mixture in mushroom caps, sprinkle with crumbs and dot with butter.

Heat about 3 tablespoons butter in a shallow skillet, arrange the filled mushroom caps in the pan and cook over low heat for 5 minutes.

After top-of-stove cooking, put the mushrooms in the broiler about 5 inches from the heat. Grill until puffed and browned.

Serve on toast with pan liquid poured over.

RUMAKI
Oriental-style chicken livers with bacon

12 chicken livers

12 canned water chestnuts

12 slices bacon

1 tablespoon minced onion

½ cup soy sauce

⅓ cup Sherry

1 garlic clove, crushed

1 finger green ginger, minced

½ teaspoon red pepper flakes

Makes 24 hors d'oeuvres

Halve the livers, water chestnuts and bacon.

Fold a piece of chicken liver around a piece of water chestnut, then wrap this little bundle in a half slice of bacon. Secure with a toothpick (be sure the toothpick goes through the water chestnut).

Combine the remaining ingredients in a bowl. Put prepared appetizers in mixture and let them marinate at room temperature for 1 hour.

Drain on paper towels. Broil until bacon is crisp, turning to brown all sides. Serve hot.

PETITES QUICHES LORRAINES

Pastry

24 slices Swiss cheese

6 slices boiled ham, halved

4 eggs

2 cups light cream

½ teaspoon salt

Dash of cayenne

Grated nutmeg

Makes 12 little tarts

Butter 12 individual tart pans and line them with Pie Pastry* or Puff Pastry*. Put a square of foil or wax paper in each shell and fill with dried beans.

Bake the shells in a hot oven, 450°, for 10 minutes. Remove from oven and discard paper and beans. Reduce oven heat to moderate, 350°.

Cut the cheese and ham into rounds to fit into tart shells. Fill each shell with a piece of cheese, a piece of ham, another piece of cheese.

Beat together the eggs, cream and seasonings. Fill the tart shells right to the top with this mixture. Dot tops with butter.

Return the filled tarts to oven and bake 20 to 25 minutes, until filling is set and shell a golden brown.

Slip the baked tarts from pans and serve hot.

SHRIMP REMOULADE

1 pound cooked, shelled and cleaned shrimp

Lettuce

1 tablespoon drained chopped capers

1 tablespoon drained sweet pickle

1 tablespoon minced parsley

1 tablespoon shallots

1 tablespoon prepared mustard

1 cup mayonnaise

Makes 6 servings

Arrange the chilled shrimp in lettuce cups or on shredded lettuce.

Be sure all the moisture is pressed out of the chopped ingredients, then stir them, with the mustard, into the mayonnaise. Mix well.

Spoon the sauce generously over the shrimp and serve with picks. Or serve sauce in bowl and surround with shrimp for dipping.

PLAZA PIZZA

Pastry (see Samosas* pastry)

3-4 tablespoons butter

3 large ripe tomatoes, chopped

1 large sweet onion, minced

2 anchovies, drained and chopped (optional)

¼ pound imported salami, chopped

3 pitted green olives, minced

1 small clove garlic, minced

1 tablespoon minced parsley

¼ pound Swiss OR Mozzarella cheese, diced

Makes 12 to 18 "pies" depending on size

Prepare pastry. Roll out and line tiny pie pans or tart shells. (Pastry may be rolled thick or thin according to taste.) Prick shells with a fork, dot with butter and chill ½ hour.

Arrange shells on a cookie tin or shallow baking pan for ease of handling. Bake in a hot oven, 425°, about 4 minutes.

Combine remaining ingredients, except cheese. Cook and stir over moderate heat for 2 to 3 minutes. Stir in cheese.

Fill shells and return to oven. Bake in a moderate oven, 375°, about 15 to 20 minutes, or until shells are golden brown and filling is cooked.

I often make this recipe in a 9-inch pie shell and cut in wedges to serve 5 to 6 friends. Add a salad, fresh fruit and cheese tray, black coffee and a liqueur for a more than satisfying "little" meal. E.B.

OEUFS A LA ROYALE

6 fresh eggs

½ cup tarragon, white OR wine vinegar

6 very thin slices boiled ham (Danish if possible)

1 large ripe tomato, peeled

Garden lettuce

Mayonnaise

Makes 6 servings

Poach the eggs in boiling water plus ½ cup vinegar. Use a slotted spoon to remove eggs, cool and trim into rounds or ovals. (Use kitchen shears for this— they do a neat quick job.)

Wrap each egg in a thin slice of ham and place on a slice of tomato. This, in turn, is bedded in a cup of tender garden lettuce leaves. Chill.

Serve with a garnish of good mayonnaise and pass more to be added to taste.

I can't think of anything better to serve on a hot August day. E.B.

ROULADE OF HAM AND CHEESE

1 cake (3 ounces) cream cheese

1 tablespoon minced fresh dill

¼ teaspoon coarse-grind black pepper

Dash of cayenne

6 slices Danish ham

Minced parsley

Makes 2 dozen

Soften the cream cheese. Add seasonings and blend until smooth.

Place the ham slices on a flat surface and divide the cheese mixture evenly among them.

Spread cheese over ham and roll up firmly, making 6 rolls. Chill.

Slice each roll into 4 portions. Press cut side into minced parsley.

PLAZA MARINATED HERRING

18 fresh herrings

2½ cups dry white wine

1½ cups cider vinegar

2 medium-size onions, thinly sliced

2 large carrots, thinly sliced

1 teaspoon salt

1 bay leaf

Sprig of leaf thyme

Sprig of parsley

1 whole peppercorn

Pickled beets

Chopped sweet onions

Sliced dill pickle

Sour cream

Makes 8–10 servings

Arrange herrings in a large enamel kettle.

Combine wine, vinegar, sliced onions and carrots, salt, bay leaf, thyme, parsley and peppercorn in a saucepan.

Heat to boiling and simmer until carrots are tender. Pour over herrings.

Heat herrings to boiling and simmer 10 minutes. Chill in marinade.

Serve with pickled beets, chopped onions, pickles and sour cream.

PIROJKI

2 cups flour

1 package active dry yeast

¼ teaspoon sugar

¼ teaspoon salt

½ cup milk, heated

½ cup butter

2 eggs

Filling (recipe follows)

Makes about 4 dozen appetizers

Stir flour, yeast, sugar and salt together in large bowl of electric mixer.

Scald milk and stir in butter until melted. Cool to lukewarm.

On medium speed, beat liquid into dry ingredients. Then beat in eggs one at a time.

Continue mixing until dough is smooth and stiff enough to pull from sides of bowl. If dough is too soft or wet to do this, add an additional ½ cup flour about 2 tablespoons at a time.

Shape dough into a ball, rub with a little oil, place in a bowl and let stand in a warm place for about 1 hour.

Prepare filling and cool to room temperature before using.

Divide the dough in half and roll out 1 portion at a time. Roll dough ⅛ inch thick and cut into 2½-inch rounds.

Place a spoonful of filling in center of each round and bring dough up to cover filling and make a ball. Arrange balls, seam side down, on lightly greased baking sheet.

Bake in a moderately hot oven, 375°, for about 10 minutes, or until browned. Serve hot.

FILLING

1 tablespoon chopped onion

2 tablespoons butter

½ pound ground beef

½ teaspoon salt

Freshly ground black pepper

Pinch of thyme

3-4 tablespoons dairy sour cream, OR Brown Sauce*, OR Bottled chili sauce

Sauté onion in hot butter. Shape ground meat into a flat cake and brown on both sides.

When cake is well browned but not crusty, use a fork to crumble meat. Stir in seasonings and simmer a few minutes.

Bind the filling with sour cream, brown sauce or chili sauce.

FILLINGS FOR FINGER SANDWICHES

Puree artichoke hearts in blender with a little butter and lemon juice. Stir in mayonnaise and season with Tabasco and curry.

Mash a small wedge of ripe Roquefort cheese with ½ of a ripe avocado. Season with lemon juice and a dash of cayenne pepper.

Puree cooked ham in blender with a little vegetable juice to moisten. Mix with an equal amount pâté de foie gras and blend until reduced to a spreadable paste.

Mash cream cheese with an equal amount soft wine Cheddar. Blend in few chopped walnuts. Add heavy cream for spreadability.

Drain sardines and mash with butter, Worcestershire, lemon juice and mayonnaise.

Mince cooked shrimp and mix with sieved egg, chopped chives, lemon juice and Russian dressing.

Mix sour or sweet pickle relish, chopped cooked bacon and minced shallot with mayonnaise to bind.

Combine minced chicken, finely chopped pecans, grated fresh pineapple and mayonnaise.

Flake canned crabmeat and mix with enough Sauce Remick* to bind.

Mash tuna (or other fish) with chopped chives, chopped capers, chopped cucumber, seasonings and mayonnaise.

Soften cream cheese, blend with dairy sour cream. Add finely chopped raw mushrooms. Season with black pepper and curry.

Grate medium-sharp Cheddar cheese. Blend in minced ham and Brandy. Season with pepper.

Blend together butter, cream cheese, blue cheese and anchovy paste. Season with mustard and a few drops vinegar.

Mix red caviar, dairy sour cream, chopped egg yolk, lemon juice and Tabasco.

Blend cream cheese, minced tongue, fresh grated horseradish and beer.

TERRINE FOIE GRAS

½ pound thinly sliced pork fat

1 pound cubed veal

1 pound cubed pork

1 pound chicken livers

4 eggs, beaten

⅓ cup Cognac

½ cup chopped truffles

¼ cup flour

3 teaspoons salt

½ teaspoon freshly ground pepper

½ teaspoon allspice

¼ teaspoon cloves

1 8-ounce can pâté de foie gras

Puff Pastry*

† Egg wash–Beat one egg with 3 tablespoons cold water. Apply with pastry brush.

Makes 20 servings

Line an 8-cup loaf pan with part of the thinly sliced pork fat.

Process veal, pork and chicken livers through a meat grinder twice, using a fine blade.

Beat eggs in a large bowl and blend in ground meat, Cognac, truffles, flour, salt, pepper, allspice, and cloves until smooth. Cut pâté de foie gras into thin slices.

Layer ground-meat mixture and sliced pâté in prepared loaf pan. Top with remaining sliced pork. Cover loaf with a double thickness of aluminum foil. Place in a pan and fill with hot water to a depth of 2 inches.

Bake in hot oven, 400°, for 3 hours, or until pâté is firm. Remove foil from pâté and top with a pan, just smaller than pâté, and fill with heavy object to weigh down until mold is cold.

Prepare Puff Pastry and roll out on a floured pastry cloth to a rectangle large enough to encase pâté. Place pâté loaf on pastry rectangle and fold pastry so that pâté is completely covered. Brush all edges with egg wash† and press together to seal. Place seam side down on cookie sheet. Brush pastry with egg wash. Cut pastry trimmings into fancy shapes and arrange on loaf. Brush with egg wash.

Bake in very hot oven, 450°, for 10 minutes. Then lower heat to moderate 375° and bake 20 minutes longer, or until pastry is golden.

ENDIVE WITH HAM AND CHEESE

Imported canned endive

1 slice imported Swiss cheese

1 slice boiled ham

Cheese Sauce (recipe follows)

Makes 1 serving

Drain endive and pat between two paper towels to remove moisture.

Roll the drained endive in the slice of cheese, then in the slice of ham, making a firm little packet.

Place the roll in an individual baking dish and top with ½ cup cheese sauce. Broil until cheese sauce is golden brown and puffy. Serve hot.

CHEESE SAUCE

1 cup milk

1 cup grated sharp Cheddar cheese

¾ cup grated process American cheese

¼ teaspoon dry mustard

½ teaspoon paprika

¼ teaspoon Worcestershire sauce

3 tablespoons butter

3 tablespoons flour

Salt and pepper

Makes 3 cups

Combine milk, cheeses and seasonings in top of double boiler. Heat until cheeses melt.

Make a roux with butter and flour. Cook about 3 to 4 minutes but do not brown.

Add roux to cheese mixture, a little at a time. Whip in after each addition until mixture is smooth.

Cook sauce just to a boil, remove from heat and strain.

LEGUMES VARIES

Raw Carrot
Cut carrot in fine slivers (julienne). Season with salt, pepper, sugar, nutmeg, lemon juice, olive oil.

Fresh Celery Knob
Peel and cut in fine julienne strips directly into white vinegar. Drain and mix with salt, pepper, prepared mustard, mayonnaise and a little oil.

Pickled Beets
Slice cooked beets and mix with raw onion rings, few garlic cloves, salt, pepper, sugar, vinegar and very little oil.

Pressed Cucumber
Peel cucumber, remove seeds, then cut in thin slices. Mix in a generous amount of salt and let stand for 15 minutes. Rinse away salt and place cucumber slices in a clean kitchen towel. Wring out excess liquid. Season with pepper, lemon juice, a little oil and vinegar, chopped chives.

Hearts of Artichokes
Marinate cooked artichoke hearts in a light olive oil with 2 to 3 cloves garlic, salt, pepper and vinegar. Partially drain. Serve with anchovies on top.

Belgian Endive
Pull the endive into separate leaves, rinse and dry on paper towels. Combine mayonnaise, heavy cream, prepared mustard, Worcestershire sauce and fresh lemon juice. Drizzle mixture over the endive. Sprinkle with salt, pepper and hot pepper sauce.

Cauliflower flowerets
Rinse cauliflower and break into flowerets. Soak in French dressing for several hours. Drain and sprinkle with salad salt and seasoned pepper.

Raw Mushrooms
Rinse and peel mushrooms, trim stem end. Slice mushroom through cap and stem to make little "umbrellas." Mix with salt, pepper, lemon juice, olive oil and chopped fresh tarragon or dill.

SOUPS

AIGO A LA MENAGERE

BEEF CONSOMME

BONGO BONGO

CREAM OF AVOCADO

CREAM OF ASPARAGUS, ARGENTEUIL

CREAM OF SPINACH FLORENTINE

CREAM OF LETTUCE

CREAM OF CELERY

CREAM OF BROCCOLI

CREAM OF CARROTS VELOUR

CHICKEN GUMBO

CREAM OF CHESTNUT

CREAM OF CAULIFLOWER DUBARRY

BOULA BOULA GRATINE

BLACK BEAN SOUP A L'ANGLAISE

BROWN STOCK

CONSOMME A L'ANCIENNE

CREAM OF ONION

CREAM OF MUSHROOM FORESTIERE

CHICKEN STOCK OR BROTH

WATERCRESS AND POTATO SOUP

CREAM OF BARLEY, MARIE STUART

CREAM OF WHEAT SOUP

TURTLE SOUP AMONTILLADO

VELOUTE JOINVILLE

BORSCHT

CREAM DAME BLANCHE

PLAZA HOME MADE CHICKEN SOUP

PETITE MARMITE HENRY IV

POTAGE SANTE

SORREL SOUP

POTAGE PARMENTIER

CREAM OF SORREL WITH OATMEAL

HOT VICHYSSOISE

ONION SOUP

COCKIE-LEEKIE

FISH STOCK

HUNGARIAN GOULASH SOUP

BISQUE OF LOBSTER

POT-AU-FEU

SCOTCH LAMB BROTH

POTAGE ANDALOUSE

CULTIVATEUR LIE

OXTAIL SOUP

PHILADELPHIA PEPPER POT

ROSSELNICK

POTAGE SAVOYARDE

GAZPACHO

CREME SENEGALAISE

ENGLISH GIBLET SOUP

MANHATTAN CLAM CHOWDER

WHITE STOCK

AIGO A LA MENAGERE
Savory Egg Soup

2 tablespoons butter	Melt butter in large skillet. Sauté onion until clear. Add other vegetables, seasonings and broth. Simmer 20 minutes. Correct seasonings and bring soup to a rapid boil. Break each egg into a cup, then slip it gently into the bubbling soup. Poach 4 eggs this way.
½ Spanish onion, minced	
1 raw potato, peeled and minced	
1 ripe tomato, peeled, seeded, and minced	Lay a slice of hot buttered toast in each soup plate and place a poached egg on each slice. Pour soup into bowls and serve at once.
1 sprig parsley, minced	
1 sprig celery leaves, minced	A small meal in itself. Dieters like it for lunch with a cup of black coffee. E.B.
1-inch strip dried orange peel, minced	
Pinch of crushed garlic	
Salt and pepper	
1 quart hot broth*	
4 eggs	
4 slices hot buttered toast	
Makes 4 servings	

BEEF CONSOMME

Pot-au-Feu*	Strain Pot-au-Feu. Allow to cool and remove all the fat.
1 pound chopped raw beef rump	Combine stock with chopped beef in large pot. Add egg whites, leek and carrot.
2 egg whites	
1 leek (white part only), chopped	Heat to a simmer. (This is very important or the clarification will fail.) Simmer for 1½ hours.
1 carrot, thinly sliced	
	Skim off any fat very gently, then strain through cheesecloth or very fine sieve.
	This consommé is very light and clear, with a delicious "beefy" taste. All sorts of garnishes may
Makes 8 servings	be added. E.B.

BONGO BONGO
A Plaza Favorite

4 tablespoons butter	Melt butter in a heavy kettle, add shallots and simmer few minutes. Stir in wine and bring to a boil. Cook until liquid is reduced by half.
4 shallots, minced	
½ cup dry white wine	Finely chop oysters, or process in blender, and add to wine mixture with liquor. Stir in salt and pepper. Cook and stir over moderate heat for 4 to 5 minutes. Remove from heat.
1 pint raw oysters	
1 teaspoon salt	
⅛ teaspoon white pepper	In a separate saucepan combine spinach and Chicken Broth or Stock. Bring to a boil. Reduce heat and cook until spinach is tender. Add the light cream and simmer until heated through.
½ package (about 5 ounces) frozen chopped spinach	
2 cups Chicken Broth* or Stock*	Combine the two mixtures and let stand until cooled.
4 cups light cream	Process soup in blender on high speed for a few seconds. Return to heavy kettle over low heat.
2 tablespoons cornstarch	Dissolve cornstarch in a little cold water. Stir into soup. Continue stirring until soup is thickened and thoroughly blended.
1 teaspoon Worcestershire sauce	
Dash of cayenne pepper	Add remaining ingredients. Correct seasoning and serve hot.
	This is an unusual and delicious party soup. I dress it up with whipped cream and just a hint of lemon zest. E.B.
Makes 8–10 servings	

CREAM OF AVOCADO
A Chilled Soup

4 large ripe avocados	Quarter, pit and peel avocados. Cut into small pieces.
1 quart cold Chicken Broth*	Process avocados with Chicken Broth and cream in a blender, a little at a time. Blend well to a smooth, velvety texture.
1 quart light cream	
3 teaspoons salt	Correct seasoning and chill. Serve in chilled cups.
Few drops of Tabasco	This is a delightful summer soup. Try it with a spoonful of yogurt on top. E.B.
Makes 10 servings	

CREAM OF ASPARAGUS, ARGENTEUIL

½ cup butter

1 medium onion, chopped

2 stalks celery, chopped

1 cup flour

2 quarts White Stock* OR
2 quarts of water

1½ pounds fresh or frozen
asparagus, cut in 1-inch pieces

1 tablespoon salt

Dash of pepper

2 egg yolks

2 cups light cream

Makes 8–10 servings

Melt butter in a large flame-proof casserole. Add onion and celery, cover and simmer for a few minutes. Stir flour into casserole. Cook over medium heat, stirring constantly.

Stir in stock or water until blended. Add asparagus and seasonings.

Bring to a slow boil and simmer 45 minutes. Remove from heat and rub through a fine sieve, or use a blender. Then pass through very fine strainer.

Beat egg yolks and blend in cream. Fold into asparagus mixture. Correct seasonings. Finish the soup by adding a few pats of butter. Serve hot.

CREAM OF SPINACH FLORENTINE

Proceed for this soup as for *Cream of Asparagus**, replacing the asparagus with 1 pound chopped spinach leaves. Makes 8–10 servings.

CREAM OF LETTUCE

Proceed for this soup as for *Cream of Asparagus**, replacing the asparagus with same amount lettuce. Finish soup with 2 tablespoons finely shredded green lettuce leaves blanched and smothered with 1 tablespoon butter. Makes 8–10 servings.

CREAM OF CELERY

Proceed for this soup as for *Cream of Asparagus**, replacing the asparagus with same amount celery. Finish soup with ½ cup cooked diced celery and ½ tablespoon chopped white celery leaves. Makes 8–10 servings.

CREAM OF BROCCOLI

Proceed for this soup as for *Cream of Asparagus**, replacing the asparagus with ½ pound fresh or frozen broccoli. Cooked vermicelli, alphabet noodles or tapioca may be added to this soup as a garnish. Makes 8 servings.

CREAM OF CARROTS VELOUR

Proceed for this soup as for *Cream of Asparagus**, replacing asparagus with 2 cups sliced carrots. Cooked minute tapioca may be added. Makes 8 servings.

CHICKEN GUMBO

¼ cup chicken fat OR butter

3 green peppers, diced

3 leeks (white part only), diced

2 stalks celery, diced

1 medium-size onion, diced

1 cup fresh okra, sliced OR
1 can (1 pound) okra, drained

1 teaspoon salt

2 quarts Chicken Broth*

12 peppercorns

2 bay leaves

¼ teaspoon leaf thyme

2 chicken breasts, cooked and diced

3 ripe tomatoes, peeled, seeded and diced

1 cup boiled rice

Makes 10 servings

Melt chicken fat or butter in a large kettle. Add prepared vegetables and salt. Stew the vegetables together for a few minutes, but do not allow to brown.

Add Chicken Stock, and seasonings tied in a cheese-cloth bag. Bring to a boil, then reduce heat and simmer until the vegetables are almost done.

Add chicken, tomatoes and rice to soup. Simmer for another 10 minutes. Remove herb bag. Correct the seasonings and serve at once while piping hot.

CREAM OF CHESTNUT

¼ pound fresh chestnuts

3 quarts White Stock* OR
3 quarts water

¼-pound piece salt pork

2 large carrots, peeled and chopped

1 large potato, peeled and chopped

1 teaspoon sugar

1 bay leaf

Pinch of salt and pepper

Croutons

Makes 8–10 servings

To skin and shell chestnuts: place chestnuts in a saucepan large enough to fill up to ¾ height. Cover with cold water and add a pinch of salt. Heat to boiling and boil 5 minutes. Remove from heat, drain and cool. When chestnuts are cold, peel with a sharp-pointed vegetable knife.

Put peeled chestnuts with stock or water, salt pork, vegetables and seasonings in good-size kettle.

Bring to a boil. Reduce heat and simmer for 40 minutes or until the salt pork is soft. Remove salt pork and drain, then dice. Put soup through a fine strainer. Correct seasonings and return the diced pork to soup.

If a thicker soup is desired, thicken with a little cornstarch mixed to a paste with cold water. For a thinner soup, stir in a little more broth or warm milk. Heat well before serving. Croutons are passed separately, to be added to taste.

CREAM OF CAULIFLOWER DUBARRY

1 small cauliflower, about 1 pound

¾ cup butter

1½ teaspoons chopped onion

1½ teaspoons chopped celery

¾ cup flour

2 quarts White Stock* OR
2 quarts chicken broth

2 teaspoons salt

½ teaspoon white pepper

½ cup cream

Makes 10 servings

Break cauliflower into flowerettes and blanch in lightly salted water for 10 minutes. Drain.

Melt ½ cup butter in a flameproof casserole. Stir in onion and celery and smother for 4 minutes. Stir in flour and cook, over very low heat, for 10 minutes. Blend stock or broth into roux with a whip until roux has completely dissolved into the liquid. Add blanched cauliflower and seasonings.

Cook over very low heat 45 minutes, stirring several times. Put soup through a fine sieve. Blend in remaining butter and cream and simmer a minute or two over low heat. Cooked cauliflowerettes may be added before serving, if desired.

PHEASANT SOUVAROFF

BOULA BOULA GRATINE

1 quart Pea Soup

1 pinch turtle herbs†

1 cup cooked green peas

⅓ cup dry Sherry

3 tablespoons diced turtle meat

1 cup whipped cream

*† Turtle herbs can be purchased in
gourmet food stores.*

Makes 10 servings

Heat Pea Soup slowly with turtle herbs.

Add peas, Sherry and turtle meat. Simmer for
10 minutes.

Serve in heated soup bowls with a spoonful of
whipped cream on top.

BLACK BEAN SOUP
A L'ANGLAISE

1 pound black beans

3 quarts water

1 ham bone

1 large onion, peeled

1 stalk celery

1½ teaspoons salt

Dash of pepper

1 small lemon

½ small grapefruit

½ cup dry Sherry

2 hard-cooked eggs, chopped

Makes 8–10 servings

Soak beans overnight. Drain and place in large soup
kettle. Add water, ham bone, onion, celery and
seasonings.

Bring to a boil, cover and reduce heat. Simmer
over low heat about 2½ hours, or until beans
are very soft.

Remove kettle from heat. Discard ham bone, onion
and celery. Pass the soup through a vegetable masher
and then through a strainer. Correct seasonings.

Peel the lemon and grapefruit and cut away all
membranes. Use the pulp only. Stir in chopped or
crushed lemon and grapefruit pulp, and Sherry wine.
Serve hot, garnished with chopped egg.

Note the way Chef André has used citrus pulp in
this recipe. This is a very different and very good
version of Black Bean Soup. E.B.

ARROZ CON POLLO

BROWN STOCK

3 pounds beef shin

4 pounds beef and veal bones, cracked

2-3 carrots, cut up

2 onions, halved

1 leek

2 celery stalks with leaves

1 tablespoon salt

1 bay leaf

½ cup parsley sprigs

2 garlic cloves

3 whole cloves

Makes about 3½ quarts

Put the meat, bones and vegetables in a roasting pan. Roast in a hot oven, 450°, for 40 minutes, or until the meat and bones are well browned.

Drain off fat and turn the browned ingredients into a large kettle.

Rinse out the roasting pan with 2 cups of boiling water, scraping and stirring to get all the juices adhering to pan. Pour this liquid into kettle.

Add cold water to cover by at least 3 inches. Cook to a simmer over moderate heat.

As the liquid begins to simmer, skim continuously until scum ceases to form on top.

Add the salt, then the remaining seasonings tied in a piece of cheesecloth.

Partially cover the kettle, leaving a small opening for steam to escape. Cook at a simmer for about 5 hours. Skim as necessary. Add boiling water when liquid evaporates.

Cool and strain. Chill stock until fat hardens on top, then lift or scrape off.

CONSOMME A L'ANCIENNE

Pot-au-Feu*

GARNITURES

2 large carrots, diced

1 small turnip, diced

2 leeks, diced

1 cup chopped cabbage

Toasted bread rounds

Makes 12 servings

Strain Pot-au-Feu into soup kettle. Add vegetables and simmer until tender.

Ladle into consommé cups and top with toasted bread rounds.

CREAM OF ONION

6 tablespoons butter	Melt butter in a heavy saucepan. Add chopped onions and simmer over medium heat until soft, without browning onions.
4 large onions, finely chopped	
¾ cup flour	Add flour and stir with a wooden spoon until the flour has cooked and the roux is a very, very light tan color–just off-white.
*2 quarts Chicken Broth**	
1 teaspoon salt	Remove from heat and blend in chicken broth, salt and peppercorns. Use a wire whip to blend until smooth.
8 whole peppercorns	
1 cup light cream	Return to heat and bring to a boil, then lower heat and simmer gently 30 minutes, stirring at frequent intervals.
1 tablespoon chopped chives	
	Remove from heat and allow to cool for 15 minutes, then fold in cream. Strain and correct seasonings. Bring back to serving heat, but do not boil. Add
Makes 8–10 servings	chives just before serving.

CREAM OF MUSHROOM FORESTIERE

½ cup butter	Melt butter in a flameproof casserole. Add onion and celery and smother for several minutes. Stir in flour and cook over low heat, but do not let flour brown. Blend in stock until smooth. Add mushrooms, salt and pepper.
1 medium-size onion, diced	
2 stalks celery, diced	
¾ cup flour	Heat slowly to boiling, then simmer 40 minutes. Remove from heat and rub through a coarse sieve, then strain through a fine sieve.
*2 quarts Chicken Stock**	
1 pound mushrooms, sliced	Blend in heavy cream and lemon juice. Correct seasonings. Finish soup by adding a few pats of butter, if you wish. Serve hot.
Salt and pepper	
2 cups heavy cream	For a garniture, you may reserve 6 mushrooms and dice finely. Sauté in butter and few drops lemon juice E.B.
Few drops of lemon juice	
Makes 8–10 servings	

CHICKEN STOCK OR BROTH

5-pound fowl

Water

1 pound veal bones

3 stalks celery, chopped

2 leeks, chopped

1 large carrot, chopped

1 onion stuck with a clove

3 sprigs parsley

3 teaspoons salt

Makes about 3 quarts

Place the trussed fowl in a large soup kettle. Cover with water and heat to boiling. Simmer 5 minutes. Remove fowl and pour off water from kettle.

Return fowl to kettle and add 4½ quarts water, veal bones and remaining ingredients. Cover kettle, lower heat and simmer 1 hour. Remove fowl and keep for chicken salad. Strain the stock through a sieve lined with cheesecloth.

WATERCRESS AND POTATO SOUP
Cressonnière

1 bunch watercress

2 tablespoons butter

1 cup chopped onion

½ cup chopped celery

2 quarts White Stock* OR 2 quarts water

6 medium-size potatoes, peeled and quartered

2 teaspoons salt

½ teaspoon white pepper

1 cup light cream, warmed

½ cup milk, warmed

Makes 8 servings

Remove watercress leaves from stems. Blanch leaves and stems separately in lightly salted water for 3 to 4 minutes.

Melt butter in a large kettle and add onion and celery. Cover and stew for about 10 minutes.

Add stock or water and heat to boiling. Add potatoes, blanched watercress stems and seasonings. Cook slowly over low heat for about 45 minutes.

Put soup through a fine sieve. Reheat slowly to a boil. Stir in cream and milk. Correct seasonings. Garnish with the blanched watercress leaves.

CREAM OF BARLEY, MARIE STUART

4 tablespoons butter

½ cup barley flour

2 quarts hot Chicken Broth°

4 leeks (white only), chopped

2 stalks celery, chopped

1 veal knuckle, parboiled

BRUNOISE OF VEGETABLES

1 stalk celery, diced

2 leeks (white only), diced

1 large carrot, diced

1 medium-size onion, diced

2 tablespoons butter

¼ cup pearl barley

2 cups consommé

Makes 8 servings

Melt butter in a large heavy saucepan. Add barley flour and cook slowly, just until roux begins to turn golden.

Stir in hot broth and cook until mixture thickens. Add leeks, celery and veal knuckle. Cook, skimming when necessary, for 2 hours. Press mixture through a sieve.

Add the Brunoise of Vegetables to melted butter, cover and simmer until lightly browned.

Cook pearl barley in consommé until done, then drain.

Add the Brunoise of Vegetables and the cooked barley to the first mixture. Reheat before serving.

CREAM OF WHEAT SOUP

½ cup butter

¼ cup finely chopped onion

½ cup Cream of Wheat

1½ quarts Chicken Stock°

Salt and white pepper

½ cup light cream

Makes 6 servings

Melt ¼ cup of the butter in a heavy saucepan. Sauté onion until soft. Stir in Cream of Wheat. Cook, stirring constantly, until wheat turns golden.

Stir in chicken stock, salt and pepper and heat to a boil. Simmer, stirring several times, for 8 to 10 minutes.

Fold in light cream and heat just to a boil. Correct seasonings. Finish with remaining ¼ cup butter, cut into pats. Serve at once.

TURTLE SOUP AMONTILLADO

1 can (1 pound) prepared turtle meat

4½ cups Beef Consommé

1 cup Amontillado Sherry

Pinch of sweet marjoram

Pinch of sage

Pinch of rosemary

Pinch of sweet basil

Tiny pinch of mint leaves

2 teaspoons arrowroot (cornstarch)

Makes 8 servings

Cut the turtle meat into tiny pieces. Combine with Beef Consommé and heat to a simmer.

Heat Sherry to boiling and stir in all the herbs. Let stand a few minutes, then strain infusion into the soup. Thicken soup with arrowroot mixed with a little cold water.

This thick soup is highly seasoned and has a fragrant aroma. Add more Sherry to your liking right at the table. E.B.

VELOUTE JOINVILLE

2 cups milk

½ cup soft white bread crumbs

Salt and pepper

2 tablespoons butter

2 tablespoons chopped onion

½ pound fillet of sole, chopped

3 smelt fillets, chopped

1 tablespoon lemon juice

3 tablespoons Shrimp Butter (recipe follows)

6 crayfish or large shrimp

Truffles

Makes 6 servings

Scald milk in a heavy saucepan. Stir in bread crumbs, salt and pepper until smooth.

Melt butter in small skillet and sauté onion 2 minutes. Add fish and cook 5 minutes. Pound mixture with lemon juice until smooth.

Add mixture to saucepan and simmer 5 minutes. Press through a sieve and blend in shrimp butter.

Ladle into cream soup bowls and garnish with cooked crayfish or shrimp and chopped truffles.

SHRIMP BUTTER

½ cup cooked unpeeled shrimp
(about 6 large)

Rinse the blender container several times with very hot water. When container is heated, shake dry.

½ cup sweet butter, melted

Immediately add the shrimp and the hot butter. Process at highest speed.

As soon as the butter stiffens, pour the mixture from container into a saucepan. Heat gently until butter melts. Return to container and process again.

Makes about ½ cup

Repeat this action as many times as necessary to achieve a smooth paste. Season with salt and pepper to taste.

BORSCHT

2 pounds chicken wings and necks

Combine chicken wings and necks and beef with water in a stock pot. Simmer 3 hours, skimming when necessary. Strain stock and return to stock pot. Boil until liquid is reduced to 2½ quarts.

1 pound lean beef

3 quarts water

1½ pounds cabbage, julienne

Sauté cabbage, onions, celery, beets and carrots in butter in large kettle for 10 minutes, but do not brown.

1 pound onions, julienne

1 bunch celery, julienne

Add prepared stock and simmer 30 minutes, or until vegetables are almost done. Add tomato paste and simmer for another 15 minutes, or until vegetables are done. Season with salt and pepper.

½ pound beets, julienne

½ pound carrots, julienne

½ pound butter

When ready to serve, garnish each plate with a Pirojki and a spoonful of sour cream.

1 can (6 ounces) tomato paste

Salt and pepper

*Pirojki**

1 cup sour cream

Makes 10 servings

CREAM DAME BLANCHE

4 tablespoons butter

½ cup rice flour

2 quarts hot Chicken Broth*

4 leeks (white only), chopped

2 stalks celery, chopped

1 veal knuckle, parboiled

¼ cup blanched almonds

½ cup water

1 cup diced cooked chicken breast

Makes 8 servings

Melt butter in a large heavy saucepan. Add rice flour and cook slowly, just until roux begins to turn golden.

Stir in hot broth and cook until mixture thickens. Add leeks, celery and veal knuckle. Cook, skimming when necessary, for 2 hours. Press mixture through a sieve, or process in blender until smooth.

Process almonds and water in a blender until smooth. Stir into soup mixture and reheat. Ladle into cream soup bowls and garnish with cooked chicken.

PLAZA HOME MADE CHICKEN SOUP
A Plaza Favorite

½ cup butter

1 stalk celery, chopped

½ leek (white only), chopped

¼ cup flour

1½ quarts Chicken Broth*

1 cup heavy cream

1 cup diced cooked chicken, white meat only

½ cup cooked rice

¼ cup finely chopped celery

Salt and pepper

Makes 8 servings

Melt ¼ cup butter in a large saucepan. Add celery and leek and allow to "seethe" in the foaming butter for several minutes. Stir in flour and cook a little, but do not allow to brown. Remove saucepan from heat and use a wire whip to blend in hot Chicken Broth. When soup is smooth and creamy, return to low heat and simmer for 20 minutes, stirring often. Remove from heat, cool slightly and strain.

Blend in heavy cream and add chicken, rice, celery and seasonings. Simmer a few minutes to heat through. Do not allow to boil. When hot enough, correct seasonings. Finish by stirring in remaining butter. Serve immediately.

PETITE MARMITE HENRY IV

1 4-pound fowl

3 pounds beef shoulder

½ pound chicken wings

1 pound soup bones

Carcass of 1 chicken (optional)

6 quarts cold water

2 large carrots

3 leeks

2 stalks celery

1 white turnip

1 large onion stuck with 6 cloves

1 browned onion, cut in half

1 bunch parsley stems

2 cloves of garlic

2 tablespoons salt

15 peppercorns

1 bay leaf

GARNITURES   4 medium-size carrots

1 stalk celery, diced

2 leeks, sliced

2 small white turnips, peeled

Toasted croutons

Grated cheese

Makes 12 servings

Place fowl, beef, chicken wings, soup bones and chicken carcass (if used) in large soup pot with water. Heat slowly to a boil, skimming well.

Add vegetables and seasonings. Heat to boiling and skim again. Cover pot and simmer 3 hours. At end of this time, remove fowl and beef. Let cool enough to handle, then slice or cut in julienne pieces and set aside.

Strain Pot-au-Feu through a fine sieve and correct seasonings. Cut garniture vegetables into julienne strips and cook in salted water until tender. Drain. Add prepared meats and vegetables to strained Pot-au-Feu, reheat. Serve with croutons and grated cheese.

Serve this generous soup "family style" from an earthenware tureen. E.B.

POTAGE SANTE
Health Soup

½ *pound sorrel leaves* OR

½ *pound spinach*

¼ *cup butter*

½ *cup chopped onions*

¼ *cup chopped celery*

3 *cups parsley stems*

2 *quarts White Stock** OR
2 *quarts water*

2½ *pounds potatoes, peeled
and quartered*

2 *teaspoons salt*

½ *teaspoon white pepper*

1 *cup warm milk*

Makes 8 servings

Remove leaves from stems of sorrel or spinach. Cut leaves into fine julienne strips and smother with 2 tablespoons butter in a small saucepan for about 10 minutes. Set aside.

Melt 2 tablespoons butter in a flameproof casserole. Smother onions, celery, parsley and sorrel or spinach stems and cook 10 minutes.

Add stock or water, potatoes and seasonings. Bring to a boil. Cook slowly for about 45 minutes. Pass soup through a fine sieve.

Bring soup to a boil once again. Add warm milk. Correct seasonings. Add smothered sorrel or spinach leaves.

SORREL SOUP

1 *cup fresh sorrel, cleaned
and shredded*

2 *tablespoons butter*

1 *tablespoon flour*

4 *cups water*

½ *teaspoon salt*

1 *cup milk*

1 *cup light cream*

1 *egg, beaten*

Makes 4-6 servings

Put the sorrel in a saucepan with the butter. Cover and cook over low heat until the sorrel is soft and "cooked down" to about ½ cup.

Stir in the flour and blend well. Stir in the water and salt. Continue cooking over low heat for 15 to 20 minutes.

Beat the milk, cream and egg together. Stir into soup. Raise the heat to moderate and bring soup just to a boil, stirring constantly. Remove from heat immediately.

Correct seasonings and serve with croutons.

POTAGE PARMENTIER

¼ cup butter

6 leeks (white only), diced

2 large onions, diced

8 large potatoes, diced

1½ quarts White Stock* OR

1½ quarts water

2 cups milk

1 teaspoon salt

1 bay leaf

6 white peppercorns, crushed

2 cups cream

Makes 10 servings

Melt butter in heavy kettle. Add leeks and onions and smother well for about 5 minutes on medium heat. Add potatoes, stock or water, milk and seasonings.

Bring to a boil, then reduce heat and simmer for 30 minutes.

Fold in cream and correct seasonings.

CREAM OF SORREL WITH OATMEAL

1 cup regular oatmeal

2 cups water

4 cups milk

2 teaspoons salt

Dash of white pepper

½ pound fresh sorrel

6 tablespoons butter

1 cup light cream

Makes 8 servings

Stir oatmeal into cold water in a large saucepan. Add milk with seasonings. Heat to boiling, stirring constantly. Reduce heat and simmer for 1¼ hours, stirring occasionally.

Chop sorrel very fine, discarding coarse stems and leaves. Heat butter in a heavy frying pan. Add sorrel and stir over low heat until sorrel is wilted and soft and liquid is completely evaporated.

Add sorrel to soup and simmer 15 minutes, stirring often. Remove from heat and cool slightly. Process in blender or rub through a sieve, then strain. Reheat to a simmer, stir in cream and correct seasonings. Serve at once.

A very tangy, refreshing soup well worth making. E.B.

HOT VICHYSSOISE

¼ cup butter

5 medium-size onions, sliced

12 large leeks, diced

5 medium-size potatoes, sliced

1½ quarts strong Chicken Stock*

1 teaspoon salt

Dash of white pepper

2 cups heavy cream

2 bunches chives, finely chopped

Makes 6 servings

Melt butter in large saucepan. Add onions and leeks and simmer for 10 minutes. Add potatoes, chicken stock and seasonings.

Bring to a boil, then reduce heat and simmer 45 minutes. Remove from heat.

Strain through medium sieve and blend in cream. Pour into saucepan to heat, but do not allow to boil.

Serve hot. Pass chives separately.

ONION SOUP

1 cup butter

4 large onions, sliced

½ clove garlic, crushed

1 sprig parsley, chopped

Pinch of chervil

Pinch of salt

Pinch of black pepper

1 teaspoon flour

1½ quarts chicken or beef broth

Thinly sliced French bread, toasted

2 cups grated Parmesan cheese

Makes 6 servings

Melt ½ cup butter in a large saucepan. Sauté onion until golden brown.

Add garlic, parsley, chervil, seasonings and flour. Simmer over very low heat, stirring constantly, for 2 to 3 minutes. Add broth gradually and boil gently for about 15 minutes.

Pour into an oven-proof soup tureen or large oven-proof dish. Place thin slices of toasted French bread on top. Sprinkle with Parmesan cheese and dot with remaining ½ cup butter.

Put tureen in a pan of hot water and place in moderately hot oven, 375°, for 15 minutes.

COCKIE-LEEKIE

2 tablespoons butter

6 leeks (white only), cut in julienne pieces

2 quarts Chicken Broth°

1½ cups cooked chicken, cut in julienne pieces

8 prunes, presoaked and cut in julienne pieces

Salt and pepper

Chives

Makes 8–10 servings

Melt butter in a large heavy saucepan. Add leeks and simmer on medium heat for 5 minutes.

Add remaining ingredients, mix well and bring to a boil. Reduce heat to moderate and simmer 25 minutes. Correct seasonings and serve very hot. Sprinkle with chives before serving.

A Scottish contribution to our cuisine. E.B.

FISH STOCK

Bones and trimmings of 8 whitefish OR other white-fleshed fish

3 quarts water

1½ cups white wine

2 carrots, chopped

2 onions, sliced

2 sprigs parsley

1 bay leaf

Pinch of leaf thyme

8 peppercorns

2 teaspoons salt

Makes 2½ quarts

Place fish bones and trimmings in a large soup kettle. Add remaining ingredients. Heat slowly to boiling and skim well. Simmer 30 minutes. Strain the stock through a sieve lined with cheesecloth.

HUNGARIAN GOULASH SOUP

2 tablespoons shortening

1½ pounds lean beef, cut in
1-inch cubes

1 tablespoon paprika

¼ cup tomato puree

3 quarts Brown Stock* OR
3 quarts water

1⅛ teaspoons caraway seeds

1 teaspoon salt

¼ teaspoon pepper

2 cups diced potatoes

2 cups diced onions

1 cup diced celery

1 cup diced carrots

1 tablespoon chopped parsley

Makes 8 servings

Melt shortening in large kettle. Add beef cubes and stir over high heat for 5 minutes.

Add paprika and mix well. Stir in tomato puree and cover with stock or water. Add seasonings.

Bring to a boil, then reduce heat and simmer for 30 minutes.

Add potatoes, onions, celery and carrots. Simmer 1 hour, or until meat is done.

Remove kettle from heat. Correct seasonings and sprinkle with freshly chopped parsley.

This goulash soup will make a wonderful main course. E.B.

BISQUE OF LOBSTER

1 fresh lobster, about 2 pounds

10 tablespoons butter

1 medium-size onion, diced

1 large carrot, diced

2 shallots, diced

1 stalk celery, diced

1 bunch parsley, chopped

1 tablespoon peppercorns

⅓ cup white wine

¼ cup Cognac

2 tablespoons flour

1 cup chopped tomatoes

1 quart Fish Stock*

2 cups light cream

Pinch of salt and pepper

Makes 8 servings

Cook live lobster in boiling water for 3 minutes. Remove lobster from kettle and cut, shell and all, into large pieces.

Brown 4 tablespoons of the butter in a deep saucepan over high heat. Add onion, carrot, shallots, celery, parsley and peppercorns. Reduce heat and simmer for 10 minutes.

Add white wine, 2 tablespoons of the Cognac and flour. Stir constantly until sauce has thickened. Add tomatoes, lobster, and Fish Stock and simmer for 30 minutes, stirring several times to prevent burning. Remove saucepan from heat and lift out lobster pieces with slotted spoon.

Strain liquid through cheesecloth and pour into saucepan. Add cream, remaining butter and Cognac. Stir over low heat until well blended. Season with salt and pepper.

Remove lobster meat from shell and dice. Add to saucepan. Heat until hot enough to serve.

POT-AU-FEU

3 pounds beef shoulder or flank

1 pound marrow bones, tied in a piece of cheesecloth

1 broiler-fryer, split OR *carcass from roasting chicken*

½ pound chicken wings

5 quarts cold water

3 large carrots, peeled and chopped

3 leeks, chopped

1 white turnip, peeled and chopped

2 stalks celery, chopped

1 large onion, stuck with 6 cloves

1 onion, well browned in butter

1 bunch of parsley stems

2 garlic cloves

2 tablespoons salt

15 whole peppercorns

1 bay leaf

Makes 10 servings

Place beef, bones, chicken and chicken wings in a large kettle with water. Cook to a boil. Throw 3 or 4 ice cubes into broth (this will bring all the scum to the surface) and skim very well.

Add vegetables and seasonings. Return to the boil and skim again. Cover kettle and simmer over low heat for 3 hours, or until beef is very tender.

Lift out the marrow bones and remove marrow. (This makes a delicious appetizer or snack spread on thin crisp toast.) Strain soup and remove all fat.

Serve the clear, amber broth in bouillon cups as a first course. Slice the beef and serve with freshly boiled whole vegetables on the side as the entrée.

SCOTCH LAMB BROTH

2 pounds lamb bones

1 leek, chopped

1 stalk celery, chopped

1 large carrot, chopped

1 medium onion, chopped

3 quarts water

1 teaspoon salt

6 whole peppercorns

1 cup pearl barley

2 tablespoons butter

BRUNOISE OF VEGETABLES

3 stalks celery, diced

2 leeks (white only), diced

1 large carrot, diced

1 medium onion, diced

1 cup cream

1 teaspoon chopped parsley

Makes 10 servings

Parboil lamb bones for a few minutes in a kettle and drain. Place lamb bones in kettle with chopped leek, celery, carrot and onion. Add water, salt and peppercorns and bring to a boil.

Cook slowly for 2 hours, skimming as necessary. Strain the broth.

Presoak the barley in cold water for 1 hour and drain.

Sweat the Brunoise of Vegetables in butter until lightly browned. Pour lamb broth over vegetables and add barley.

Heat to boiling and simmer for 1 hour. Correct seasonings. Fold in the cream and parsley before serving.

POTAGE ANDALOUSE

4 tablespoons butter

2 large carrots, chopped

2 large onions, chopped

¾ cup flour

2 quarts Chicken Stock*

*1 can (1-pound, 13-ounces)
Italian tomatoes*

3 leeks, chopped

6 large tomatoes, chopped

1 clove garlic, minced

8 white peppercorns

1 tablespoon sugar

2 teaspoons salt

1 cup quick-cooking tapioca

1 quart consommé

Makes 12 servings

Melt butter in stock pot. Add carrots and onions and sauté until soft. Stir in flour and cook 3 minutes.

Stir in hot Chicken Stock and cook, stirring constantly, until mixture thickens. Add canned tomatoes, leeks, fresh tomatoes, garlic, peppercorns, sugar and salt.

Simmer 2 hours, skimming as necessary. Force the soup through a sieve.

Cook tapioca in consommé until tender. Drain. Add to soup and serve in cream soup bowls.

CULTIVATEUR LIE

8 tablespoons butter

1 cup shredded leeks (white only)

1 cup shredded celery

1 cup shredded carrots

1 cup shredded cabbage

½ cup shredded onion

⅓ cup flour

1½ quarts Chicken Broth*

⅔ cup shredded white turnip

1 cup shredded potatoes

½ cup fresh green peas

½ cup fresh lima beans

½ cup light cream

Salt and pepper

Makes 8 servings

Melt 6 tablespoons butter in a large saucepan. Slowly simmer the leeks, celery, carrots, cabbage and onion for 3 minutes.

Stir in flour until well blended. Blend in broth with wire whip. Heat to boiling.

Add turnip and boil 5 minutes. Add potatoes, peas and lima beans. Cook 25 minutes.

Fold in light cream and remaining butter. Add salt and pepper to taste. Serve at once.

OXTAIL SOUP

2½ pounds oxtails, cut in
2-inch pieces

2 large carrots, diced

1 medium-size onion, sliced

½ cup shortening

2 tablespoons flour

2 quarts Beef Stock* OR
2 quarts water

1 cup Madeira wine

Pinch of sweet marjoram

Pinch of sage

Pinch of rosemary

Pinch of sweet basil

Cooked meat from oxtails, diced

GARNITURES

3 large carrots, diced

2 medium-size white turnips, diced

2 stalks celery, diced

Makes 8 servings

Blanch oxtails in boiling water for 3 minutes. Cool.

In a deep kettle sauté oxtails, carrots and onion in hot shortening. Sprinkle flour over the meat and vegetables and stir in. Cook until mixture reaches a rich brown color.

Add stock or water and heat to boiling. Cover. Simmer very slowly for 3 hours. At the end of this cooking time the soup should be very thick and gelatinous. Strain the soup while it is hot.

Heat Madeira wine to boiling and mix in herbs. Let stand 10 minutes, then strain into the soup. Adjust seasonings.

Cook garniture vegetables in salted boiling water until done. Drain. Add to soup with diced oxtail meat. Serve very hot.

A rich, highly seasoned soup much liked by men dining alone. E.B.

PHILADELPHIA PEPPER POT

½ cup diced salt pork

3 leeks, diced

1 medium-size onion, diced

3 green peppers, diced

2 stalks celery, diced

1 tablespoon flour

1 cup diced parboiled tripe

2 quarts Brown Stock*

1 tablespoon salt

10 peppercorns, crushed

1 bay leaf

1 pinch thyme

2 medium-size potatoes, diced

3 tomatoes, peeled, diced,
seeds removed

Freshly ground pepper

Chopped parsley

Makes 8 servings

Place salt pork in a heavy kettle and fry. Add leeks, onion, green peppers and celery. Sauté the vegetables, stirring with a wooden spoon, until they are golden brown.

Remove kettle from heat and stir in flour until mixed and smooth. Add tripe, Stock and seasonings.

Heat to boiling and simmer 30 minutes. Add potatoes and tomatoes and simmer 45 minutes longer. Remove from heat and correct seasonings. Finish off with freshly ground pepper and chopped parsley.

ROSSELNICK
A Chilled Soup

6 tablespoons butter

¾ cup flour

2 large cucumbers, peeled and chopped

½ medium-size onion, chopped

1 leek, chopped

1 stalk celery, chopped

2 quarts Chicken Broth*

½ teaspoon salt

¼ teaspoon pepper

1 cup heavy cream

1 cup diced cooked cucumber

1 tablespoon chopped fresh dill

Makes 8 servings

Melt butter in a large heavy kettle. Stir in flour and cook over medium heat for a few minutes. Do not allow to brown.

Add chopped raw cucumbers, onion, leek, celery, chicken broth, salt and pepper. Use a wire whip to smooth ingredients.

Bring to a boil, then reduce heat and simmer 30 minutes. Strain through a fine sieve. Cool.

Fold in cream and diced cooked cucumber. If too thick, add some cold chicken broth or milk. Correct seasonings and add dill. Serve chilled.

POTAGE SAVOYARDE

¼ *cup butter*

6 *leeks (white only), diced*

2 *large onions, diced*

½ *pound parboiled salt pork, diced*

1 *ham bone*

8 *large potatoes, diced*

1½ *quarts White Stock** OR
1½ *quarts water*

2 *cups milk*

1 *teaspoon salt*

1 *bay leaf*

6 *white peppercorns, crushed*

2 *cups light cream*

2 *teaspoons chopped chives*

Makes 10 servings

Melt butter in heavy kettle. Add leeks and onions and smother for 4 to 5 minutes on medium heat. Add salt pork and cook a few minutes more.

Add ham bone, potatoes, stock or water, milk and seasonings. Bring to a boil, then reduce heat and simmer for 30 minutes.

Remove the ham bone. Gradually fold in cream.

Correct seasonings and add the chopped chives.

This is an excellent rich soup. You can make a meal out of it. E.B.

GAZPACHO
A Chilled Soup

8 ripe tomatoes, peeled

2 green peppers, halved and seeded

2 medium-size cucumbers, peeled

2 medium-size onions, peeled

2 cloves garlic

1 cup canned tomato puree

¾ cup tomato juice

¾ cup red wine vinegar

½ cup olive oil OR
½ cup salad oil

1½ teaspoons Ac'cent

10 drops Tabasco

Pinch of cayenne pepper

Makes 8 servings

Coarsely chop raw vegetables and process in blender until smooth.

Combine remaining ingredients in a large bowl. Stir in blended vegetables with a wire whip. Chill several hours before serving.

Garnish each serving with a sprinkle of finely diced green pepper and onion.

CREME SENEGALAISE
A Favorite Plaza Chilled Soup

½ cup butter

¾ cup flour

½ cup chopped onion

½ cup chopped leeks

½ cup chopped celery

4 teaspoons curry powder

2 large ripe tomatoes, chopped

2 quarts hot Chicken Broth*

Salt to taste

1 small piece cracked ginger

1 small piece stick cinnamon

Light cream

Makes 10 servings

Melt 6 tablespoons butter in a heavy saucepan and stir in flour. Cook the roux over very low heat (or place in a slow oven) for 10 minutes, but do not allow roux to brown.

Melt 2 tablespoons butter in a large saucepan and sauté onion, leek, celery and garlic until translucent, about 7 to 8 minutes. Blend in the curry powder. Cook and stir over very low heat for 2 minutes (do not allow curry powder to burn). Stir in tomatoes, hot broth, salt, ginger and cinnamon.

Bring to the boil and keep bubbling briskly for 10 minutes. Gradually add spoonfuls of the roux, blending well with a wire whip.

Simmer the thickened soup over low heat for 30 minutes. Strain twice through cheesecloth. Chill until almost cold. Stir in cream to desired consistency and correct seasonings. Chill until very cold. If soup is too thick, add additional cream.

ENGLISH GIBLET SOUP

1 pound chicken necks

1 pound chicken wings

½ cup butter

½ pound chicken gizzards

½ cup flour

3 quarts Chicken Stock* OR
3 quarts water

2 teaspoons salt

¼ teaspoon pepper

1 Bouquet Garni (parsley stems,
celery, bay leaf)

½ cup diced white celery

¾ cup raw rice, parboiled

Makes 8 servings

Cut up chicken necks and wings into chunky pieces. Heat half the butter in heavy kettle. Add chicken necks, wings and gizzards and brown well. Sprinkle with flour and fry until lightly browned. Stir continuously to avoid burning flour.

Add chicken stock or water, seasonings and Bouquet Garni. Bring to a boil, then lower heat and simmer 1½ hours. Remove gizzards (use a slotted spoon) and let cool. Trim gizzards by cutting away gristle and membranes. Dice remaining portion of gizzards. Strain soup.

Sauté celery and diced gizzards in remaining butter. Add to strained soup with parboiled rice.

Simmer for 15 minutes. Correct seasonings, being sure soup has a strong pepper taste. Serve hot.

This is a "peppery" soup–very good on cold windy days. E.B.

MANHATTAN CLAM CHOWDER

¼ cup diced salt pork

3 onions, chopped

3 leeks, chopped

3 potatoes, peeled and diced

1 can (1 pound) stewed tomatoes

1 cup chopped celery

2 quarts White Stock*

½ cup chopped parsley

½ teaspoon leaf thyme

Salt and pepper

12 hard-shelled clams

2 tablespoons Worcestershire sauce

Makes 6 servings

Brown salt pork in large kettle. Sauté onions and leeks in fat until golden.

Add potatoes, tomatoes, celery, stock, parsley, thyme, salt and pepper. Heat to boiling. Simmer for 30 minutes, or until potatoes are tender.

Open clams, reserving liquid. Chop clams and add to soup with reserved liquid. Add Worcestershire sauce and simmer 5 minutes longer.

WHITE STOCK

3 pounds chicken necks, backs, skinned feet and bones

2 pounds veal bones

Water

3 leeks, chopped

3 medium-size onions, chopped

1 large carrot, chopped

2 teaspoons salt

1 stalk celery

3 sprigs parsley

1 bay leaf

Few sprigs fresh thyme

Makes 2½ quarts

Place chicken pieces and veal bones in a large soup kettle. Cover with water and heat to boiling. Simmer until scum rises to top. Skim well.

Add more water to make about 4 quarts. Add leeks, onions, carrot and salt. Make a fagot by tying together celery, parsley, bay leaf and thyme. Add to kettle.

Cover kettle, lower heat and simmer 3 hours. Do not stir.

Ladle out as much of the stock as possible without disturbing bones and vegetables. Strain the stock through a sieve lined with cheesecloth.

SALADS

ASSORTED SALADS SERVED AT THE PLAZA

ORANGE GROVE SALAD

ORGANIC SALAD

LEEKS VINAIGRETTE

CHEF'S SALAD, PLAZA

VEGETABLE SALAD

FLAKED HALIBUT SALAD

AVOCADO–SHRIMP SALAD

SALADE NICOISE

SPINACH SALAD PLAZA

PLAZA CHICKEN SALAD

CELERY VICTOR

PEAR CORONATION SALAD

PALM COURT SPINACH SALAD

ASSORTED SALADS
SERVED AT THE PLAZA

Aida Grapefruit segments and fresh pineapple slices arranged in alternate layers on lettuce hearts, garnished with walnuts. French Dressing.

Aiglon Lettuce in chiffonade, tomatoes, cooked French-cut string beans and truffles in julienne mixed with light cream mayonnaise. Combine with anchovy sauce and serve in a bowl.

Albert A green combination of chicory, romaine and escarole, sprinkled with crisp shredded bacon and fines herbes. French Dressing.

Alda Slices of Bartlett pear, layered with cream cheese between the slices. Garnish with dice of fresh fruit, berries or maraschino cherries. French Dressing.

Alice Segments of grapefruit and orange slices on hearts of romaine. Top with mixture of chopped green peppers and walnuts. French Dressing.

Barrett Hollowed tomatoes stuffed with diced pineapple and celery mixed with mayonnaise. Topped with nuts and watercress.

Black-eyed Susan On one-inch thick slice of head lettuce arrange orange sections petal fashion. Center with a cube of cream cheese, top with a slice of pickled walnut, and sprinkle with chopped walnuts. French Dressing.

Colchester On base of Belgian endive arrange slices of orange, grapefruit segments, red and green peppers and pickled walnuts.

Cole Slaw, Hawaiian Shredded pineapple, shredded cabbage and nuts. Mousseline Dressing.

Combination Torn-up lettuce, romaine, chicory, radishes, beets, watercress and tomato. French Dressing.

Comtesse Chicory and romaine, artichoke slices, cucumbers and quartered tomatoes in bowl.

Cordon Rouge Heart of lettuce and sliced celery knobs. Border with diced beets.

Creole	Half hearts of celery and tomato quarters with timbale of cooked rice in center. Decorate with fancy-cut green peppers. Russian Dressing.
Cucumber Japonaise	Matchlike strips of cucumber, chopped shallots and strips of sweet pepper, served on lettuce leaves. Sour Cream Dressing.
Cupid	Alternate slices of alligator pear and grapefruit segments on lettuce heart. Flank with bits of green and red peppers and top with sprinkling of chopped watercress.
Dee-Lite	Equal parts chopped celery, shredded pineapple, diced orange and diced apple, mixed with mayonnaise on lettuce. Top with whipped cream, chopped nuts and maraschino cherry.
Dejanire	Heart of lettuce with diced pineapple, orange and tomatoes. Red dressing.
Demidoff	Lettuce, slice of pineapple, apples, celery and endive with julienne-cut truffles.
Diana	Bartlett pear halves, stuffed with pineapple, orange and strawberries. Carnation Dressing.
Diplomate	Heart of lettuce, pineapple, apples and celery in with chopped walnuts.
Dolly	Romaine, endive, sliced pear and sliced beet. Mayonnaise.
Dorothy	Romaine with slices of orange, grapefruit and alligator pear. Crisscross with red pepper.
Duchesse	Cooked asparagus tips on leaves of lettuce. Add slices of apple and celery in julienne. Top with finely chopped truffles.
Elsie	Lettuce, pineapple, orange, grapes and chopped nuts.
Emily	Heart of romaine, asparagus tips, grapefruit segments and red and green pepper strips.

Endive Astoria   Belgian endive, grapefruit segments, orange slices and pepper rings.

Equitaine   On crisp lettuce fill a ring of alligator pear with sliced figs and kumquats. French Dressing.

Eva   Heart of romaine, sliced artichoke bottoms, asparagus tips and chopped truffles.

Excelsior   Apple is scooped out, filled with chopped celery and nuts and served on slice of pineapple. Top with mayonnaise and sprinkle with paprika.

Favorite   Lettuce, slices of alligator pear, celery, pimientos and ripe olives.

Floral   Peeled tomato, stuffed with chopped marinated cucumber. Garnish with radish rose. French Dressing.

Florida   Fill a banana shell with celery in julienne, diced bananas and grapefruit segments. Mayonnaise with cream and paprika.

Floridienne   Romaine, grapefruit and orange segments, maraschino cherries.

Frou-Frou   Chicory, escarole, celery, beets, truffles and white of hard-cooked eggs, all julienne, with chervil, in a bowl.

Gauloise   Heart of romaine, asparagus tips, celery, mushrooms, truffles, all julienne.

Geneva   Slices of romaine, alternate sliced eggs and beets.

Gertrude   Heart of endive, watercress, julienne of mushrooms. Red Dressing.

Giant Asparagus   Lettuce, jumbo peeled asparagus, strip of pimiento.

Gourmand   Heart of lettuce, sections of orange, apple and pear.

Guillaume   Watercress, diced potatoes and artichoke, slices of hard-cooked eggs and radishes in bowl. French Dressing (paprika).

Hawaiian   Lettuce, sliced pineapple, cream cheese, grapes and sprigs of watercress.

A BOILED CORNED BEEF PLATTE

Herman Senn	Scoop out a half grapefruit and fill shell with lettuce, sections of orange and grapefruit and artichoke heart strips cut in eight pieces. Decorate with star of red pepper.
Hortense	Heart of romaine, julienne strips of celery, apples, and carrots. French Dressing.
Imperiale	Heart of romaine, asparagus tips, anchovy fillets, truffles in julienne.
Isabella	Lettuce, sliced cucumber, sliced radish, chopped celery on rings of green pepper, red pepper in center.
Jockey Club	Heart of romaine, celery knobs, truffles and artichoke bottoms in julienne.
Julienne	Chicory, escarole, carrots, turnips, celery knobs, haricots verte, green peas mixed with French Dressing in bowl. Mayonnaise.
Juliette	Lettuce, French-cut string beans, celery in julienne, celery knobs, artichokes and truffles.
Kentucky	Fill hollowed halves of green peppers with grapefruit segments, diced apple and walnuts. Mayonnaise.
Knickerbocker	Romaine, orange and grapefruit sections. Garnish with fresh strawberries and whipped cream. French Dressing.
Kuroki	Heart of romaine, orange, grapefruit and apples. Decorate with red peppers.
Ladies Delight	Lettuce hearts, grapefruit and orange sections, cream cheese, red and green cherries.
Lamm	Lettuce, slices of banana on slice pineapple, chopped nuts, red cherries.
Lettuce Chiffonade	Hearts of lettuce. Chiffonade dressing.
Lily	Lettuce cup, balls of cream cheese, red Bar-le-duc.
Lorenzo	Lettuce and watercress, quartered pears, chopped English walnuts.

Loretta	Belgian endive, grapefruit sections, maraschino cherries.
Louise	Heart of lettuce, chopped celery and apple, pieces of orange and grapes, cherry.
Maggie Pepper	Cabbage, apples, beets and celery in julienne, chopped green peppers, pimientos and chives. French Dressing. Let stand 2 hours before serving.
Marguerite	Lettuce, chicory, Belgian endive, chopped yolks of eggs, few sprigs of watercress.
Marie	Lettuce, asparagus tips, julienne of celery, pickled walnuts in bowl.
Marie-Jose	Heart of lettuce, asparagus tips, French-cut string beans. French Dressing.
Marquis	Tomato shell with pearl onions, diced celery and lettuce. Red dressing.
Mathilde	Romaine, sliced alligator pear, apples and cucumbers, chopped walnuts.
Matschische	Shredded cabbage, pineapple, apple, maraschino cherries, chopped walnut. Mayonnaise-Sour Cream Dressing.
Melba	Endive, finely cut apples, currant jelly. French Dressing.
Mercedes	Heart of lettuce, celery, beets and truffles. Cream Mayonnaise.
Merry Widow	Lettuce, cream cheese layered between pineapple slices, fresh strawberries.
Mexican	Cole slaw, red and green peppers, strips of pimientos.
My Fancy	Heart of romaine and sliced oranges.
My Lady	Lettuce, slice of pineapple, orange and grapefruit sections, apple slices, maraschino cherries. Whipped Cream Mayonnaise.

Narragansett	Sliced lettuce, sliced tomato, sliced egg, fancy cut beets.
Niçoise	Lettuce, diced potatoes, tomato quarters, green beans, pinolas in bowl.
Orange Avocado	Shredded lettuce, ring of alligator pear, orange sections. Garnish with cherries.
Oregon	Shredded lettuce, Oregon cherries pitted and stuffed with hazelnuts.
Orientale	Endive, lettuce, tomatoes, red peppers and pineapple. Cream mayonnaise with paprika.
Oscar	Romaine, grapefruit sections, sliced banana. Garnish with strawberries, pecans and pickled walnuts. Chatelaine dressing.
Palm Beach	Head lettuce, slice of pineapple, cream cheese, strawberry or raspberry preserve. Garnish with red and green cherries.
Plaza	Heart of endive, pears and grapefruit sections. Plaza dressing.
Pommes d'Eve	Apple shell filled with a macédoine of asparagus tips, French-cut string beans, green peas, red and green peppers, mayonnaise. Garnish with chopped truffles.
Port Au Prince	Red apple shell filled with diced grapefruit and oranges. Creamed mayonnaise dressing.
Princesse	Tomato slice, lettuce, asparagus tips, crisscross of red and green peppers.
Printemps	Romaine, escarole, tomatoes, asparagus tips.
Priola	Chicory, tomatoes, diced celery, cut artichoke bottoms, diced potatoes, chopped truffles, in a bowl.
Romaine Astoria	Romaine, grapefruit and orange sections, pickled walnut, green pepper ring and diced pimiento.
Roof Garden	Lettuce, cantaloupe ring, fresh fruits. Garnish with fresh berries and maraschino cherries.

Royale	Romaine, watercress, slice tomato, celery in julienne. French Dressing.
St. George	Chicory and apples in julienne in bowl. Horseradish cream dressing.
Saratoga	Heart of romaine, grapefruit sections, banana slices, diced green peppers, cherries.
Serena	Romaine, alligator pear, tomato, celery. Cream mayonnaise, paprika.
Sevillane	Orange shell, filled with diced apples, celery, pineapple, nuts, truffles and pimientos. Cream mayonnaise, decorate.
Spring	Shredded lettuce, sliced cucumbers, sliced tomatoes. French Dressing.
Stuffed Apple	Pare and core small apples. Cook until tender in a syrup of sugar and cinnamon red hots. Cool apple, stuff with cream cheese and pecans and mask with mayonnaise mixed with little whipped cream. Serve on crisp lettuce cups.
Stuffed Pear	Lettuce, Bartlett pear halves stuffed with cheese, nuts. Mayonnaise.
Therese	Romaine, celery, apples and potatoes all in julienne in bowl. Cream Mayonnaise.
Tomatoes Stevens	Whole peeled tomato split in center about ⅔ way through. Insert two slices of beets and one slice of cucumber with fancy cut edge in center between beet slices.
Tomato Surprise	Small peeled tomato stuffed with diced celery, apples, green peppers. Mayonnaise.
Tomato With Cheese	Lettuce, tomato slices, grated Parmesan cheese.
Touraine	Cantaloupe round, grapefruit sections, Heart of romaine, asparagus tips, green and red peppers. French Dressing.
Trianon	Orange slices, pickled beets, pickled walnuts, French endive. Lorenzo dressing.

Turquoise	Escarole, celery, pineapple and pimientos in julienne. Mayonnaise.
Valenciennes	Heart of lettuce, diced celery, sliced hard-cooked eggs, strips of truffles.
Venitienne	Lettuce, beets, celery knobs, French-cut string beans, apples in julienne, in a bowl. French dressing with paprika.
Vera	Heart of lettuce or romaine, quartered small tomatoes, artichoke bottoms, red and green peppers. Lemon-Cream Dressing.
Victoria	Shredded lettuce, tiny asparagus tips, artichoke bottoms, chopped eggs.
Viennoise	Heart of lettuce, diced celery, slices of hard-cooked eggs, truffles in julienne. French Dressing.

ORANGE GROVE SALAD

6 California oranges

6 grapefruit

4 half grapefruit shells

Boston or Bibb lettuce

½ cup coarsely chopped pecans

Citrus Mayonnaise (recipe follows)

Makes 4 salads

Peel the oranges and grapefruit. Use a sharp knife to section both fruits.

Line the grapefruit shells with lettuce and fill with alternate sections of grapefruit and orange.

Sprinkle each salad with chopped nuts. Serve with Citrus Mayonnaise.

CITRUS MAYONNAISE

1½ cups Mayonnaise*

¼ cup orange juice†

⅛ teaspoon very fine sugar

1 teaspoon grated lemon rind

Makes about 1⅔ cups

† Or use the orange and grapefruit juice drained from sections.

Stir ingredients together. Chill until ready to use.

ORGANIC SALAD
Green Tulip Room Specialty

6 slices cucumber

½ large ripe tomato, sliced

2 large onion slices, broken into rings

¼ cup grated carrot

¼ cup alfalfa sprouts

¼ cup bean sprouts

¼ cup sliced celery

3 raw mushrooms, sliced

Few fresh spinach leaves

3-4 radish roses

Makes 1 serving

Arrange the cucumber slices, tomato slices and onion rings around the edge of a shallow salad bowl.

Arrange the carrots, sprouts, celery and mushrooms in the bowl "spoke fashion." Center with a rosette of spinach leaves and radish roses.

LEEKS VINAIGRETTE

12 leeks

2 cups consommé*

½ cup olive oil

¼ cup lemon juice

1 teaspoon salt

¼ teaspoon pepper

1 tablespoon chopped capers

½ teaspoon English mustard

1 teaspoon chopped parsley

1 teaspoon chopped chives

Makes 6 servings

Halve and trim leeks. Wash thoroughly under running water. Tie leeks into bundles with string and lay in large skillet.

Pour consommé over leeks and cover skillet. Heat to boiling. Reduce heat and simmer 10 minutes, or until leeks are tender.

Remove leeks to a shallow dish with a slotted spoon and cut strings.

Combine remaining ingredients in a small bowl and beat with a wire whip. Pour over hot leeks.

VEGETABLE SALAD

1 pound green beans, tipped
and cooked

1 pound fresh lima beans, shelled
and cooked

1 pound fresh peas, shelled
and cooked

1 small cauliflower, cooked
and diced

2 large carrots, cooked and diced

French Dressing II*

Salad greens

Makes 6 servings

Drain all vegetables well and chill thoroughly before making salad.

Toss chilled vegetables with enough French Dressing to thoroughly moisten all ingredients.

Serve in individual salad bowls lined with salad greens.

CHEF'S SALAD, PLAZA
A Plaza Favorite

½ head iceberg lettuce

¼ head each chicory, escarole
and romaine

1 teaspoon salt

¾ cup julienne strips of chicken,
both white and dark meat

¾ cup julienne strips beef tongue

¾ cup julienne strips Swiss cheese

¾ cup julienne strips boiled ham

¾ cup julienne strips raw carrot

½ cup shredded cabbage

Russian Dressing*

2 hard-cooked eggs, chopped
very fine

Makes 6 servings

Discard damaged leaves from greens and cut or tear remainder into bite-size pieces. Place greens in a large pan. Cover with cold water and sprinkle with salt.

Wash and rinse greens thoroughly to remove foreign particles. Drain in salad basket or strainer. (If you are preparing greens ahead of time, just put the strainer with greens in refrigerator until ready to use.)

To serve, place greens in a large bowl. Add chicken, tongue, cheese, ham, carrots and cabbage and mix well.

Add Russian Dressing and serve in individual salad bowls on beds of lettuce leaves. Garnish with chopped egg.

FLAKED HALIBUT SALAD

1 pound cooked halibut,
boned and flaked

1 cup mayonnaise

⅓ cup diced celery

2 teaspoons capers

1 teaspoon French mustard

1 teaspoon chopped parsley

Salt and pepper

½ head Boston lettuce

1 ripe tomato, quartered

1 hard-cooked egg, quartered

1 lemon, quartered

Makes 2 servings

Combine flaked halibut, mayonnaise, celery, capers, mustard, parsley, salt and pepper in a bowl. Chill several hours to develop flavors.

Line 2 chilled salad plates with Boston lettuce. Mound fish salad in center of greens. Garnish plates with tomato, egg and lemon quarters.

AVOCADO–SHRIMP SALAD

2 firm-ripe avocados

1 pound cooked shrimp, diced

¾ cup mayonnaise

Salt and pepper

2 large canned pimientos,
cut into strips

Large ripe olives

Boston or leaf lettuce

Hot toasted saltines

Makes 4 servings

Halve and peel avocados, remove pits. Scoop a generous quantity of the avocado meat from each half and dice.

Combine avocados, shrimp, ½ cup mayonnaise and salt and pepper to taste.

Fill avocado halves with salad mixture and garnish with crisscross strips of pimiento and ripe olives.

Place on individual salad plates, lined with lettuce. Serve with remaining mayonnaise and hot toasted saltines.

SALADE NICOISE

1 pound green beans, tipped and cooked

French Dressing*

2 large ripe tomatoes, cut into wedges

1 medium-size red onion, thinly sliced

½ cup halved pitted ripe olives

1 can (2 ounces) anchovy fillets, drained

2 cans (7 ounces each) solid-pack tuna, drained and broken into chunks

2 hard-cooked eggs, shelled and sliced

Makes 6 servings

Drizzle hot green beans with ½ cup of the French Dressing. Chill for at least 2 hours. Chill remaining dressing and salad ingredients at same time.

To serve, spoon green beans into a large chilled salad bowl. Add tomato wedges, onion slices, olives and anchovy fillets, reserving a few of each for garnish. Toss gently.

Add tuna and egg slices and toss again. Garnish with reserved tomato, onion, olives and anchovy.

Drizzle with remaining French Dressing and serve at once.

SPINACH SALAD PLAZA

1 pound fresh young spinach

6 strips bacon, diced

3 shallots, minced

1 clove garlic, minced

1 small white onion, chopped

3 tablespoons wine vinegar

¼ teaspoon English mustard

Freshly ground pepper

Sieved hard-cooked egg yolk

Makes 6 servings

Wash spinach well in several changes of warm water. Trim all stems and break spinach into tiny pieces. Drain well and chill.

Fry bacon in small skillet. Remove bacon with slotted spoon and drain on paper towels.

Sauté shallots, garlic and onion in fat in skillet until soft. Add vinegar, mustard and pepper. Heat to boiling.

Place spinach in salad bowl. Pour hot dressing over and toss well. Top with bacon bits and sieved hard-cooked egg.

PLAZA CHICKEN SALAD
A Plaza Favorite

1 fowl, 4 to 5 pounds	Simmer the fowl until tender and allow to cool in broth. Remove skin and slip meat from bones. Cut in large dice. (Reserve broth for soup.)
1 cup diced celery	
⅓ cup cider vinegar	Combine diced chicken, celery, vinegar, ¼ cup mayonnaise, salt and pepper in a bowl. Allow to stand in the refrigerator several hours, or even overnight, mixing salad several times to blend flavors.
1 cup mayonnaise	
Salt and pepper	
1 head lettuce	To serve, separate lettuce into leaves. Wash and dry well. Line one large salad bowl or 6 individual salad bowls with lettuce.
2 hard-cooked eggs, shelled and quartered	Spoon chicken mixture into lettuce leaves. Add quartered eggs, sliced olives and a sprinkling of capers. Top with remaining mayonnaise. Serve at once.
6 stuffed olives sliced	
1 tablespoon capers	
	Chef André says that in making chicken salad it is always better to use boiled chicken because the meat is always more tender and moist. And, of course,
Makes 6 servings	you have all that lovely broth to use as soup. E.B.

CELERY VICTOR

2 hearts of celery	Wash the celery well (it should be white, not green), trim the root and cut off all but the small end to reach leaves in the center of the heart.
1 onion, sliced	
2½ cups beef or chicken broth	Put the celery hearts and the sliced onion in a saucepan, add the broth. Cover and cook until tender, 15 to 20 minutes.
1 cup garlic-flavored French dressing	
Shredded lettuce	Let the hearts cool in cooking liquid. Then remove, cut in half lengthwise and put in a shallow dish. Pour over French dressing and chill 3 to 4 hours.
Coarsely ground black pepper	
Anchovy fillets	To serve, drain off the dressing and place celery on a bed of shredded lettuce. Sprinkle with pepper.
Pimiento	Garnish with anchovy fillets, pimiento strips and chopped watercress.
Watercress	
	One of my favorite salads. I often serve it, too, as a
Makes 4 servings	cold vegetable with ham or lamb. E.B.

PEAR CORONATION SALAD
A Plaza Favorite

1 large ripe pear (Bosc or Bartlett)

Lemon juice

¼ cup crumbled Roquefort cheese

⅓ cup whipped cream

Leaf or Boston lettuce

2 tablespoons Bar-le-duc

Makes 1 serving

Halve, core and peel pear. Sprinkle pear halves with lemon juice.

Combine crumbled cheese and 2 tablespoons whipped cream to make a mixture of molding consistency. Fill the pear cavity with mixture and press halves together to restore whole pear shape.

Place pear on a salad plate lined with leaf or Boston lettuce.

Fold Bar-le-duc into remaining whipped cream and spoon over salad.

This delicious salad is something to write home about. E.B.

PALM COURT SPINACH SALAD

3 pounds fresh spinach

1 bunch watercress

Spinach Salad Dressing (recipe follows)

6–8 slices bacon, crisply fried and crumbled

Makes 6–8 servings

Choose tender young spinach with velvety-textured leaves. Remove and discard stems from the spinach and watercress. Wash thoroughly several times. Dry greens well and chop or break into small pieces.

Place spinach salad dressing in a large salad bowl. Add prepared greens. Toss to coat leaves evenly.

Sprinkle crisp bacon pieces over greens and serve very cold.

This is a great favorite in our Palm Court. E.B.

SPINACH SALAD DRESSING

3 tablespoons olive oil

Juice of ½ lemon

1 tablespoon red wine vinegar

1 teaspoon dry English OR French mustard

Pinch of salt and pepper

Makes about ⅓ cup

Combine all ingredients and mix vigorously until thoroughly blended.

DRESSINGS

CLASSIC FRENCH DRESSING

¼ cup wine vinegar, cider vinegar OR fresh lemon juice

Combine ingredients in a screw-top jar. Shake vigorously until blended. Keep cold.

¾ cup olive oil (or other salad oil if preferred)

Stir or shake before using.

1½ teaspoons salad salt

Freshly ground black pepper

1 clove garlic (optional)

Makes 1 cup

VARIATIONS

Anchovy

Omit salt from dressing. Drain and mash anchovy fillets from 1 small flat can. Add to dressing with extra lemon juice is desired.

Fines Herbes

Use tarragon vinegar in dressing. Add ½ teaspoon dried basil, crumbled; 1 teaspoon pakrika; ½ teaspoon dry mustard; ¼ cup finely minced parsley.

FRENCH DRESSING I

½ clove of garlic

Rub the inside of mixing bowl with the garlic. Add seasonings and egg yolks.

1 teaspoon French mustard

½ teaspoon sweet paprika

Beat vigorously with wire whip until well blended. Add salad oil very slowly, beating until all oil is added. Then add vinegar and mix for a few seconds.

½ teaspoon salt

Pinch of sugar

This is the classic dressing for tossed greens. A good marinade for cold vegetables, too. E.B.

Dash of freshly ground white pepper

2 egg yolks

1 cup salad oil

2½ tablespoons red wine vinegar

Makes about 1 cup

FRENCH DRESSING II

¼ cup mayonnaise

½ teaspoon salt

½ teaspoon paprika

Pinch of freshly ground white pepper

Pinch of sugar

¼ clove garlic, crushed

½ cup salad oil

¼ cup red wine vinegar

Makes about 1 cup

Combine mayonnaise, salt, paprika, white pepper, sugar and garlic in mixing bowl. Blend thoroughly with a small wire whip.

Add salad oil slowly, beating constantly with wire whip. Then beat in vinegar, a little at a time, until no separation occurs.

GREEN TULIP DRESSING

½ cup wine vinegar

1½ teaspoons salt

⅛ teaspoon white pepper

1 tablespoon Dijon mustard

2 tablespoons hot prepared horseradish

½ teaspoon minced chives

½ teaspoon minced dill

2 tablespoons Worcestershire sauce

2 cups mayonnaise

2 egg yolks

1 cup salad oil

½ pint large curd cottage cheese

Makes about 1 quart

Combine vinegar, seasonings and Worcestershire sauce in large mixer bowl. Blend on low speed.

Add mayonnaise and egg yolks and mix until smooth.

Slowly add oil while continuing to mix on low speed. Fold in cheese by hand.

ORGANIC SALAD DRESSING
Green Tulip Specialty

¼ cup wine vinegar

⅓ cup pine nut oil

1 tablespoon chopped sour pickle

1 tablespoon minced onion

1 teaspoon chopped parsley

½ hard cooked egg, chopped

1 teaspoon prepared Dijon mustard

½ teaspoon salt

⅛ teaspoon pepper

Makes about ⅔ cup dressing OR *2 servings*

Combine all ingredients and mix well. Chill until ready to serve.

Shake very well before serving.

LEMON MAYONNAISE

1 egg yolk, slightly beaten

½ teaspoon salt

2 tablespoons lemon juice (possibly more)

2 cups olive oil

Beat egg yolk with salt and then with 1 tablespoon of the lemon juice.

Put mixture into a chilled mixing bowl. Blend in ¼ cup of oil, a little at a time. (If you use an electric mixer, be sure the beaters are chilled too.) Then whip in another ¼ cup of oil more rapidly. Then more oil until the 2 cups have been used.

As the mixture thickens with the addition of the oil, add another tablespoon of lemon juice. Just before serving, if a very tart dressing is desired, add more lemon juice.

Sometimes salads can be enhanced with a pale green or pink dressing. *For green,* crush parsley or watercress in a piece of cheesecloth and squeeze juice into mayonnaise. *For pink,* add a bright colored paprika, crushed lobster coral or a little tomato puree. E.B.

Makes about 2 cups

CHEF ANDRE'S SALAD DRESSING

1 tablespoon mayonnaise

¼ teaspoon dry English mustard

¼ teaspoon prepared mustard

¼ teaspoon Worcestershire sauce

¼ teaspoon strained chili sauce

Pinch of salt and pepper

Pinch of paprika

Dash of sugar

Dash of A-1 sauce

Dash of tarragon vinegar

Dash of onion juice

2 cups olive oil

Makes about 2 cups

Combine all ingredients, except oil, in a chilled bowl.

Beat in oil very gradually, adding ¼ cup at a time and blending thoroughly with a wire whip or electric beater with each addition of oil.

Continue until all oil has been used. Adjust salt. Chill until ready to use. Shake or beat before using.

This dressing will keep in the refrigerator for a week or more–but in my house it never lasts that long. E.B.

GOLDEN SALAD DRESSING

2 whole eggs

¼ cup pineapple, apple or other light-colored fruit juice

¼ cup lemon juice

⅓ cup sugar

Makes about 1 cup

In a very heavy saucepan *or* top of a double boiler, beat eggs until well blended, but not foamy. Blend in fruit juices and sugar.

Cook mixture in saucepan over very low heat or place top of double boiler over simmering water. Continue cooking, stirring constantly, until mixture thickens.

Pour dressing into a bowl and chill. Serve with fresh fruit salad or a tossed salad with fruits.

This dressing is similar to a cooked dressing. A good way to use up left-over fruit juices. E.B.

RUSSIAN DRESSING

½ cup French Dressing I*

5 tablespoons mayonnaise

2 tablespoons chili sauce

1 tablespoon diced pimiento

1 tablespoon chopped watercress

1 tablespoon red vinegar

1 teaspoon finely chopped chives

Makes about 1 cup

Put all ingredients into mixing bowl and beat with a wire whip to blend thoroughly.

Store until serving time in refrigerator. Give a light beating to dressing with wire whip before using.

Serve with hearts of lettuce, hard-cooked eggs, seafood or thick slices of tomato on iceberg lettuce.

You can substitute a good bottled French dressing in these recipes. E.B.

MAYONNAISE

2 egg yolks

½ teaspoon salt

Dash of white pepper

½ teaspoon dry mustard

2 teaspoons lemon juice

1 cup light olive oil

Makes about 1 cup

Rinse a deep bowl with hot water and dry well. With electric mixer set at medium speed, beat egg yolks with salt, pepper, dry mustard and 1 teaspoon lemon juice until well blended.

Begin to add oil, a drop at a time, until about ¼ cup has been added. Then add ½ teaspoon more of the lemon juice. Continue to beat and add oil until mayonnaise is thick.

Beat in remaining lemon juice and correct seasonings. (If mayonnaise should curdle, beat 1 egg yolk in a small bowl and slowly beat into curdled mayonnaise.)

FRUIT DRESSING

½ cup raspberry jam OR
stewed raspberries
drained of their liquid

2 tablespoons mayonnaise

2 tablespoons lemon juice

Dash of salt

¼ cup heavy cream, whipped

Makes about 1 cup or 8 servings

Mash raspberries with a fork in mixing bowl. Blend in mayonnaise, lemon juice and salt until thoroughly mixed.

Fold in whipped cream until blended. Chill for several hours.

When a fruit salad is topped with this dressing, it can be used for the salad course or for a refreshing dessert. E.B.

SAUCES

BROWN SAUCE

MORNAY SAUCE

MEAT SAUCE

BECHAMEL

GLACE DE VIANDE

CURRY SAUCE BASE FOR MEAT OR FISH

CREAM SAUCE

HOLLANDAISE SAUCE

MOUSSELINE SAUCE

SAUCE AIGRE-DOUX

SAUCE CHASSEUR I

SAUCE AUX CORNICHONS

SAUCE BORDELAISE

SAUCE CHASSEUR II

SAUCE BRETONNE

SAUCE ITALIENNE

CELERY SAUCE

SAUCE BOURGUIGNONNE

TOMATO SAUCE A LA PLAZA

SCAMPI SAUCE PLAZA

SAUCE AU PORTO

HONGROISE SAUCE

SAUCE REMICK

VELOUTE SAUCE

STROGANOFF SAUCE

SAUCE MARSEILLAISE

SAUCE SUPREME

DEMI-GLACE

BROWN SAUCE
Sauce Espagnole

½ cup fat (beef or pork)

1 carrot, chopped

2 onions, chopped

½ cup flour

2 quarts Brown Stock*

1 clove garlic

2 stalks celery

Few sprigs parsley

1 bay leaf

Few sprigs fresh thyme (if available)

½ cup tomato puree

Makes about 1 quart

Melt the fat in a heavy saucepan and cook the carrot and onions until lightly browned. Stir in the flour and continue cooking until the flour is browned, stirring continuously.

Add about 3 cups of boiling stock, the garlic and the next 4 ingredients tied in a bundle (fagot).

Cook and stir over moderate heat until mixture thickens. Add 3 more cups hot stock.

Cook over low heat, stirring occasionally, for 1 hour. Skim off fat as it comes to the surface.

Stir in the tomato puree and cook 10 minutes. Strain through a fine sieve.

Add the remaining hot stock (2 cups) and cook slowly over low heat for 1 hour. Skim as needed. At this point the sauce should be reduced to about 4 cups. Strain again and cool.

Store, covered, in refrigerator. The sauce should be used within 8 to 9 days.

MORNAY SAUCE

2 tablespoons butter

1 tablespoon minced onion

¼ cup flour

3 cups hot milk

Salt and white pepper

Few sprigs parsley

1 cup grated Gruyère OR Swiss cheese

1 teaspoon English mustard

Makes about 2 cups

Melt the butter and add onion in a saucepan. Simmer a few minutes.

Stir in the flour and cook over low heat until flour begins to turn golden.

Add the hot milk stirring all the time with a wire whip.

Add salt, white pepper and parsley and cook over low heat stirring often, for 30 minutes.

Strain through a fine sieve into a second saucepan. Add cheese and mustard. Heat slowly until cheese melts.

MEAT SAUCE

1 tablespoon salad oil

½ cup minced onion

½ clove garlic, crushed

½ pound chopped lean beef

⅓ cup white wine

1 cup chopped fresh tomato pulp

1½ cups Tomato Sauce*

1½ cups Demi-Glace*

2 tablespoons sugar

1 small bay leaf

¼ teaspoon oregano

⅛ teaspoon crushed Italian
red pepper

1 teaspoon salt

Makes approximately 4 cups

Heat oil in a heavy skillet. Fry onion and garlic until yellow. Add beef shaped into a round patty. Fry until beef loses redness, breaking up patty as meat cooks. Skim out any excess fat.

Add wine and simmer 3 to 4 minutes. Stir in remaining ingredients and mix well. Simmer for 1 hour, stirring occasionally.

If sauce becomes too thick, thin to desired consistency with a little broth or stock. Let stand a few minutes before serving; then skim off any fat and adjust seasonings.

BECHAMEL SAUCE

¼ cup butter

1 tablespoon minced onion

½ cup flour

6 cups hot milk

Salt and white pepper

Few sprigs parsley

Pinch of nutmeg

Makes about 1 quart

Melt the butter and add onion. Simmer a few minutes.

Stir in the flour and cook over low heat until flour begins to turn golden.

Add the hot milk, 2 cups at a time, stirring all the while with a wire whip.

Add remaining ingredients and cook over low heat, stirring often, for about 40 minutes.

Strain through a fine sieve.

GLACE DE VIANDE
Meat Glaze

1 gallon (4 quarts) veal Broth OR *chicken Broth**

Use a heavy pot or Dutch oven, over low heat. Bring broth to a boil, then reduce heat to low and simmer until only about 1 quart of broth remains. This will take about 2 hours.

Strain broth into a small saucepan and continue to simmer over low heat until the liquid remaining in the saucepan is brown in color and of a syrupy consistency. Strain into a bowl or jar and refrigerate to use as needed.

Meat or chicken glaze is used most often to improve the flavor of soups and sauces. When glaze is refrigerated it becomes jellylike. The amount to be used should be melted in a double boiler, or over very low heat.

Makes about 1 cup

Whenever you boil a chicken for salad or other dishes, save and freeze the broth until you have one gallon. E.B.

CURRY SAUCE BASE FOR MEAT OR FISH

¼ cup butter

1 onion, chopped

1 carrot, chopped

1 unpeeled green apple, chopped

3–4 tablespoons good fresh curry powder

1 clove garlic

1 bay leaf

1 tablespoon shredded fresh coconut

2 cups water, stock or broth

Salt and pepper

Makes approximately 2 cups

Heat the butter in a heavy covered skillet. Stir in onion, carrot and apple. Cover and simmer 5 minutes. Mix in curry powder, garlic, bay leaf and coconut. Cover and simmer 5 minutes.

Add water, stock or broth. Simmer uncovered for about 40 minutes. Strain. Add salt and pepper to taste.

Use curry sauce base in the following proportions: ¼ cup curry sauce to ½ or ¾ cup Cream Sauce (see Béchamel*) or Fish Velouté (see Velouté*). For a mild curry flavor, reduce amount of curry sauce used; for a stronger flavor, increase the amount of curry sauce used. Stir in 2 to 3 tablespoons heavy cream for a smooth finish. Serve with chutney.

CREAM SAUCE
Sauce Crème

2 cups Béchamel Sauce*

½ cup light cream

¼ cup heavy cream

Makes about 2 cups

Combine Béchamel and light cream in a heavy saucepan. Stir with a wire whip over moderate heat until reduced and thickened.

Let sauce cool for a few minutes, then strain and correct seasonings.

Gently stir in heavy cream. Sauce may be reheated, but do not allow it to boil.

HOLLANDAISE SAUCE

3 egg yolks

1 tablespoon cold water

½ cup butter, cut into 8 pieces

1 teaspoon lemon juice

Dash of salt

Makes 1 cup

Combine egg yolks and cold water in top of double boiler and beat with a wire whip until smooth.

Place top of double boiler over simmering, not boiling water on low heat. Beat egg yolks with wire whip until mixture is fluffy.

Add butter, a few pieces at a time and continue to beat with wire whip until butter melts before adding more. When all butter is added and sauce thickens, add lemon juice and salt.

Note: If sauce should begin to curdle take sauce from heat and gradually beat in 1 tablespoon boiling water.

MOUSSELINE SAUCE

3 egg yolks

1 tablespoon cold water

½ cup butter, cut into 8 pieces

1 teaspoon lemon juice

Dash of salt

¼ cup heavy cream, whipped

Makes about 1½ cups

Combine egg yolks and cold water in top of double boiler and beat with a wire whip until smooth.

Place top of double boiler over simmering, not boiling, water on low heat. Beat egg yolks with wire whip until mixture is fluffy.

Add butter, a few pieces at a time, and continue to beat with wire whip until butter melts before adding more. When all butter is added and sauce thickens, add lemon juice and salt.

Just before serving, fold in whipped cream.

SAUCE AIGRE-DOUX
Sweet and Sour

½ cup sugar

¾ cup chopped onion

½ cup cider vinegar

10 peppercorns, crushed

½ cup currant jelly

1½ cups Demi-Glace*

1 tablespoon fresh lemon juice

Makes 3-4 servings

Melt the sugar in a heavy skillet over low heat.

When the sugar is completely melted and starts to take on a yellow-brown color, carefully stir in onions (mixture may spatter). Cook 2 to 3 minutes.

Carefully stir in cider vinegar and crushed peppercorns. Simmer over low heat until mixture is reduced to about one fourth its original volume. Stir in jelly and Demi-Glace.

Simmer sauce for 15 minutes. Add lemon juice and strain.

I find this sauce especially good with ham and pork dishes. E.B.

SAUCE CHASSEUR I

⅓ cup salad oil

1 medium onion, sliced

10 large mushroom caps, sliced

3 firm tomatoes, peeled and sliced

½ cup white wine

1 clove garlic, mashed

1 teaspoon salt

1 bay leaf

⅛ teaspoon freshly ground
black pepper

Few leaves fresh tarragon

2 cups Brown Sauce*

Chopped parsley

Makes about 4 cups

Mix oil, onion and mushrooms. Cover and cook over low heat 5 minutes.

Mix in tomatoes, wine and garlic. Cover and cook another 5 minutes, or until slightly reduced.

Add remaining ingredients except parsley. Mix well. Bring to a boil, then reduce heat, cover and simmer for about 20 minutes, or until sauce is thickness desired.

Correct seasonings, strain and serve garnished with chopped parsley.

SAUCE AUX CORNICHONS
Sauce with Tiny Sour Gherkins

4 teaspoons chopped shallots

2 tablespoons butter

⅓ cup dry white wine

⅓ cup cider vinegar

2 cups Demi-Glace*

1 small sour pickle, slivered

1 teaspoon chopped parsley

1 teaspoon chopped fresh tarragon

1 teaspoon chopped fresh chervil

1 teaspoon chopped fresh dill
(optional)

Makes about 2 cups

Sauté shallots in hot butter. Stir in wine and vinegar and cook until reduced to about ⅓ cup.

Add Demi-Glace and simmer for 10 minutes.

Stir in slivered pickle and chopped herbs. Serve hot.

SAUCE BORDELAISE

1 tablespoon chopped shallots

2 tablespoons butter

⅛ teaspoon leaf thyme

¼ piece bay leaf

8 peppercorns, crushed

⅔ cup red Bordeaux wine

2 cups Demi-Glace*

Juice of ½ lemon

¼ cup poached diced marrow

Makes about 1½ cups

Simmer shallots in hot butter. Stir in seasonings and wine. Bring to a boil and cook until reduced to about ⅓ cup.

Add Demi-Glace and simmer for 15 minutes. Strain.

Stir in lemon juice and prepared marrow. Heat through.

SAUCE CHASSEUR II
Hunter-Style Sauce

2 tablespoons butter or salad oil	Heat butter or oil in a heavy saucepan. Add mushrooms, shallots and garlic. Cook 5 minutes.
1 cup sliced fresh mushrooms	
1 tablespoon chopped shallots	Add wine and simmer until reduced to about half original volume.
½ clove of garlic, crushed	
½ cup dry white wine	Stir in remaining ingredients except parsley or chervil. Simmer 15 to 20 minutes. Correct seasonings and sprinkle with chopped parsley or chervil.
1 tablespoon tomato puree	
2 fresh tomatoes, peeled, seeded and chopped	
2 cups Demi-Glace*	
2 teaspoons chopped parsley OR chervil	
Makes about 3 cups	

SAUCE BRETONNE

4 tablespoons butter	Heat butter in a heavy saucepan. Add onions and garlic. Simmer until onions are yellow and translucent.
½ cup chopped onions	
1 clove garlic, crushed	Add wine and continue to simmer for about 20 minutes, or until reduced to half the original volume.
½ cup good white wine	
3 ripe tomatoes	Peel tomatoes and press out seeds. Chop pulp and add with remaining ingredients (except parsley).
1½ cups Tomato Sauce*	
1 bay leaf	Cover and simmer for about 25 minutes, stirring occasionally. Correct seasonings, remove bay leaf. Do not strain. Sprinkle with parsley.
Salt and pepper to taste	
2 teaspoons chopped parsley	A good sauce with fresh green beans. Delicious with tender green limas, too. E.B.
Makes about 3½ cups	

SAUCE ITALIENNE

2 tablespoons olive oil

1 tablespoon chopped shallots

¼ cup diced cooked ham

¼ cup diced raw mushrooms

½ clove garlic, crushed

½ cup dry white wine

2 ripe tomatoes, peeled and chopped

2 teaspoons tomato puree

1 cup Tomato Sauce*

1 cup Demi-Glace*

Salt and pepper

1 teaspoon minced fresh parsley

1 teaspoon minced fresh chervil OR basil

Makes 2 cups

Heat oil in a heavy pan. Add shallots, ham, mushrooms and garlic. Stir over moderate heat 5 to 6 minutes. Add wine and continue to cook and stir until volume is reduced by half.

Add tomatoes, puree, Tomato Sauce and Demi-Glace. Simmer 15 to 20 minutes, stirring occasionally. Strain. Correct seasonings and stir in minced herbs.

CELERY SAUCE

⅓ cup finely diced white celery

¼ teaspoon salt

2 cups Velouté Sauce*

¼ cup heavy cream

½ tablespoon finely minced white celery leaves

Makes approximately 2 cups

Scrape or peel celery to remove all strings before dicing. Put about 3 tablespoons celery in a small saucepan with salt and water to cover. Cook until tender, drain.

Add remaining diced celery to white Velouté Sauce. Simmer 15 minutes, strain. Stir in cream, the cooked celery and the minced celery leaves. Adjust seasonings and serve hot.

SAUCE BOURGUIGNONNE

1 fresh fish head

¼ cup chopped carrots

¼ cup chopped celery

¼ cup chopped onion

¼ cup parsley sprigs

¼ cup chopped mushrooms

2 cups Burgundy wine

8–10 peppercorns

½ teaspoon salt

½ bay leaf

1 tablespoon butter

1 tablespoon flour

Makes 2-3 servings

Put all ingredients except butter and flour into a heavy saucepan. Bring to a boil. Reduce heat and simmer mixture for about 40 minutes, or long enough to reduce liquid to one third the original amount.

Strain through a fine sieve and return liquid to low heat.

Blend butter and flour to a paste and drop bits of mixture into hot liquid. Use a wire whip to blend smooth.

When sauce is smooth and thickened to taste, adjust seasonings.

Serve hot with fish dishes.

This sauce really starts with half a fresh salmon head, but these aren't easily come by—so any fish head will do. E.B.

TOMATO SAUCE A LA PLAZA

1 medium-size onion, chopped

½ cup butter

½ clove garlic, crushed

2 cups tomato puree

Salt and pepper

1 teaspoon sugar

¼ bay leaf

Ham bone, or small piece cooked ham

Makes about 1⅓ cups (4 servings)

Brown onion in butter. Add garlic and simmer for a minute or two.

Add remaining ingredients and simmer over low heat for about 45 minutes, stirring frequently. Adjust seasonings, strain and serve hot.

SCAMPI SAUCE PLAZA

¼ cup olive oil

1 clove garlic, mashed

1 tablespoon chopped leek

1 tablespoon chopped onion

1 tablespoon chopped celery

1 cup red wine vinegar

1 small bay leaf

⅛ teaspoon leaf thyme

⅛ teaspoon oregano

1 teaspoon coarsely ground
black pepper

1 teaspoon salt

1 cup beef bouillon

2 cups tomato puree

Juice of 1 small lemon

1 tablespoon prepared mustard

¼ cup minced parsley

Makes about 3½ cups

Heat oil in a heavy saucepan. Add garlic and chopped vegetables. Simmer 5 minutes.

Add wine vinegar, bring to a boil. Reduce heat to low moderate and cook until reduced to about half the original volume.

Stir in seasonings, bouillon, tomato puree and lemon juice. Cover and simmer over very low heat for about 1 hour. Stir often to prevent scorching.

Strain sauce, blend in mustard and parsley. Correct seasoning. Cool and store in refrigerator to use as needed.

SAUCE AU PORTO

⅔ cup Ruby Port wine

2 cups Demi-Glace*

Juice of ½ lemon

Makes about 1½ cups

Stir wine over moderate heat until it is reduced to about ⅓ cup. Stir in Demi-Glace and simmer 10 minutes.

Strain, stir in lemon juice and heat through.

An excellent sauce with beef and game. E.B.

SAUCES   145

HONGROISE SAUCE

1 small onion, minced

5 tablespoons butter

½ cup dry white wine

1 tablespoon Hungarian paprika

Pinch of salt

Few sprigs parsley

Pinch of leaf thyme

1½ cups Velouté Sauce*

Makes about 2 cups

Sauté onion in 2 tablespoons butter in saucepan until soft. Add white wine, paprika, salt, and parsley. Heat to the boil and cook until liquid is reduced by one half.

Blend in Velouté Sauce and simmer for 5 minutes.

Strain through a fine sieve into a second saucepan. Add remaining 3 tablespoons butter and simmer 2 minutes.

SAUCE REMICK

1 teaspoon dry English mustard

Pinch of celery salt

1 teaspoon Worcestershire sauce

½ teaspoon paprika

Dash of Tabasco

2 cups chili sauce

2 cups good mayonnaise

Tarragon vinegar

Makes 4 cups

Thoroughly blend seasonings with chili sauce and mayonnaise. Thin to desired consistency with 1 to 2 tablespoons vinegar.

The perfect sauce with shrimp. E.B.

VELOUTE SAUCE

¼ cup butter

½ cup flour

6 cups White Stock*

Few white peppercorns

½ teaspoon salt

1 cup mushroom peelings

Melt the butter. Stir in flour and cook very slowly until flour starts to change color.

Heat the stock, then add to roux a cup at a time, mixing all the time with a wire whip.

Add the remaining ingredients and cook very slowly for 1 hour, stirring often. Skim when necessary.

When the sauce is the consistency of heavy cream, remove from heat. Strain through a fine sieve and cool. Stir occasionally while cooling to prevent a skin from forming on top.

Cover and store in refrigerator. Use within 1 week.

Note: For Fish Velouté use 5 bottles Doxsee clam broth *or* 6 cups court bouillon (fish stock).

Makes about 1 quart

STROGANOFF SAUCE

1 cup white wine vinegar

½ cup chopped onion

2 bay leaves

¼ teaspoon coarsely ground black pepper

1 teaspoon prepared hot mustard

3 tablespoons tomato paste

3 cups Béchamel Sauce*

1 cup dairy sour cream

Makes about 1 quart

Combine vinegar, onion, bay leaves and pepper in a heavy saucepan. Bring to a boil. Reduce heat and simmer until liquid is reduced to about ½ cup.

Use a wire whip to beat in mustard and tomato paste. Blend in Béchamel Sauce. Bring to a boil, stirring all the time with a wire whip.

Correct seasonings and strain through a fine sieve. Allow to cool for 10 minutes before blending in sour cream.

SAUCE MARSEILLAISE

2 tablespoons olive oil

1 tablespoon each: minced carrot
minced celery
minced onion
minced fennel
minced leek (white only)

1 clove garlic, crushed

Generous pinch of saffron

2 cups chopped tomato pulp

1 teaspoon tomato puree

½ cup good white wine

1 bay leaf

2½ cups white consommé OR
Fish Stock*

⅛ teaspoon white pepper

1 teaspoon salt

12 cherrystone clams

2 teaspoons chopped parsley

2 teaspoons chopped dill

Makes about 1 quart

Simmer olive oil, minced vegetables and garlic in a heavy saucepan. After about 5 minutes add saffron, tomato pulp, puree and wine.

Cook and stir over low heat until very thick. Add bay leaf, consommé or stock, pepper and salt. Bring to a boil.

Reduce heat and simmer 20 minutes. Strain.

Open clams and mince in blender, or chop very fine. Add to sauce with liquor. Heat about 10 minutes. Stir in parsley and dill.

If you like Bouillabaise you'll enjoy this sauce with fish dishes. E.B.

BELUGA CAVIAR WITH ITS
TRADITIONAL GARNITURES

SAUCE SUPREME

2 cups Chicken Stock*

¼ cup chopped fresh mushrooms

1 cup Velouté Sauce*

1 cup heavy cream

Salt

Cayenne pepper

Makes about 2 cups

Heat Chicken Stock and chopped mushrooms to the boil in a saucepan. Boil until mixture is reduced by one-half.

Add Velouté Sauce and stir to blend well. Continue to cook until mixture is reduced by one half. Reduce heat and slowly blend in heavy cream. Season with salt and cayenne pepper.

Strain through a fine sieve.

DEMI-GLACE

Stems and peelings from ½ pound mushrooms

½ cup dry Sherry

2 cups Brown Sauce*

1 tablespoon Glace de Viande*

Makes about 1½ cups

Chop mushroom stems and peelings. Simmer with Sherry until reduced about one half.
Stir in Brown Sauce and Glace de Viande. Bring to a boil.

Reduce heat to a simmer and cook 10 to 15 minutes. Strain.

PRIME RIBS OF BEEF WITH POPOVERS

ENTREE-EGGS

CHEF'S RAREBIT

EGGS EN COCOTTE

QUICK SPINACH OMELETTE

SCRAMBLED EGGS GEORGETTE

CHEESE AND POTATOES SAVOYARDE

EGGS BENEDICT

SPANISH EGGS

POACHED EGGS ON CREAMED CHICKEN
     IN PATTY SHELLS

EGG NESTS

EGGS NORMANDIE

HAM AND OYSTER PLANT RISSOLE

EGGS FLORENTINE

FRANCOIS' FRENCH TOAST

EGG BALLS

EGGS LORRAINE

POACHED EGGS BOURGUIGNONNE

EGGS MAXIMILIENNE

POACHED EGGS ARCHIDUC

EGGS EN BORDURE CHIMAY

EGGS CAREME

OMELETTE MAISON

CHEF'S RAREBIT

2 cups grated sharp American cheese

¼ cup beer

⅛ teaspoon paprika

⅛ teaspoon dry mustard

1 teaspoon Worcestershire sauce

1 egg yolk, beaten

4 slices fresh hot toast

Makes 2 servings

Mix cheese and beer in a very heavy saucepan, or in the top of a double boiler over hot water.

Blend paprika, mustard and Worcestershire sauce with 1 tablespoon hot water. Stir into cheese.

Stir over low heat—or, if using double boiler, over simmering water—until cheese is melted and smooth.

Remove from heat and immediately stir in beaten egg yolk, using a wire whip. Pour at once over hot toast slices.

The beaten egg yolk stirred in at the last minute is the master touch. Prepared this way, your Rarebit will be creamy smooth, never stringy. E.B.

EGGS EN COCOTTE

½ cup heavy cream, heated

4 eggs

Salt and pepper

1 teaspoon butter

Warm 2 individual earthenware ramekins by filling them with boiling water and letting stand 10 minutes. Empty and dry before using.

Divide the warm cream between the 2 ramekins.

Break 2 eggs into a small shallow dish and gently slide them onto the cream. Repeat for second dish.

Sprinkle with salt and pepper and dot each dish with ½ teaspoon butter.

Set ramekins in a shallow baking pan and fill pan with hot water to half an inch from top of ramekins.

Cover pan with a piece of heavy foil, pressing it down firmly and sealing it around the edges. With the point of a small knife, make a little slit in each corner to allow steam to escape.

Bake in a moderate oven, 350°, for about 8 to 10 minutes, or until whites are set.

Makes 2 servings

A lovely way to serve eggs, but only when they are fresh, fresh, fresh! E.B.

QUICK SPINACH OMELETTE

4 eggs

¼ cup light cream

¼ teaspoon salt

Dash white pepper

2 tablespoons butter

1 cup cooked spinach, well drained and chopped

1 teaspoon grated onion

2 tablespoons grated Parmesan cheese

Chopped parsley

Makes 2 servings

Beat eggs with cream and seasonings until very light and fluffy.

Heat butter in omelette pan until it just begins to brown. Reduce heat and add spinach mixed with grated onion. Simmer 1 minute.

Pour in beaten eggs and sprinkle with grated cheese. Turn heat to moderate.

As mixture begins to set, lift around edges with spatula and let liquid egg run under to cook.

When top of omelette begins to set–it should be moist and fairly loose, not firm–use spatula to roll omelette to side of pan opposite handle. Reduce heat and cook for a few seconds.

Lift handle and with the spatula roll omelette onto a warm serving dish.
Garnish with parsley and serve.

I vary this dish by using shredded Swiss cheese–about ¼ cup–in place of grated Parmesan. E.B.

SCRAMBLED EGGS GEORGETTE

2 large baking potatoes

8 eggs

3 tablespoons cream

Salt and pepper

4 tablespoons butter

½ pound cooked, cleaned, and shelled shrimp

Parsley

Makes 4 servings

Scrub potatoes and bake in hot oven, 425°, for 1 hour. Halve potatoes, scoop out and mash pulp. Season to taste with cream, butter, salt and pepper. Pipe mixture back into potato shells and bake in hot oven, 425°, 5 minutes, or just until golden.

Beat eggs until well mixed but not too light. Blend in cream, salt and pepper.

Melt butter in a heavy skillet. Add beaten eggs. Stir with a wooden spoon over low heat until eggs are softly set.

Spoon eggs into potato shells and top with cooked shrimp. Garnish with parsley.

CHEESE AND POTATOES SAVOYARDE

3 eggs

¼ cup finely diced Swiss cheese

¼ cup finely diced cooked potatoes

Salt and pepper

4 tablespoons butter

Makes 1 serving

Mix the eggs lightly with a fork. Add cheese, potatoes, salt and pepper being careful not to overmix.

Heat butter in a medium-size omelette pan until it becomes hazelnut brown.

Pour the egg mixture into the butter. Stir briskly with a fork to make sure the eggs do not stick to the pan.

As soon as the eggs congeal, roll the omelette by moving the skillet and folding both sides with a fork. Invert onto heated serving dish. Serve at once.

EGGS BENEDICT

4 poached eggs

2 English muffins, split and toasted

4 slices broiled Virginia ham

⅔ cup Hollandaise Sauce*

Sliced truffles

Glace de Viande*, melted

Makes 2 servings

Drain poached eggs well on paper towels. Place toasted muffins on heated serving plate. Top muffins with ham slices and poached eggs.

Heat Hollandaise Sauce over simmering water and spoon over eggs. Top with sliced truffles and Glace de Viande.

SPANISH EGGS

4 large firm ripe tomatoes

Salt and pepper

Fresh basil, minced

8 eggs

3–4 tablespoons butter

2 white onions, sliced

Makes 4 servings

Cut tomatoes in half. Sprinkle with salt, pepper and just a hint of minced fresh basil. Broil, cut side up, about 8 minutes.

Fry eggs in hot butter until whites are set and yolks are still soft. Trim whites to conform to size of tomato halves.

Fry onion in same buttered pan used for eggs. Separate slices into rings as onion cooks.

Place an egg on each tomato half and garnish with fried onion rings.

POACHED EGGS ON CREAMED CHICKEN IN PATTY SHELLS

2 cups diced cooked breast of chicken

Combine diced chicken and Béchamel Sauce in a heavy saucepan. Heat until bubbly, stirring often.

2 cups Béchamel Sauce*

4 hot patty shells

Spoon chicken mixture into hot patty shells and arrange on shallow baking dish.

4 poached eggs

Arrange one trimmed poached egg in each patty shell and top with 2 crossed pimiento strips.

8 pimiento strips

Bake in moderate oven, 375°, 5 minutes. Serve hot.

Makes 4 servings

EGG NESTS

4 eggs, separated

Beat egg whites until stiff but still moist.

4 slices buttered toast

Butter

Place toast in baking dish and mound each slice with egg white. Shape the stiffly beaten white with a teaspoon into a round "nest" with a hollow in the center.

Salt and pepper

Drop a dot of butter and a whole unbroken egg yolk into each "nest." Sprinkle with salt and pepper to taste.

Bake in a moderate oven, 350°, for about 8 to 10 minutes, or until yolk is set to taste and white is delicately browned.

Makes 2 servings

EGGS NORMANDIE

¾ cup heavy cream

Measure 3 tablespoons heavy cream into each of 4 individual baking dishes or ramekins. Sprinkle with salt and pepper.

Salt and pepper

20 raw oysters, shucked

Add 5 raw oysters and a little oyster liquor to each dish. Top the oysters with an egg, being careful not to break yolk.

4 eggs

1 cup rich Cream Sauce*

Bake in a hot oven, 400°, for 8 to 10 minutes.

½ teaspoon anchovy paste

Gently heat Cream Sauce. Stir in anchovy paste. Spoon sauce over eggs and serve at once.

Makes 4 servings

HAM AND OYSTER PLANT RISSOLE

3 eggs

2 tablespoons finely diced cooked ham

2 tablespoons finely diced cooked oyster plant

Salt and pepper

4 tablespoons butter

Makes 1 serving

Mix the eggs lightly with a fork. Add ham, oyster plant, salt and pepper, but do not overmix.

Heat butter in a medium-size omelette pan until it becomes hazelnut brown.

Pour the egg mixture into the butter and stir briskly with a fork to make sure the eggs do not stick to the pan.

As soon as the eggs congeal, roll the omelette by moving the skillet and folding both sides with a fork. Invert onto heated serving dish. Serve at once.

EGGS FLORENTINE

1 pound fresh spinach, cooked and chopped

Salt and pepper

Pinch of nutmeg

1 cup heavy cream

8 eggs

⅓ cup grated Parmesan cheese

Makes 4 servings

Be sure cooked spinach is thoroughly drained. Drain again after chopping. Add salt and pepper, nutmeg and ⅓ cup cream to spinach. Mix well.

Divide the spinach among 4 individual buttered baking dishes.

Break 2 eggs into each dish and spread with some of the remaining cream. Sprinkle each dish lightly with grated cheese.

Bake in a moderate oven, 375°, for about 10 minutes, or until eggs are set to taste.

This is a very popular luncheon dish. It can be made in advance by lightly poaching the eggs and reheating in a hot oven for quick serving. E.B.

FRANÇOIS' FRENCH TOAST

1 large egg

1½ cups light cream

¼ cup powdered sugar

Pinch of salt

½ teaspoon vanilla

⅓ cup Rum, Brandy or Curaçao

8 thick slices French OR
Italian bread, cut on a slant

6 tablespoons butter

¼ cup applesauce

¾ cup thin custard (recipe follows)

Makes 4 servings

Beat together egg, cream, 1 tablespoon powdered sugar, salt, vanilla and liquor. Dip bread slices in mixture, turning to coat sides and edges.

Sauté the slices in about 6 tablespoons hot butter, turning once.

When bread is golden brown, arrange in a single layer in a shallow buttered casserole. Mix the applesauce and custard and pour over toast.

Sprinkle remaining powdered sugar over top. Bake in a hot oven, 400°, for 15 minutes, or until browned and bubbly.

THIN CUSTARD

1½ cups milk

3 egg yolks

¼ cup sugar

Pinch of salt

½ teaspoon vanilla

Makes 1½ cups

Heat milk in top of double boiler, over direct heat.

Use a wire whip to beat egg yolks, sugar and salt until well mixed. Slowly pour hot milk into mixture, beating all the time.

Return mixture to first pan and place over hot water. Cook, stirring constantly, until a thin coating forms on metal spoon. This takes about 10 minutes.

Pour custard into a bowl and cool before using.

EGG BALLS

6 hard-cooked eggs, shelled

¼ cup chopped raw mushrooms

1 tablespoon butter

½ teaspoon salt

⅛ teaspoon pepper

1 cup thick Cream Sauce*

Batter for dipping (recipe follows)

Oil

Tomato Sauce*

Makes 3 servings

Finely chop eggs. Sauté mushrooms until tender in hot butter.

Thoroughly mix eggs, mushrooms, seasonings and thick Cream Sauce. Chill mixture in refrigerator for several hours; it should be very stiff. Shape into balls about the size of a walnut.

Dip the egg balls into batter until they are completely coated. Drop into deep hot fat and fry to a golden brown.

Drain on paper towels. Serve hot with Tomato Sauce.

BATTER

1½ cups all-purpose flour

2¼ teaspoons baking powder

½ teaspoon salt

1 egg white

2 egg yolks

⅔ cup milk

2 tablespoons salad oil

Stir dry ingredients together.

Beat egg white until moist stiff peaks form. Whip egg yolks, milk and oil together.

Gradually add flour mixture to milk mixture, beating smooth with a wire whip. Fold in egg white.

A delicious luncheon idea. Add a salad, hot rolls and a simple dessert. E.B.

EGGS LORRAINE

16 slices grilled bacon	Use individual baking dishes or casseroles. Place 4 slices bacon in each dish.
8 slices good Gruyère cheese	
8 eggs	Top the bacon with 2 slices cheese and add 2 eggs (be sure the yolks do not break!) to each dish.
Salt and pepper	Sprinkle eggs with salt, pepper and the barest touch of cayenne.
Dash of cayenne	
1 cup heavy cream	Whip cream until it just begins to thicken. It should drop, not run, from the spoon. Divide into 4 portions.
	Spread a portion of cream over each filled egg dish.
	Bake in a moderate oven, 350°, for 10 to 12 minutes.
Makes 4 servings	A favorite brunch dish with many friends. E.B.

POACHED EGGS BOURGUIGNONNE
Chef André Special

2 cups California Burgundy	Heat the wine and poach the eggs in the hot wine. Remove the eggs, place on buttered toast and keep warm.
6 eggs	
*½ cup Demi-Glace**	Cook the wine until it is reduced to less than 1 cup. Stir in Demi-Glace and simmer over low heat for 5 to 6 minutes.
2 tablespoons butter, melted	
1 tablespoon flour	Make a paste with the melted butter and flour. Stir into hot sauce. Stir and simmer until slightly thickened. Spoon sauce over eggs and serve at once.
Makes 3 servings	

EGGS MAXIMILIENNE

2 large firm ripe tomatoes

2 tablespoons chopped parsley

½ small garlic clove, crushed

2 tablespoons grated Parmesan cheese

Butter

4 eggs

½ cup buttered soft bread crumbs

Makes 2 servings

Cut the tomatoes in half. Scoop out pulp. Sprinkle the inside of the tomato shells with mixed parsley, garlic and cheese.

Drop a bit of butter into each shell, then break an egg into each. Sprinkle crumbs generously over egg.

Bake in a moderate oven, 375°, for 10 minutes.

A fanciful dish–not at all difficult to prepare. E.B.

POACHED EGGS ARCHIDUC

3 tablespoons butter

6 chicken livers, halved

8 large mushrooms, diced

Salt and pepper

4 warm tartlettes OR
4 patty shells

4 freshly poached eggs

Hongroise Sauce*

Makes 2 servings

Heat butter but do not allow to brown.

Sauté halved livers and mushrooms in hot butter. When livers are cooked to taste, spoon mixture into tartlettes or patty shells.

Trim eggs so white conforms to shape of patty shell. Top each shell with a poached egg.

Spoon about 3 tablespoons hot sauce over each egg. Serve at once.

EGGS EN BORDURE CHIMAY

12 hard-cooked eggs, shelled

½ pound mushrooms, diced

6 tablespoons butter

2 cups sautéed spinach leaves

Duchess Potatoes*

Mornay Sauce*

Makes 6 servings

Cut eggs in half lengthwise. Remove yolks and pound into a paste in a bowl.

Sauté mushrooms in butter in a skillet until soft. Stir into egg yolks until well blended. Divide mushroom-egg yolk mixture among egg whites.

Line 6 buttered au gratin dishes with sautéed spinach. Arrange 4 filled egg whites in each au gratin dish.

Pipe Duchess Potatoes around border of each au gratin dish. Spoon Mornay Sauce over eggs.

Place dishes under very hot broiler, just until sauce and potatoes are golden.

EGGS CAREME

4 eggs

2 tablespoons butter

1 medium-size salmon steak, cooked, boned and flaked

3 tablespoons rich mayonnaise

Seasoning

4 tartlettes or patty shells

Caviar

Makes 2 servings

Lightly fry eggs in hot butter (yolks should remain soft). Trim whites with a round cutter. Let stand on a clean towel until ready to use.

Toss flaked salmon with mayonnaise (add more if you wish) and seasonings to taste.

Fill tartlettes or patty shells with salmon mixture and place an egg on each one.

Garnish with caviar and serve.

OMELETTE MAISON

2 large mushrooms, sliced

4 tablespoons butter

½ cup grated aged American cheese

¼ cup milk

½ cup heavy cream, softly whipped

2 eggs, separated

¼ teaspoon chopped parsley

¼ teaspoon chopped chives

Salt and pepper

10–12 cooked or canned asparagus tips

Makes 2 servings

Sauté mushrooms in half the butter until they are golden and soft. Keep warm.

Combine cheese and milk in top of double boiler over hot water. Stir until cheese melts and mixture is smooth. Remove from heat and cool. Fold in ⅓ cup whipped cream.

Beat the egg whites until they stand in soft peaks. Add the slightly beaten egg yolks, fold together.

Fold in mushrooms, seasonings to taste and remaining whipped cream.

Heat the remaining butter in an omelette pan, pour in the egg mixture and cook until surface is set but still soft.

Fold omelette and slide onto a heat-proof serving platter. Arrange asparagus spears around omelette and carefully spoon cheese sauce over both. Place under preheated broiler for 1 minute. Serve immediately.

A delightful suggestion for after-theatre supper or Sunday brunch. E.B.

ENTREE~BEEF

BOUCHEES OF SWEETBREADS
    FINANCIERE
BOEUF A LA MODE EN ASPIC
BEEF AND KIDNEY PIE
BEEF STEAK APLATI BONNEFOY
BROILED SALISBURY STEAK, STANLEY
BOILED CORNED BRISKET OF BEEF
BRAISED BEEF BOURGEOISE
GLAZED CORNED BEEF
CARBONADE A LA FLAMANDE
BROWN ROAST BEEF HASH
FILLET OF BEEF WITH STUFFED
    MUSHROOMS
CHIPPED BEEF IN CREAM WITH
    PHILADELPHIA SCRAPPLE
LARDED ROAST FILLET OF BEEF,
    "CHORON" JARDINIERE
TOURNEDOS RICHELIEU
CHATEAUBRIAND PRINCE RAINIER III
EMINCEE OF TENDERLOIN CAFE MARTIN
BEEF LYONNAISE
PRIME BEEF STEAK SAUTE BORDELAISE
LONDON BROIL BORDELAISE
ROAST FILLET OF BEEF
BEEF WELLINGTON
MEDAILLONS OF BEEF TENDERLOIN,
    SMITANE
3-DECKER HAMBURGER A LA PLAZA
OPEN FACE SEARED TARTAR STEAK

BOUCHEES OF SWEETBREADS FINANCIERE

Puff Pastry*

1 egg, beaten

2 cups cooked diced calf sweetbreads

1 cup Béchamel Sauce*

½ cup sliced olives

Black truffles, cut in strips

Makes 24

Roll out Puff Pastry to a ¼-inch thickness on a lightly floured pastry cloth or board. Cut out pastry with a 3-inch round cutter. Cut 1-inch centers out of half the rounds.

Place rounds on cookie sheet and moisten edges with water. Place rims on rounds and place centers on second cookie sheet. Brush pastry with beaten egg. Chill at least 1 hour.

Bake in very hot oven, 450°, for 10 minutes, or until puffed. Reduce oven to moderate, 375°, and bake 10 minutes longer, or until golden.

Combine sweetbreads, Béchamel Sauce and olives and heat slowly.

Spoon into prepared bouchée. Garnish with truffle strips and top each bouchée with a baked pastry center.

BOEUF A LA MODE EN ASPIC

3 cups Beef Consommé*

1 cup dry red wine

1 egg white and shell

2 envelopes unflavored gelatin

12 slices cold Roast Fillet of Beef*

Cooked whole green beans

Cooked baby carrots

Tomato wedges

Hard-cooked egg slices

Sliced truffles

Makes 6 servings

Combine Beef Consommé, red wine and egg white and shell. Heat to boiling and simmer 5 minutes. Cool. Strain through double thickness of cheesecloth.

Soften gelatin in ½ cup cold water and stir into Beef Consommé until gelatin dissolves. Chill until mixture begins to set, about 20 minutes.

Cover the bottom of a chilled platter with thickened gelatin. Arrange beef slices down the center. Arrange vegetables and eggs in an attractive pattern around edge. Top beef slices with truffles. Spoon remaining aspic over meat and vegetables. Let set.

This is a perfect dish for a small gathering of friends on a midsummer's eve. E.B.

BEEF AND KIDNEY PIE

2 pounds round steak

1 pound beef kidney

¼ cup beef suet

1 large onion, chopped

1½ cups Beef Stock*

2 tablespoons Worcestershire sauce

Freshly ground pepper

4 tablespoons flour

½ cup cold water

Pie Crust* (⅓ of recipe)

Makes 8 servings

Cut steak and kidney, well trimmed, into 1-inch cubes.

Render suet in a heavy kettle and remove cracklings. Sauté onion in fat until soft. Brown meat cubes in same kettle. Add Beef Stock, Worcestershire and pepper. Cover kettle.

Cook, stirring occasionally, 1½ hours, or until meat is tender. Heat to boiling.

Blend flour and cold water. Stir into boiling liquid until sauce thickens. Boil for 1 minute.

Pour into an 8-cup shallow baking dish. Cool to lukewarm.

Roll out pastry to a diameter 1-inch wider than diameter of casserole. Place over meat and flute edge. Make several slits for steam to escape.

Bake in a hot oven, 400°, for 30 minutes, or until crust is golden.

BEEF STEAK APLATI BONNEFOY

½ cup minced shallots

1 cup dry white wine

½ cup Velouté Sauce*

4 minute steaks, about 6 ounces each

6 tablespoons butter

Chopped tarragon

Parsley

Sliced cooked marrow

Makes 4 servings

Heat shallots and white wine to a boil in small heavy saucepan. Reduce liquid to ¼ cup. Add Velouté Sauce and simmer for 20 minutes.

Rub sauce through a fine sieve and stir in 4 table-spoons of butter. Heat, but do not allow to boil.

Sauté steaks in remaining 2 tablespoons butter in a heavy skillet, until done to your taste.

Serve steaks with sauce and garnish with chopped tarragon and parsley and slices of marrow.

BROILED SALISBURY STEAK, STANLEY

2 pounds ground sirloin

½ cup soft white bread crumbs

2 tablespoons grated onion

1 tablespoon chopped parsley

Salt and pepper

Paprika

6 split bananas, sautéed

Horseradish Sauce*

Makes 6 servings

Combine ground sirloin, bread crumbs, onion, parsley and seasonings, *very lightly*, in a bowl. Shape into six small steaks, about ¾-inch thick.

Broil 3 inches from the heat in a preheated grill, 5 minutes on each side, or until done as you like.

Serve with bananas and Horseradish Sauce.

BOILED CORNED BRISKET OF BEEF
A Plaza Specialty

5-pound corned brisket of beef

1 tablespoon pickling spices

1 bay leaf

1 clove garlic, sliced

6 whole peppercorns

6 steamed cabbage wedges

6 boiled potatoes

6 boiled carrots

Horseradish sauce

Makes 6-8 servings

Place corned beef in a large kettle. Cover with water. Add pickling spices, bay leaf, garlic and peppercorns.

Heat to boiling, skimming the surface if necessary. Simmer 3 hours, or until meat is tender. Allow beef to stand in broth 1 hour. Preheat in broth before serving.

Cut the beef into thin slices and serve with cooked cabbage wedges, potatoes and carrots on platter. Pass the horseradish sauce in a sauce dish.

BRAISED BEEF BOURGEOISE

1 carrot, sliced

1 onion, sliced

3-pound top round of beef

1 stalk celery

4 sprigs parsley

1 bay leaf

Few sprigs thyme

Salt and pepper

1 cup consommé

2 cups Bordelaise Sauce*

Bourgeoise Vegetables
(recipe follows)

Makes 8 servings

Place sliced carrot and onion in bottom of a casserole. Lay beef over vegetables. Add a fagot of celery, parsley, bay leaf and thyme. Season with salt and pepper.

Roast in a hot oven, 425°, for 20 minutes, or until beef has browned. Pour consommé over and cover casserole.

Reduce oven to 375° and continue cooking 1½ hours, basting several times.

Remove meat from casserole. Press juices through a sieve and combine with Bordelaise Sauce. Return beef to casserole and add Bourgeoise Vegetables. Add sauce and cover casserole.

Cook 1 hour longer, or until meat is tender.

Short ribs, cut into serving pieces, may be substituted for top round in this recipe. E.B.

BOURGEOISE VEGETABLES

1 pound small white onions, peeled

2 tablespoons butter

1 pound tiny carrots, pared

2 white turnips, peeled and cubed

3 stalks celery, cut in 3-inch pieces

½ cup Beef Consommé*

In a large skillet sauté onions in butter until golden. Add remaining ingredients. Cover and simmer 5 minutes.

GLAZED CORNED BEEF

5-pound piece corned beef
(mild-cure preferred)

2 tablespoons whole cloves

1 tablespoon minced onion

6 peppercorns

⅓ cup ketchup

1 teaspoon dry mustard

1 teaspoon prepared horseradish

2 tablespoons butter

3 tablespoons vinegar

⅓ cup sugar

Mustard Cream Sauce
(recipe follows)

Makes 8 servings

Rinse the corned beef well under running cold water. Place it in a heavy kettle and add cold water to cover generously. Bring to a rapid boil and cook 5 minutes. Reduce heat and skim very well.

Cover the kettle and simmer the beef over low heat until tender, about 3 hours more or less depending on cure and cut of beef. Let the beef cool in its cooking water, then drain.

Place the meat on a rack in a shallow roasting pan. Stud all over with whole cloves. Place in a moderate oven, 350°, for 15 minutes.

Combine the remaining ingredients in a small saucepan. Cook and stir over low heat for 5 to 6 minutes.

Spread some of the glaze over the corned beef and return to a moderate oven for 35 to 40 minutes. Spoon remaining glaze over beef at intervals until it is used up.

Remove the glazed beef to a hot platter and let stand 10 minutes before carving. Serve with Mustard Cream Sauce.

MUSTARD CREAM SAUCE

2 tablespoons dry English mustard

1 teaspoon flour

¼ teaspoon salt

¼ cup sugar

1 egg yolk

1 cup light cream

½ cup cider vinegar, heated

Makes about 2 cups

Thoroughly mix the dry ingredients. In a small heavy saucepan blend the egg yolk and light cream together with a wire whip.

Over low heat gradually blend the dry mixture into the cream mixture. Continue to cook and stir over low heat until sauce is thickened and very smooth.

Still using the wire whip, rapidly and vigorously stir the hot vinegar into the thickened sauce. Cook and stir another minute or two. Cool and refrigerate overnight. Serve hot or cold. To serve hot, reheat in a double boiler over simmering water.

CARBONADE A LA FLAMANDE

3 pounds bottom round

2 tablespoons beef suet

1 12-ounce can beer

3 cups Beef Consommé*

3 large onions, sliced

3 tablespoons butter

1 stalk celery

3 sprigs parsley

1 bay leaf

Few sprigs thyme

Steamed red cabbage wedges

Makes 8 servings

Cut beef into thin slices and flatten with a mallet. Brown beef, a few pieces at a time, in suet in a skillet. Deglaze skillet with beer and stir in beef consommé.

In a second skillet, sauté onions in butter until golden.

Layer browned beef slices and onion slices in a casserole. Pour consommé sauce mixture over and add a fagot of celery, parsley, bay leaf and thyme. Cover casserole.

Bake in a slow oven, 325°, for 2 hours. Serve with red cabbage wedges.

BROWN ROAST BEEF HASH

3 cups diced cold roast beef

2 cups diced cooked potatoes

1 green pepper, finely chopped

3 tablespoons grated onion

Salt and pepper

1 cup Beef Stock*

¼ cup tomato puree

3 tablespoons salad oil

Makes 4 servings

Run beef through a meat chopper, using a fine blade. Combine in a bowl with potatoes, green pepper, onion, salt and pepper. Stir in beef stock and tomato puree.

Heat oil in a large skillet. Add beef mixture and cook until brown and crusty on one side. Turn. Brown on other side. Serve on a heated platter.

A big favorite with men, and women, too. E.B.

FILLET OF BEEF WITH STUFFED MUSHROOMS

4 slices fillet of beef,
¼- to ½-inch thick

Salad oil

1 tablespoon butter

2 teaspoons minced parsley

1 teaspoon minced onion

4 large mushrooms

1½ cups seasoned Brown Sauce*

¼ cup buttered soft bread crumbs

1 sweet red pepper, seeded

1 sweet green pepper, seeded

Makes 4 servings

Brush the fillets with salad oil and pan broil in a heated dry heavy skillet over high heat. Cook for about 6 minutes, turning once. Remove to a shallow baking dish and keep warm.

Heat butter. Add parsley, onion and chopped mushroom stems. Cook a few minutes, then stir in 3 tablespoons Brown Sauce. Use this mixture to stuff the mushroom caps.

Place a stuffed mushroom cap on each side of fillet. Sprinkle with bread crumbs.

Roast in a hot oven, 425°, for about 8 to 10 minutes, until fillets are browned. Pour hot brown sauce around fillets and top with red and green peppers cut into very thin slices.

A beef-lover's dream. E.B.

CHIPPED BEEF IN CREAM WITH PHILADELPHIA SCRAPPLE

6 tablespoons butter

6 tablespoons flour

2½ cups cream, scalded

¼ cup dry white wine

Salt and pepper

½ pound shredded chipped beef

4 tablespoons butter

1 pound Philadelphia scrapple

Makes 4 servings

Melt 6 tablespoons butter in heavy saucepan. Stir in flour and cook roux 3 minutes, but do not allow to brown. Stir in cream and heat to boiling. Add wine, and salt and pepper to taste. Add chipped beef and simmer 5 minutes.

Heat 4 tablespoons butter in a skillet. Cut scrapple into thick slices. Brown in hot butter.

Arrange scrapple on heated serving platter and spoon beef over.

LARDED ROAST FILLET OF BEEF, "CHORON" JARDINIERE

4-pound fillet of beef

½ pound sliced pork fat

1 cup dry red Burgundy

½ cup tarragon vinegar

Freshly ground pepper

1 onion, thinly sliced

"CHORON" JARDINIERE

Fluted carrots, cooked

Fluted white turnip, cooked

French-cut green beans, cooked

Cauliflowerettes, cooked

½ cup melted butter

Makes 4-6 servings

Lard fillet with matchlike strips of pork fat. Place in an earthenware casserole and cover with a mixture of Burgundy, vinegar, pepper and onion slices. Cover casserole and chill 3 days, turning meat each day.

Remove fillet from marinade and wipe dry with paper towels.

Roast in a moderate oven, 375°, for 30 minutes, or just until rare. Baste with marinade.

Place fillet on heated serving platter and surround with bundles of carrots, turnip, green beans and cauliflowerettes. Drizzle vegetables with melted butter.

TOURNEDOS RICHELIEU

6 filets mignons, about 6 ounces each

2 tablespoons butter

2 tablespoons olive oil

6 round croutons

Potato balls

Leaf lettuce

Tomato wedges

2½ cups Bordelaise Sauce*

Makes 6 servings

Sauté filets mignons in butter and olive oil in a heavy skillet over medium heat for 3 minutes on each side, or until done as you like. Place on croutons and arrange on a heated platter.

Garnish platter with potato balls and leaf lettuce nests with tomato wedges. Spoon Bordelaise Sauce over the meat just before serving.

CHATEAUBRIAND PRINCE RAINIER III

1 châteaubriand, about 1½ pounds

2 tablespoons softened butter

Salt and pepper

Béarnaise Sauce*

Pommes Soufflé*

French Peas*

Makes 2 servings

Rub châteaubriand with soft butter. Grill 4 inches from heat for 4 minutes, or just until beef is rare. Season with salt and pepper.

Place on heated platter and serve with Béarnaise Sauce, Pommes Soufflé and French Peas.

EMINCEE OF TENDERLOIN CAFE MARTIN

12 slices Roast Fillet of Beef*

Poached beef bone marrow, cut into strips

Bordelaise Sauce*

Makes 4 servings

Arrange beef slices and beef bone marrow in an au gratin dish. Heat Bordelaise Sauce in a saucepan and pour over beef.

Heat in a slow oven, 325°, for 10 minutes. Serve immediately.

BEEF LYONNAISE

Shortening or beef fat

4 thick slices rare roast beef

2 large onions, sliced

2 tablespoons wine vinegar

1 tablespoon sweet butter

2 tablespoons chopped fresh tarragon leaves

Makes 4 servings

Use a deep heavy skillet to heat a little shortening or beef fat. When the fat is sizzling hot, add the beef slices and fry as you would steak, turning once. Remove meat and keep warm.

Add onions to the skillet and fry lightly, separating into rings.

Return the meat to the hot skillet for a minute or two, then arrange on warm serving dish and sprinkle with vinegar.

Cover the meat with hot onion rings and top with tarragon butter made by creaming sweet butter with chopped tarragon leaves.

PRIME BEEF STEAK SAUTE BORDELAISE

4 club steaks, 12 ounces each

4 tablespoons clarified butter*

2 tablespoons salad oil

Salt and pepper

2 cups Bordelaise Sauce*

Watercress

Broiled mushroom caps

Makes 4 servings

Sauté steaks in butter and oil in a heavy skillet over medium heat 4 minutes on each side, or until done as you like. Season with salt and pepper.

Arrange on heated serving platter and spoon Bordelaise Sauce over. Serve with watercress and mushroom caps.

LONDON BROIL BORDELAISE

12 slices freshly roasted Fillet of Beef*

6 slices white toast, trimmed

Bordelaise Sauce*

Broiled tomatoes

Watercress

Makes 6 servings

Arrange 2 slices Fillet of Beef on each slice of toast on a heated serving dish.

Cover with Bordelaise Sauce. Serve with broiled tomatoes and watercress.

ROAST FILLET OF BEEF

4-pound fillet of beef

2 tablespoons butter, softened

Freshly grated pepper

1 cup Beef Consommé*

Makes 8–10 servings

Place beef in a shallow roasting pan. Rub with butter and season with pepper.

Roast in a moderate oven, 350°, for 30 minutes, or just until rare. Baste with consommé.

BEEF WELLINGTON

3 pound fillet of beef, well trimmed

2 tablespoons salad oil

2 cups finely diced mushrooms

1 cup finely diced onion

2 tablespoons butter

¾ cup finely diced ham

½ pound finely chopped
cooked goose livers

Salt and pepper

Puff Pastry*

Perigourdine Sauce (recipe follows)

Makes 8–10 servings

Brown fillet well on all sides in salad oil in large skillet. Allow to cool.

Sauté mushrooms and onion in butter in large saucepan until golden. Remove from heat and blend in ham and goose livers. Season with salt and pepper and cool completely.

Roll out Puff Pastry to a rectangle and place cooled fillet in center. Spread liver mixture over fillet to coat evenly.

Fold pastry over filling to completely encase fillet. Place seam side down on baking sheet. Cut pastry trims into fancy shapes and decorate fillet with them, using beaten egg to keep pastry pieces in place. Brush pastry with beaten egg. Make slits in pastry for steam to escape.

Bake in a moderate oven, 350°, for 40 minutes, or until pastry is golden. Serve in thick slices with Perigourdine Sauce.

This recipe is certain to make a hit at any dinner party. E.B.

PERIGOURDINE SAUCE

1 can (2 ounces) truffles

½ cup Madeira wine

2 cups Brown Sauce*

Salt

Cayenne

Makes about 2 cups

Slice truffles and add to Madeira in a small heavy saucepan. Boil until liquid is almost completely reduced.

Heat Brown Sauce and add truffle mixture. Season with salt and cayenne.

MEDAILLONS OF BEEF TENDERLOIN, SMITANE

6 tournedos of beef, about 9-ounces each

2 tablespoons clarified butter*

2 tablespoons olive oil

6 round croutons

Sauce Smitane (recipe follows)

Watercress

Makes 6 servings

Sauté tournedos in butter and oil in a heavy skillet for 3 minutes on each side, or until done as you like. Place on croutons and arrange on a heated platter.

Spoon Sauce Smitane over and garnish platter with watercress.

SAUCE SMITANE

½ cup chopped onion

½ cup wine vinegar

½ cup dry red wine

½ teaspoon freshly grated pepper

1 bay leaf

3 tablespoons butter

6 tablespoons flour

½ cup heavy cream

1 teaspoon salt

½ cup sour cream

Makes about 2½ cups

Combine onion, vinegar, wine, pepper and bay leaf in a heavy saucepan. Heat to boiling and simmer until liquid is reduced by one third.

Melt butter in a saucepan. Stir in flour and cook roux 3 minutes. Strain onion mixture into roux. Add cream and salt. Simmer 5 minutes. Stir in sour cream.

3-DECKER HAMBURGER
A LA PLAZA

1 teaspoon salt

¼ teaspoon pepper

1½ pounds ground top round of beef

8 slices Swiss cheese

4 slices boiled ham

Makes 4 servings

Work salt and pepper gently into ground beef. Divide beef into four equal portions, then shape three flat patties from each portion of meat. For each serving, place a slice of cheese on first patty, add the second patty and top with a slice of ham, add the third patty and top with another slice of cheese. Broil and serve as is, or with Tomato Sauce*.

This is *not* a run-of-the-mill "burger." Divine served with Tomato Sauce à la Plaza. E.B.

OPEN FACE SEARED
TARTAR STEAK
Green Tulip Specialty

½ pound chopped beef sirloin

1 tablespoon freshly grated horseradish

1 teaspoon Worcestershire sauce

1 tablespoon chili sauce

1 tablespoon finely chopped onion

Salt and pepper

1 large slice rye bread

2 tablespoons butter

GARNISH

1 hard cooked egg, sliced

3–4 fillets of anchovies

1 tablespoon capers

1 tablespoon freshly grated horseradish

Lettuce

Makes 1 serving

Mix the ground beef and seasonings. Shape into a flat cake.

Place the meat cake on the slice of rye bread and use a small spatula to spread the meat into an even layer on the bread.

Score the surface of the meat with the spatula.

Heat 1 tablespoon butter in a small skillet. Place the bread, meat side down, in the hot butter. Sear for 1 minute.

Add remaining butter to the pan and turn the bread over so meat side is up.

Fry the bread until golden brown. Drain on a paper towel.

Place the open face tartar steak on a small platter and arrange sliced egg on top. Surround with remaining garnishes arranged on lettuce leaves. Serve at once.

ENTRÉE~VEAL

LA COTE DE "PLUME DE VEAU" PLAZA

NOISETTE OF MILK-FED VEAL AU MADERE

BREAST OF VEAL HUNGARIAN STYLE

VEAL KIDNEY FLAMBE

VEAL GOULASH AUSTRIAN

LIVER WITH BASIL IN WINE

MILK-FED VEAL CUTLET A LA STRESA

VEAL MARENGO

VEAL FRICASSEE L'ANCIENNE

SWEETBREADS PARISIENNE

LA COTE DE "PLUME DE VEAU" PLAZA

Juice of 1 lemon

6 veal rib chops, cut thick

1 cup flour

½ teaspoon salt

¼ teaspoon white pepper

½ cup Clarified Butter*

1 cup dry white wine

1 cup heavy cream

¼ cup puree of white truffles

Makes 6 servings

Brush the lemon juice over the chops on both sides. Roll the chops in mixed flour, salt and pepper.

Heat the clarified butter in a large heavy skillet. Add the chops and sauté quickly over high heat, turning to brown both sides.

Put the skillet with chops into a slow oven, 325°, for 15 minutes. Remove chops and keep warm. Pour off the butter.

Add the wine to the skillet and reduce to about ½ cup over moderate heat. Stir in the cream and cook until sauce is reduced to about ¾ cup.

Blend in the truffle puree and correct seasonings.

Spoon some of the sauce onto a warmed serving platter and arrange chops in platter. Surround the chops with a "bouquetière" of vegetables. Serve remaining sauce from a small boat.

NOISETTE OF MILK-FED VEAL AU MADERE

1 medium onion, chopped

1 large carrot, chopped

1 stalk celery, chopped

1 clove garlic, minced

½ cup diced smoked ham

3 tablespoons butter

5-pound rolled loin of veal

1 cup Beef Consommé*

2 cups Brown Sauce*

⅓ cup Madeira wine

Makes 8 servings

Sauté onion, carrot, celery, garlic and ham in butter in a flameproof casserole until lightly golden. Place veal roast on vegetables.

Roast in a hot oven, 425°, for 20 minutes, or until roast is golden. Stir in consommé and cover casserole.

Reduce oven to 325° and continue roasting 2½ hours, or until veal is tender. Transfer to a heated serving platter and keep warm.

Press sauce through a sieve into a saucepan. Stir in Brown Sauce and heat to boiling. Add Madeira wine and simmer 5 minutes. Serve sauce with sliced veal.

BREAST OF VEAL
HUNGARIAN STYLE

1 veal breast, about 4 pounds

1 pound peas, shelled and cooked

3 tablespoons butter

8 cooked shelled shrimps, chopped

6 slices day-old French bread

8 cooked asparagus spears

2 egg yolks

Salt and pepper

Paprika

1 cup tomato juice

1 cup sour cream

Makes 8 servings

Have butcher prepare veal breast for stuffing.

Sauté peas in butter for 3 minutes. Add chopped shrimps and cook 2 minutes.

Soak bread slices in cold water and squeeze out excess water. Combine with pea mixture and chopped asparagus spears. Season with salt, pepper and paprika.

Spread mixture over veal breast. Roll up and tie securely. Place roast in a shallow roasting pan. Pour tomato juice over.

Roast in moderate oven, 350°, for 1½ hours, or until veal is tender. Baste often with pan juices. Transfer roast to heated serving platter.

Place sour cream in heavy saucepan. Stir in pan juices and correct seasonings. Heat slowly, just until hot.

VEAL KIDNEY FLAMBE

6 veal kidneys

6 tablespoons butter

1 cup sliced mushrooms

1 tablespoon chopped shallots

½ cup Brandy, warmed

Salt and pepper

1 teaspoon English mustard

1 cup heavy cream

Hot crisp toast

Makes 6 servings

Soak veal kidneys in cold water for 2 hours. Trim all fat from kidneys and cut into thin slices.

Heat butter in heavy skillet. Add kidney slices, mushrooms and shallots. Sauté 5 minutes, or until kidneys are browned.

Pour warmed Brandy over kidneys and ignite. When flames have died, season with salt, pepper and mustard. Stir in heavy cream. Cook slowly, until just heated through. Serve on hot crisp toast.

VEAL GOULASH AUSTRIAN

4 large onions, chopped

4 tablespoons butter

3 pounds cubed leg of veal

2 tablespoons Hungarian paprika

1 teaspoon salt

1 tomato, peeled and chopped

1 green pepper, chopped

½ cup Beef Consommé*

2 tablespoons capers

2 cups sour cream

Steamed Dumplings (recipe follows)

Makes 8 servings

Sauté onions in butter in a deep heavy skillet until golden. Add veal, paprika and salt. Stir until veal is brown.

Add tomato, green pepper and consommé. Cover skillet. Cook slowly 1 hour, or until veal is tender. Correct seasonings. Add capers and stir in sour cream. Heat slowly, but do not boil. Serve with steamed dumplings.

STEAMED DUMPLINGS

1½ cups all-purpose flour

2 teaspoons baking powder

½ teaspoon salt

1 tablespoon chopped parsley

Pinch of powdered rosemary

3 tablespoons shortening

1 teaspoon minced onion

¾ cup milk (approx.)

Sift the dry ingredients together. Stir in parsley and rosemary.

Cut in the shortening until mixture looks like fine cornmeal. Add the onion.

Stir in just enough milk to make a thick batter.

Use a wet tablespoon to pick up the dumpling batter and drop it onto the bubbling goulash. Cover tightly, reduce the heat to low and cook 15 minutes.

LIVER WITH BASIL IN WINE

2 pounds calf's liver

¾ cup milk

½ cup seasoned flour

4 tablespoons olive oil

2 tablespoons Clarified Butter*

2 cloves garlic, minced

1 leek (white only), chopped

1 cup dry white wine

1 teaspoon leaf basil

Salt and pepper

Makes 4 servings

Dip liver in milk and then into seasoned flour, pressing flour in to coat well.

Heat oil and butter in large skillet. Brown liver, a few pieces at a time. Transfer to shallow baking dish.

Sauté garlic and leek in skillet until soft. Deglaze pan with wine. Season with basil, salt and pepper. Pour over liver. Serve immediately.

MILK-FED VEAL CUTLET A LA STRESA

8 thin slices veal cutlet

4 slices Swiss cheese

4 thin slices prosciutto ham

2 eggs, beaten

¾ cup fine dry bread crumbs

¼ cup seasoned flour

4 tablespoons vegetable oil

2 tablespoons butter

Makes 4 servings

Pound veal cutlets with a wooden mallet until very thin. Top 4 cutlets with a slice of cheese and of ham, then cover with remaining cutlet. Roll up and secure with wooden food picks.

Dip veal rolls first into beaten eggs and then into a mixture of bread crumbs and seasoned flour.

Heat vegetable oil and butter in heavy skillet. Cook veal rolls on all sides until golden brown.

VEAL MARENGO

3 pounds cubed veal shoulder

Seasoned flour

4 tablespoons olive oil

1 large onion, chopped

1 clove garlic, minced

1 cup dry white wine

3 tablespoons Brandy

2 large tomatoes, peeled and chopped

1 bay leaf

2 sprigs parsley

1 teaspoon leaf thyme, crumbled

1 pound mushrooms

Chopped truffles and parsley

Makes 8 servings

Coat veal shoulder with seasoned flour. Brown in hot oil in a large skillet. Remove veal to casserole.

Sauté onion and garlic until golden in same skillet. Deglaze pan with white wine and Brandy. Stir in chopped tomatoes. Add to casserole with bay leaf, 2 sprigs parsley and thyme. Cover casserole.

Bake in moderate oven, 350°, for 45 minutes, or until veal is almost tender. Add mushroom caps. Bake 10 minutes longer, or until veal is tender.

Garnish with chopped truffles and chopped parsley.

VEAL FRICASSEE L'ANCIENNE

3 pounds cubed veal shoulder

Seasoned flour

7 tablespoons butter

3 cups Beef Consommé*

1 onion studded with 3 cloves

1 teaspoon salt

1 bay leaf

2 sprigs parsley

1 sprig thyme

12 small white onions, peeled

1 pound mushrooms, sliced

½ cup light cream

2 egg yolks

Makes 8 servings

Coat veal cubes with seasoned flour. Brown, a few pieces at a time, in 4 tablespoons butter in a heavy skillet.

In large saucepan heat consommé to boiling with onion studded with cloves, salt, bay leaf, parsley and thyme. Add browned veal.

Cover saucepan. Simmer 45 minutes, or until veal is tender.

While veal cooks, sauté onions until golden in 3 tablespoons butter in second skillet; add mushrooms and sauté several minutes. Add ¼ cup water and cover skillet. Simmer 10 minutes, or until onions are tender.

Combine veal, onions and mushrooms in a heated casserole and keep warm.

Beat together cream and egg yolks in a saucepan. Strain cooking liquid into saucepan. Beat with a wire whip until very smooth. Heat slowly until mixture thickens and just comes to a boil. Spoon over veal and garnish with chopped parsley, if you wish.

SWEETBREADS PARISIENNE

3 pair sweetbreads

¼ pound larding pork

3 tablespoons butter

1 medium-size onion, sliced

1 large carrot, sliced

3 sprigs parsley

½ teaspoon leaf thyme

1 cup Chicken Stock*

½ cup dry white wine

Cooked asparagus tips

Cooked artichoke hearts

Oven-roasted potato balls

2 tablespoons Madeira wine

Makes 6 servings

Cover sweetbreads with cold water and soak two hours. Drain. Place in large kettle and cover with salted cold water. Heat to boiling. Drain, then cover with cold water. Place on a flat dish and place a weight on top. Chill overnight.

Lard sweetbreads with matchlike pieces of larding pork.

Melt butter in a flameproof casserole. Sauté onion, carrot, parsley and leaf thyme until they turn lightly golden. Stir in chicken stock and white wine. Place prepared sweetbreads over vegetables.

Roast in moderate oven, 375°, for 45 minutes, or until sweetbreads start to break when lightly touched with a fork. Baste often with liquid in casserole.

Place sweetbreads on a heated serving platter and arrange asparagus tips, artichoke hearts and potato balls around them. Keep warm while finishing sauce.

Press sauce through a sieve into a saucepan and correct seasonings. Add Madeira and heat to boiling. Simmer 5 minutes. Spoon over sweetbreads.

ENTREE~LAMB

BAKED LAMB CHOPS EN CASSEROLE

BROCHETTE OF LAMB A L'ORIENTAL

GIGOT OF LAMB

BREADED SPRING LAMB CHOPS ZINGARA

IRISH LAMB STEW

SHASHLIK CAUCASIAN FLAMBE

CURRY OF LAMB

LAMB KIDNEY AU VIN BLANC

LAMB AND KIDNEY PIE

BROILED RACK OF LAMB

MOUSSAKA A LA TURQUE

COUS COUS

CHESSY'S CURRY OF LAMB

BAKED LAMB CHOPS EN CASSEROLE

6 shoulder lamb chops

3 tablespoons butter

Salt and pepper

6 slices onion

½ pound dried apricot halves

1 cup dry red wine

¾ cup water

4 whole cloves

1 piece stick cinnamon

Makes 6 servings

Brown chops on both sides in butter in a skillet. Transfer to a shallow baking dish. Sprinkle with salt and pepper and add onion slices and apricot halves.

Deglaze skillet with wine and water and pour over chops. Add spices. Cover baking dish.

Bake in moderate oven, 350°, for 1 hour, or until chops are tender.

BROCHETTE OF LAMB A L'ORIENTAL

4 pounds lean leg of lamb

½ cup white wine

1 teaspoon chopped shallots

½ teaspoon salt

¼ teaspoon black pepper

1 bay leaf

Juice of 1 lemon

½ cup salad oil

1 large green pepper, cut in 8 squares

1 large onion, quartered

2 firm tomatoes, quartered

Makes 4 servings

Cut lamb into 2-inch cubes, removing all fat.

Combine the wine, shallots, seasonings, lemon juice and salad oil to make a marinade. Soak the lamb cubes in the marinade for 6 to 12 hours.

When ready to broil, drain and wipe the meat on paper towels.

Thread each of 4 skewers with a square of pepper, several onion "leaves," a quarter of tomato and 5 or 6 cubes lamb pressed closely together. Finish the skewers with remaining vegetables.

Brush with a little olive oil and broil, turning often until crisp brown on the outside and pink inside. Meat cubes packed closely together will be rare and juicy.

GIGOT OF LAMB

1 leg of lamb, about 6 pounds

Trim excess fat from lamb. Season with salt and pepper.

Salt and pepper

1 large carrot, sliced

Place carrot, onion, parsley, bay leaf and mutton bone in the bottom of a large kettle. Add leg of lamb.

1 large onion, sliced

Roast lamb in hot oven, 400°, for 30 minutes, or until lamb is golden. Add hot Chicken Stock and cover kettle.

2 tablespoons chopped parsley

1 bay leaf

Reduce heat to 325° and cook 5 hours, or until lamb is ready to fall apart. Remove meat to a heated serving platter and keep warm.

Cracked mutton bone

2 cups hot Chicken Stock*

Press sauce through a sieve into a saucepan and heat to boiling.

2 tablespoons arrowroot

4 tablespoons dry Sherry

Blend arrowroot and Sherry to make a smooth paste. Beat into hot liquid with a wire whip. Cook 2 minutes. Serve with lamb.

Makes 8 servings

Gigot of Lamb is the leg of lamb you serve with a spoon—a new and different dinner treat. E.B.

BREADED SPRING LAMB CHOP ZINGARA

6 loin lamb chops, 1½ inches thick

Dip chops into beaten egg and then into seasoned flour.

1 egg, beaten

Seasoned flour

Heat oil in a large skillet and brown chops for 6 minutes on each side. Transfer to heated platter and keep warm.

3 tablespoons salad oil

Demi-Glace Sauce*

Combine Demi-Glace Sauce, ham, mushrooms and truffles in a saucepan and heat. Spoon over chops. Garnish platter with watercress.

½ cup slivered ham

½ cup chopped sautéed mushrooms

2 tablespoons chopped truffles

Watercress

Makes 6 servings

IRISH LAMB STEW

4 pounds lean shoulder of lamb

6 medium onions, peeled

6 medium potatoes, peeled

1 leek, chopped

1 cup finely chopped cabbage

1 stalk celery, chopped

Few parsley sprigs, chopped

1 small clove garlic, minced

1 bay leaf, crumbled

8 peppercorns

⅛ teaspoon leaf thyme, crumbled

Stock or water

Light cream (optional)

Makes 6 servings

Cut the meat into small cubes.

In a large casserole with a cover arrange a layer of meat, a layer of sliced onions, a layer of sliced potatoes and a layer of mixed chopped vegetables.

Sprinkle with some of the combined seasonings. Repeat the layers until the meat and vegetables are used up. The top layer should be meat. Sprinkle with the remaining seasonings.

Add stock or water to cover just over the top layer of meat. Cover and bake in a moderate oven, 350°, for about 1½ hours, or until the meat is very tender.

If desired, stir in ½ to ¾ cup light cream before serving (this is a matter of taste and is often omitted).

Serve with small boiled onions, small whole carrots and a generous sprinkle of minced parsley.

Sometimes we add fluffy potato dumplings, but I've always thought this was gilding the lily. E.B.

SHASHLIK CAUCASIAN FLAMBE

2 pounds saddle OR leg of spring lamb

½ cup salad oil

Juice of 1 lemon

1 bay leaf

4-5 small whole tomatoes

4-5 lemon wedges

Makes 4-5 servings

Cut lamb into cubes, approximately 1½ × 1½ inches. Combine oil, lemon juice and bay leaf and pour over meat in a bowl. Cover. Marinate at least 24 hours in refrigerator.

Divide marinated lamb among 4 to 5 flambé skewers. Grill until lamb is done as you like. Garnish each skewer with a tomato and a lemon wedge.

To serve, wrap a small piece of cotton around the base of each skewer. Sprinkle cotton with a few drops of alcohol and set afire.

CURRY OF LAMB

¼ cup butter

1 pound boneless lamb leg OR shoulder, cubed

4 onions, chopped

2 cloves garlic, chopped

1 cup plain yoghurt

1 teaspoon ground coriander

¼ teaspoon cinnamon

¼ teaspoon cloves

½ teaspoon ground cardamon

1 piece green ginger root, peeled and chopped

Makes 4 servings

Heat the butter in a heavy skillet. Add the lamb cut in 2-inch cubes. Brown well on all sides. Remove and keep warm.

Add the onions and garlic. Cook until onions are soft. Stir in the yoghurt and spices. Mix well. Simmer 3 to 4 minutes.

Return the lamb to the skillet and simmer until tender, about 35 minutes.

Serve with hot boiled rice and varied condiments.

LAMB KIDNEY AU VIN BLANC

4 lamb kidneys

2 tablespoons butter

1 bay leaf

Salt and pepper

1–2 tablespoons flour

½ cup dry white wine

Toast or fried bread rounds

Makes 2 servings

Remove fat and membrane from kidneys and cut in very thin slices. Melt butter in a heavy saucepan over high heat. Add sliced kidneys, bay leaf and seasonings. Cook over high heat for a few minutes, shaking pan and turning kidneys to prevent toughening and to deepen browning.

After about 8 minutes sprinkle with flour, mix well and remove from heat.

Pour wine into pan, mix well and simmer over low heat for a few minutes, stirring constantly.

Serve at once over hot buttered toast, or substitute large bread rounds that have been fried to a golden brown in hot butter.

An excellent breakfast dish on a cold snowy day. E.B.

LAMB AND KIDNEY PIE

2 pounds cubed lamb shoulder

1 pound lamb kidneys

2 tablespoons oil

1 large onion, chopped

1 clove garlic, minced

1 cup Chicken Stock*

1 teaspoon salt

Freshly ground pepper

2 tablespoons lemon juice

3 tablespoons flour

⅓ cup cold water

Pastry Shell (⅓ of Pie Crust* recipe)

Makes 6 servings

Trim and cube lamb shoulder and kidneys.

Heat oil in a heavy saucepan. Sauté onion and garlic until soft. Brown meat in saucepan. Add Chicken Stock, salt, pepper and lemon juice. Cover saucepan.

Cook, stirring occasionally, until meat is tender, about 1¼ hours. Make a paste of flour and cold water and stir into saucepan until well blended. Pour into a shallow baking dish.

Roll out pastry to an area 1 inch larger than baking dish. Place on baking dish and flute edges. Cut several vents for steam to escape.

Bake in very hot oven, 450°, for 10 minutes. Lower heat to 350° and bake 15 minutes, or until pastry is golden.

BROILED RACK OF LAMB

8-chop rack of lamb

4 tablespoons melted butter

1 teaspoon salt

1 teaspoon rosemary, crumbled

12 parboiled white onions

12 mushroom caps

Buttered baby peas

Buttered whole green beans

Makes 4 servings

Trim excess meat from lamb-rack. Brush with a mixture of melted butter, salt and rosemary.

Broil 6 inches from the heat for 20 minutes, turning several times. Arrange onions and mushrooms around lamb. Brush with remaining butter mixture.

Broil 10 minutes longer, or until lamb is done as you like. Transfer lamb to heated serving platter and arrange onions, mushrooms, peas and green beans around rack.

MOUSSAKA A LA TURQUE

1 large eggplant

½ cup olive oil

1 large onion, chopped

2–3 cloves garlic, mashed

½ pound mushrooms, chopped

¼ cup butter

3 tablespoons tomato paste

1 tablespoon flour

1½ cups water

5 firm ripe tomatoes, peeled

Salt and pepper

1 tablespoon minced parsley

¼ cup red wine

3 cups ground, cooked lamb
(about 1 pound)

½ cup grated Parmesan cheese

Makes 6 servings

It is not necessary to peel the eggplant. Cut it into thin slices and fry in hot oil until brown, turning once. Remove from pan.

Sauté the onion, garlic and mushrooms in the same oil.

Melt the butter in a saucepan and blend in tomato paste and flour. Add the water and stir over moderate heat until mixture comes to a boil. Add 1 chopped tomato. Simmer until slightly thickened.

Season with salt and pepper. Stir in parsley and wine.

Place half the eggplant slices in a single layer in a large casserole or baking pan. Cover with half of the meat, sautéed onion, garlic and mushrooms, 2 sliced tomatoes and half the sauce. Repeat the layers, using up all the prepared ingredients.

Sprinkle with cheese and dot with a little butter. Bake in a moderate oven, 350°, for 35 minutes. Brown quickly under broiler before serving.

COUS COUS
Moroccan Lamb and Vegetables

¼ cup peanut oil

2 pounds boneless lamb, cubed

1 large onion, chopped

2 firm tomatoes, cut up

1½ teaspoons salt

1 teaspoon coarsely ground
black pepper†

1 5-inch piece stick cinnamon, broken

¼ cup chopped parsley

½ teaspoon powdered coriander

¼ teaspoon crumbled saffron

3 cups cold water

2 cups canned chickpeas, drained

2 large carrots, quartered lengthwise
and cut in 2-inch pieces

2 white turnips, peeled and
cut in strips

2 sweet potatoes or yams,
peeled and sliced

1 small butternut squash,
peeled, seeded and cubed‡

2 zucchini, peeled and sliced

½ cup seedless raisins

Makes 6-8 servings

Heat the oil in a deep heavy kettle with a tight-fitting cover. Add the lamb, onion, tomatoes and seasonings. Stir and fry over high heat until lamb is well browned.

Stir in the cold water and bring to a boil. Add the chickpeas and stir again to a boil. Reduce heat to moderate, cover and cook about 25 minutes.

Add the carrots, turnips and sweet potatoes. If necessary, add boiling water to just cover vegetables. Cover and cook 15 minutes.

Add the squash, zucchini and raisins. Cover and cook 10 minutes, or until squash is tender.

† This is one third the amount of
pepper called for in the native
recipe. Add up to 1 generous
tablespoon, if desired.

‡ Firm yellow squash has been
substituted for the pumpkin
used in the native recipe.

COUS COUS

2½ cups cous cous

5 cups boiling Chicken Broth*

⅓ cup butter

1 teaspoon salt

¼ teaspoon ground cinnamon

Spread the cous cous on the bottom of a deep heavy heated saucepan with a tight-fitting cover. Stir in the boiling broth about ½ cup at a time.

When all the broth has been added, reduce the heat to low and stir in remaining ingredients. Cover.

Cook mixture for about 20 minutes, stirring once or twice.

To serve Moroccan style: Mound the cooked cous cous in the center of the heated platter. Use slotted spoon to separate the lamb cubes from the remaining ingredients and spoon them around the cous cous. Make a depression in the center of the cous cous and spoon in the vegetables and raisins.

Sprinkle a little of the hot sauce over the cous cous, and serve remaining sauce separately.

In Morocco this dish is cooked in a special pot called a "couscoussier," rather like a double boiler. The cous cous steams in the colanderlike top section, while the stew simmers in the bottom pot. E.B.

CHESSY'S CURRY OF LAMB

3 tablespoons olive oil

4 large onions, chopped

2 cloves garlic, minced

2½ pounds cubed leg of lamb

*2 tablespoons curry powder
(or more)*

3 cups Chicken Stock*

2 bay leaves

Salt and pepper

2 tablespoons tomato paste

1 chopped green apple

2 tablespoons grated coconut

2 tablespoons chopped chutney

½ cup heavy cream

Rice Pilaff*

Makes 6 servings

Heat oil in heavy kettle. Sauté onions and garlic in kettle until golden. Add lamb and brown. Stir in curry powder and cook 2 minutes.

Add Chicken Stock, bay leaves, salt and pepper. Cover kettle. Simmer 1 hour, or until lamb is tender.

Add apple, coconut and chutney. Simmer, uncovered, 30 minutes, or until sauce thickens. Stir in cream just before serving on Rice Pilaff.

ENTREE~GAME

PHEASANT SOUVAROFF WITH SAUCE
  AND FRIED HOMINY

ROAST QUAIL

ROAST QUAIL AU RISOTTO PIEDMONTAISE

ROAST SADDLE OF VENISON, POIVRADE

SAUTEED YOUNG RABBIT

MALLARD DUCK A LA PRESSE

SAUTE OF VENISON

HUNGARIAN ROAST PARTRIDGE

CIVET DE LIEVRE

ENGLISH GROUSE

GRILLED SQUAB

PHEASANT SOUVAROFF WITH SAUCE AND FRIED HOMINY

6 black truffles

¾ cup Madeira wine

½ cup Meat Glaze*

1 can (8 ounces) foie gras

4 dressed pheasants

8 slices bacon

½ cup butter

2 carrots, finely minced

2 stalks celery, finely minced

2 medium-size onions, finely minced

1 sprig thyme

½ bay leaf, crushed

¼ cup Game Gravy

Bread Sauce (recipe follows)

Fried hominy

Makes 4 servings

Simmer truffles for 5 minutes in ½ cup wine combined with Meat Glaze. Remove with slotted spoon and reserve for later. Dice foie gras and stir into wine mixture.

Stuff pheasant with foie gras mixture. Truss. Wrap 2 strips of bacon around each pheasant.

Melt butter in a baking dish just large enough to hold pheasants. Add minced vegetables, thyme and bay leaf. Cover. Allow mixture to simmer for 5 minutes. Arrange pheasants on vegetables and cover.

Roast in hot oven, 425°, for 30 minutes. Add remaining ¼ cup Madeira, Game Gravy and reserved truffles. Cover dish and cook 15 minutes longer, or until pheasants are tender. Serve with Bread Sauce and fried hominy.

BREAD SAUCE

2 cups milk

2 cups soft white bread crumbs

1 small onion stuck with 1 clove

2 tablespoons butter

Dash of salt

3 tablespoons cream

Makes about 2 cups

Heat milk to boiling in a heavy saucepan. Add bread crumbs, onion with clove, butter and salt. Simmer gently for 15 minutes.

Remove onion and beat mixture in saucepan with a wire whip until sauce is very smooth. Stir in cream and serve hot.

ROAST QUAIL

4 quail

Salt pork

Clean and drain the birds. Cover the breasts with thin slices of salt pork and place birds in a shallow roasting pan.

4 slices toast

Roast in a hot oven, 450°, for 20 minutes, basting often. Remove the salt pork to allow the breasts to brown. Return to hot oven for 10 minutes.

Serve each bird on a slice of buttered or fried toast.

Makes 4 servings

As a flavorful variation, cover the toast with slivered or chopped Virginia ham, then top with roast bird. E.B.

ROAST QUAIL AU RISOTTO PIEDMONTAISE

4 white truffles, coarsely chopped

4 tablespoons butter

4 dressed quails

Cook truffles in 2 tablespoons butter in small skillet. Stuff quails with mixed truffles and ground pork. Truss birds. Melt remaining butter and brush birds well. Place in shallow roasting pan.

¼ pound freshly ground pork fat

Roast in a very hot oven, 475°, for 15 minutes, turning and basting often, until birds are golden.

Risotto (recipe follows)

Line a timbal with Risotto, shaping nests for roasted birds. Place birds in Risotto and keep warm.

1 cup game stock

Makes 4 servings

Heat game stock in roasting pan, stirring to remove all baked pieces, until liquid boils and is reduced by half. Pour over birds and serve immediately.

RISOTTO

½ cup chopped onion

6 tablespoons butter

Sauté onion in 4 tablespoons butter in a large heavy skillet. Stir in rice and cook over low heat until the rice grains are shiny.

1 cup rice

Remove from heat and add saffron and consommé. Mix well and cover skillet.

Few strands saffron, crushed

2 cups consommé*

¼ cup freshly grated Parmesan cheese

Simmer until liquid is absorbed and rice is tender, adding more consommé if needed. When rice is cooked, stir in 2 tablespoons butter and grated Parmesan cheese.

ROAST SADDLE OF VENISON, POIVRADE

Saddle of young venison, about 6 pounds

½ cup dry Vermouth

6 shallots, chopped

1 carrot, chopped

1 bay leaf

½ teaspoon salt

Dash cayenne pepper

2 teaspoons freshly ground black pepper

1 cup beef broth

2 tablespoons butter

2 tablespoons flour

1 teaspoon lemon juice

Makes 6 servings, with about 1½ cups sauce

Meat from a young animal is usually tender enough to be cooked without using a marinade. Meat from an older animal can be improved by marinating for 24 to 48 hours before cooking.

Wipe the meat with paper towels and insert a meat thermometer in the meatiest part of the saddle. Roast in a hot oven, 450°, for 30 minutes.

Reduce the oven temperature to 350° and continue cooking until thermometer registers 135° for rare, 150° for medium.

Mix the Vermouth, seasonings and broth in a small saucepan. Bring to a boil. Reduce heat and simmer 5 minutes.

Make a paste with the butter and flour. Drop this a few bits at a time into the sauce and blend in with a wire whip.

Cook and stir the sauce until it thickens. Add lemon juice. Serve hot with the roast venison.

SAUTEED YOUNG RABBIT

Rabbit

Seasoned flour

¼ cup butter

1 cup dairy sour cream

½ teaspoon salt

2 teaspoons sweet paprika

2 tablespoons chopped parsley

Makes 3-4 servings

Wash the rabbit and cut into pieces. Roll in seasoned flour.

Heat the butter in a heavy skillet and brown the rabbit pieces on all sides. When nicely browned, reduce heat to low, cover the skillet and let cook 20 minutes, or until meat is tender.

Remove the rabbit to a hot serving dish.

Add the sour cream, salt and paprika to skillet and stir briskly to blend the cream and the pan juices. Heat sauce, but do not allow to boil.

Pour sauce over rabbit and sprinkle with parsley.

MALLARD DUCK A LA PRESSE

1 dressed wild duck

Wash and truss duck. Place in roasting pan.

½ cup dry red wine

Roast in very hot oven, 475°, for 10 minutes. Allow duck to stand 10 minutes, then remove breasts and keep warm.

5 peppercorns, cracked

1 bay leaf

Place remaining duck carcass in a duck press and process to extract all the blood and juices.

½ teaspoon leaf thyme

2 shallots, diced

Combine wine, herbs and shallots in a small heavy saucepan. Boil until mixture is reduced by two thirds.

1 tablespoon butter

Combine butter and flour until smooth and stir into hot liquid. Simmer 2 minutes and put through a fine sieve. Very gradually add duck blood to sauce and heat slowly, but do not boil.

½ teaspoon flour

Toasted bread triangles

Cut the duck breasts into thin slices and arrange on bread triangles. Pour sauce over. Serve with wild rice and red currant jelly.

Red currant jelly

Wild rice

When I serve pressed duck at home, I break up the duck carcass and run it through the meat chopper, using the coarsest blade. Then I strain the juices through cheesecloth. E.B.

Makes 2 servings

SAUTE OF VENISON

4 tablespoons butter

Heat butter until very hot in large heavy skillet. Add steaks and sauté for 5 minutes on each side, or until done as you like.

4 venison steaks, about 1-inch thick

⅓ cup dry Sherry

Stir in Sherry, salt and pepper and simmer for 2 minutes, basting steaks with sauce.

Salt and pepper

2 tablespoons chopped parsley

Place on heated serving platter and sprinkle with chopped parsley. Garnish with watercress. Serve red currant jelly on the side.

Watercress

Red currant jelly

Makes 4 servings

HUNGARIAN ROAST PARTRIDGE

4 dressed young partridges

4 tablespoons butter

Salt and pepper

Juice of 1 lemon

4 partridge livers

4 slices bacon

Hungarian Sauce (recipe follows)

Watercress

Makes 4 servings

Stuff partridges with a mixture of butter, salt, pepper and lemon juice. Add a liver to each partridge. Truss birds. Lay bacon over breasts and place birds in shallow roasting pan.

Roast in hot oven, 425°, for 30 minutes, or until golden. Baste often with pan drippings. Serve with Hungarian Sauce and garnish with watercress.

HUNGARIAN SAUCE

4 tablespoons butter

2 tablespoons finely chopped onion

½ teaspoon Hungarian paprika

Salt

½ cup dry white wine

Dash of thyme

Dash of chervil

Parsley

2 cups Velouté Sauce*

Makes about 2 cups

Heat 2 tablespoons butter in a small skillet. Sauté onion with paprika and salt until onion is soft. Add wine and herbs. Simmer until mixture is reduced by two thirds.

Strain liquid into Velouté Sauce in heavy saucepan. Simmer sauce for 5 minutes. Rub through a fine strainer and stir in remaining 2 tablespoons butter.

CIVET DE LIEVRE
Jugged Rabbit

1 hare

Have butcher prepare rabbit, reserving the blood and cutting hare into serving-size pieces.

½ pound slab bacon

Dice bacon and blanch in boiling water for 5 minutes. Drain well.

3 tablespoons butter

18 small white onions, peeled

Heat butter in a large, flameproof casserole with a cover. Sauté onions and bacon in butter until lightly browned. Remove onions and bacon and reserve.

3 tablespoons flour

Bouquet garni

Brown pieces of hare in same casserole, then add flour and cook until it turns brown. Add bouquet garni, red wine, and water just to cover. Season with salt, pepper and tomato paste. Cover casserole.
Bake in a moderate oven, 350°, for 2½ hours, or until meat is almost tender. Remove hare from casserole and strain sauce over.

1¼ cups dry red wine

Salt and pepper

2 tablespoons tomato paste

½ pound mushrooms, quartered

Rinse casserole and return hare and sauce to casserole with mushrooms and reserved onions and bacon. Cover and bake additional 20 to 25 minutes, or until hare and vegetables are tender.

2 tablespoons vinegar

Stir vinegar into reserved hare blood, then stir in a little of the hot sauce. Blend mixture into casserole and heat thoroughly, but do not allow to boil.

You can prepare this recipe using the frozen ready-to-cook rabbit now on the market. Just follow the recipe, omitting the addition of blood to sauce. E.B.

Makes 6 servings

ENGLISH GROUSE

4 dressed grouse

6 tablespoons butter

Juice of 1 lemon

Salt and pepper

4 slices bacon

Bread Sauce*

Red currant jelly

Watercress

Makes 4 servings

Stuff the grouse with a mixture of butter, lemon juice, salt and pepper. Wrap a slice of bacon around breast of each grouse. Place in shallow roasting pan.

Roast in hot oven, 425°, for 20 to 25 minutes, or just until done. Baste several times with pan drippings. Serve with Bread Sauce and red currant jelly. Garnish with watercress.

GRILLED SQUAB

3 squabs, split for broiling

Peanut oil

Freshly ground black pepper

Salt

4½ teaspoons dry mustard

4 teaspoons dry white wine

¾ cup fresh white bread crumbs

Makes 3 servings

Brush the squabs generously with oil and sprinkle with pepper and salt. Place squab skin side up on rack in broiler pan and grill about 8 inches from preheated broiler for 10 minutes. Turn, brush with oil and sprinkle with salt and pepper, grill about 8 minutes more.

Make a thin paste with mustard and wine, brush over squab halves on both sides. Coat the squabs with bread crumbs, pressing them on if necessary. Sprinkle the pieces with a little oil and return to broiler. Grill an additional 5 to 7 minutes per side. Chef André prepares this dish over a white-hot charcoal fire for wonderful flavor. E.B.

ENTREE~PORK

ROAST SMOKED LOIN OF PORK

CHOUCROUTE GARNIE STRASBOURGEOISE

SAUERKRAUT A L'ALSACIENNE

SAUCISSON EN BRIOCHE WITH HOT POTATO SALAD

ROAST SUCKLING PIG

BAKED HAM

ROAST SMOKED LOIN OF PORK

5½-6 pounds smoked pork loin

2 teaspoons freshly ground pepper

8 whole cloves

1 cup thick sweetened applesauce

Makes 8 servings

Have the butcher saw through the loin backbone lengthwise, then tie it to the loin with soft cord.

Rub the meat all over with pepper and stick with cloves. Place fat side up in a shallow roasting pan and roast in a moderate oven, 350°, for 1 hour.

Take the pork from the oven and spread with applesauce. Return to oven and roast for an additional 35 to 40 minutes, or until the applesauce has become a golden glaze.

CHOUCROUTE GARNIE STRASBOURGEOISE
Sauerkraut Garnished with Smoked Pork

1 can (1 pound, 12 ounces) sauerkraut

1 medium-size onion, sliced

1 cup dry white wine

2 tablespoons butter

3 juniper berries

3 peppercorns

2 whole cloves

½ bay leaf

6 thin pork chops

1-pound piece pickled pork OR smoked pork

½-pound piece meaty slab bacon

6 frankfurters, split

Boiled new potatoes

Makes 6 servings

Place well-drained sauerkraut in heavy kettle. Bury onion slices in sauerkraut. Add wine and butter. Tie spices in a piece of cheesecloth and add to kettle. Bring to a boil, then reduce heat, cover and simmer 25 minutes.

Sauté thin pork chops until tender. Cook pickled or smoked pork and bacon until done in boiling water. Add frankfurters. Heat through.

Remove spice bag and onion from sauerkraut. Spoon sauerkraut onto warm serving platter. Slice pork and bacon and arrange on sauerkraut with pork chops and frankfurters. Serve with boiled new potatoes.

A great informal party dish with ice cold beer and black bread. E.B.

SAUERKRAUT
A L'ALSACIENNE

1 pound slab bacon

3 pounds sauerkraut, drained

6 smoked pork loin chops

8 Strasbourgh sausages OR
8 smoked sausages

2 onions, sliced

3 cups Beef Consommé*

3 cups dry white wine

4 whole cloves

4 knackwursts, scored

Makes 8 servings

Cut bacon into thick slices. Lay half the slices in the bottom of a very large baking dish. Spoon sauerkraut over bacon. Arrange pork chops and sausages over sauerkraut and top with sliced onions. Pour Beef Consommé and wine over and add cloves. Cover baking dish.

Bake in a low oven, 350°, for 1½ hours. Add knackwurst and cook 30 minutes longer. Remove whole cloves and spoon sauerkraut on large heated platter. Arrange meats on top.

SAUCISSON EN BRIOCHE WITH
HOT POTATO SALAD
Garlic Sausage Baked in Brioche

4 tablespoons butter

2 pounds large pork sausage

2 large onions, chopped

1 cup Beef Consommé*

1 cup dry white wine

3 tablespoons tomato puree

2 tablespoons flour

Brioche (recipe follows)

Hot potato salad

Makes 6 servings

Melt 2 tablespoons butter in a large skillet. Add pork sausage and chopped onions. Brown on all sides. Drain excess fat.

Add consommé, white wine and tomato puree. Cover skillet and simmer 15 minutes.

Remove sausages from skillet with slotted spoon and place in hollowed-out Brioche. Keep warm.

Combine remaining 2 tablespoons butter and flour to make a smooth paste. Blend into hot liquid in skillet. Spoon over Brioche and serve with hot potato salad.

BRIOCHE

1 package active dry yeast

¼ cup very warm water

2 cups sifted flour

Dissolve yeast in water and blend in ½ cup flour with your fingers to make a soft sponge. Roll into a ball and cut a cross on top. Drop half into a deep bowl of warm water. When sponge rises to the surface, it is ready to make Brioche.

3 eggs, beaten

1 tablespoon sugar

½ teaspoon salt

Sift flour into a well on pastry board. Blend in eggs to make a soft dough. Scrape dough off pastry board and crash against pastry board. Repeat 100 times to make a very elastic dough that detaches itself cleanly from fingers and board.

¾ cup soft sweet butter

Knead sugar and salt into dough. Knead in butter only until blended (overworking will cause dough to loose elasticity).

Drain sponge from bowl on a towel. Knead into dough.

Place dough in a floured bowl and cover with a clean towel. Allow to rise in a warm place 3 hours, or until double in bulk.

Punch dough down and chill 6 hours or overnight. Then punch dough down and place in a large Brioche mold.

Cover and let rise in a warm place 30 minutes. Brush with beaten egg.

Makes 1 large bread

Bake in hot oven, 425°, for 30 minutes, or until brown. Remove from mold and cool completely.

ROAST SUCKLING PIG

1 young pig, about 10 pounds

1 teaspoon garlic salt

½ cup Sherry or Brandy

Stuffing

Butter

Hot stock

Apple

Thoroughly wash the pig in cold water. Dry inside and out with paper towels. Sprinkle body cavity with garlic salt. Brush inside and out with Sherry or Brandy.

Stuff the pig loosely, using favorite bread stuffing, Plaza Turkey Stuffing* or Apple Stuffing*. Lace the opening. Truss the legs separately and close under the body.

Rub the pig all over with butter and place in a shallow roasting pan. Place a ball of foil or a small block of wood in the mouth to hold it open. Cover the ears and tail with wet paper towels, then with foil, to keep them from burning.

Roast in a moderate oven, 350°, for 3½ hours, or until meat is tender and well cooked. If roast appears to be browning too quickly, "tent" the back with a piece of heavy foil.

During the roasting period, add a cup of hot stock to the pan and use the liquid in pan as a baste.

To serve, place the pig on a heated platter, remove foil from ears, tail and mouth. Place a small red apple in mouth.

Garnish platter with little spiced crab apples or pears, or with lemon cups and cranberries.

Makes 10–12 servings

Save this roast for a big party or luau. You will impress guests with your cooking ability. E.B.

BAKED HAM

1 whole smoked ham,
about 12 pounds

Cloves

1½ cups brown sugar

½ cup fine dry seasoned crumbs

2 teaspoons dry mustard

⅓ cup Brandy

Makes 8–10 servings

Use a sharp knife to loosen and remove the ham rind. Score the top in a diamond pattern and stick with cloves.

Mix the sugar, crumbs and mustard and spread over the ham.

Place ham on a rack in a roasting pan and bake in a moderate oven, 350°, for about 2 hours.

Spoon the Brandy over the ham and start basting with pan juices. Continue cooking for 1 more hour (3 hours in all), or until ham is tender.

ENTREE~POULTRY

BREAST OF CHICKEN A LA KIEV

DEVILED CHICKEN

BREAST OF CHICKEN POLYNESIAN

ARROZ CON POLLO

CHICKEN CACCIATORE

CHICKEN HASH—TRUMAN CAPOTE

CHICKEN SAUTE HUNGARIAN STYLE

GRAIN-FED CHICKEN EN CASSEROLE

SUPREME OF CHICKEN EUGENIE
    UNDER GLASS

BAKED STUFFED TOMATOES, BRESSANE,
    WITH BACON, SAUCE CHASSEUR

OLD-FASHIONED CHICKEN POT PIE

COQ AU VIN A LA BOURGUIGNONNE

PORCUPINE OF BREAST OF CHICKEN
    AUX AMANDES

CHICKEN SAUTE CYNTHIA

CHICKEN A LA CREN

PINK CHICKEN SAUTE

CHICKEN A LA REINE

SUPREME OF CHICKEN PLAZA

SUPREME DE VOLAILLE AUX
    CHAMPIGNONS

CHICKEN QUENELLES #1

CHICKEN QUENELLES #2

CHICKEN TANDOORI

BREADED CAPON LEG CUTLET

BREAST OF CAPON A LA BROCHE,
    ON HAM

GALANTINE OF DUCK

DUCK WITH ONION STUFFING

DUCKLING BIGARADE

DUCK A L'ORANGE

LONG ISLAND DUCKLING AU GRAND
    MARNIER

ROAST GOOSE

ROAST MARYLAND BABY TURKEY FILLED
    WITH WHEAT PILAFF AND APPLES

BREAST OF GUINEA HEN UNDER GLASS

ROCK CORNISH AUX PRIMEURS

BREAST OF CHICKEN
A LA KIEV

4 whole chicken breasts,
about 10 ounces each

1 cup butter

½ cup seasoned flour

1 egg, beaten

1 cup fine bread crumbs

Fat for frying

Makes 4 servings

Bone and skin chicken breasts, but keep each whole. Place each breast between pieces of wax paper and pound as flat as possible.

Divide butter into 4 parts and mold each part into a tapered "finger" shape. Chill in freezer for 30 minutes.

Wrap a butter "finger" inside each chicken breast, tucking in ends of chicken to make a neat shape.

Roll chicken rounds first in seasoned flour, then dip in beaten egg and roll in bread crumbs.

Fry in fat at 360° until a rich golden brown. Drain on paper towels. Serve immediately.

DEVILED CHICKEN

2 ready-to-cook broilers,
about 2 pounds each

½ cup soy sauce

½ cup Brandy

1 teaspoon Tabasco

½ cup olive oil

½ cup melted butter

2 cups packaged seasoned stuffing mix

1 teaspoon coarse-ground
black pepper

1 teaspoon dry mustard

¼ cup grated Parmesan cheese

Makes 4 servings

Quarter broilers. Mix soy sauce, Brandy, Tabasco and olive oil to make a marinade. Soak the chicken pieces in the marinade for 2 or 3 hours. Turn them often so all sides are well coated with mixture.

Lift the chicken from the marinade and drain, but do not allow to dry out. Place chicken, skin side down, in a shallow baking pan. Broil for 10 minutes. Turn and broil for 8 to 10 minutes more.

Remove from the broiler and brush all over with melted butter.

Crush the stuffing mix (in the blender or with a rolling pin) to fine crumbs and mix with pepper, mustard and cheese.

Coat the buttered chicken with the mixed crumbs and return to the broiler for 2 or 3 minutes. Watch carefully to avoid burning the crumbs.

Turn the chicken pieces, brush with more butter and sprinkle any bare patches with more crumbs. Broil 2 minutes.

BREAST OF CHICKEN POLYNESIAN

¼ cup freshly grated ginger root

2 cloves garlic, crushed

½ cup firmly packed brown sugar

2 cups soy sauce

4 whole chicken breasts, split

8 slices fresh or canned pineapple

4 bananas, peeled and halved

2 tablespoons butter

Makes 8 servings

Crush ginger and garlic together in mortar and pestle until well blended. Work in brown sugar to make a smooth paste. Blend into soy sauce.

Arrange chicken breasts, skin side up, in a single layer in shallow glass pan. Pour sauce over and cover. Allow chicken to marinate in refrigerator for at least 24 hours.

Broil chicken breasts 20 minutes, or until skin is a rich golden brown. Turn often and baste with marinade. Keep warm.

Sauté pineapple rings and banana halves in butter in a skillet until golden. Serve each chicken breast with a pineapple ring and banana half.

When my local Indian or Chinese market is out of fresh ginger root, I substitute 2 tablespoons ground ginger. E.B.

ARROZ CON POLLO

1 3½-pound roasting chicken, cut in 8 pieces

6 tablespoons butter

1 tablespoon salt

1 cup rice

2 onions, diced

4 hot peppers, diced

1 cup stuffed olives, cut in halves

2 cups chopped canned tomatoes

½ cup chopped green peppers

Pimiento

Makes 4 servings

Sauté chicken, including liver cut in half, in the butter heated in a large saucepan. Remove chicken to another large saucepan and add enough water to almost cover chicken. Add salt. Simmer over moderate heat until tender, about 30 minutes.

Brown rice and onions in skillet used for chicken, using butter left in pan. Stir until evenly browned all over. Add 2 cups broth from cooked chicken. Then add hot peppers, olives, tomatoes and green peppers. Mix well. Simmer until rice is tender.

Heap rice on a large warm platter. Arrange pieces of chicken on rice and garnish with pieces of pimiento.

CHICKEN CACCIATORE

2 cut up broiler-fryers,
2 pounds each

Seasoned flour

1 tablespoon olive oil

⅓ cup butter

1 medium-size onion, finely chopped

½ pound fresh mushrooms, sliced

1 large can (1 pound, 12 ounces)
solid-packed tomatoes, chopped

¾ cup dry white wine

½ cup tomato juice

1 clove of garlic, minced

Few sprigs parsley, minced

½ bay leaf

Makes 4 servings

Dredge chicken pieces in seasoned flour. Combine and heat oil and butter in heavy skillet with cover. Brown chicken pieces in hot fat. As pieces brown, remove them to make room for others. Return all the golden brown pieces to the skillet and add vegetables.

Simmer over medium heat for 5 minutes.

Add remaining ingredients. Cover and simmer over low heat for 35 minutes, or until chicken is cooked. Serve with buttered noodles.

This famous dish is called Chicken Chasseur in France, Chicken Hunter Style wherever English is spoken. E.B.

CHICKEN HASH–
TRUMAN CAPOTE

4 cups finely diced cooked chicken
(white meat only)

1½ cups heavy cream

1 cup Cream Sauce*

2 teaspoons salt

⅛ teaspoon white pepper

¼ cup dry Sherry

¼ cup Hollandaise Sauce*

Makes 4-5 servings

Mix chicken, cream, Cream Sauce and seasonings in a heavy skillet. Cook over moderate heat, stirring often, for about 10 minutes.

When moisture is slightly reduced, place skillet in a moderate oven, 350°, and bake 30 minutes.

Stir in Sherry and return to oven for 10 minutes. Lightly fold in Hollandaise Sauce and serve at once.

SUPREME OF CHICKEN EUGENIE
UNDER GLASS, COQ AU VIN
A LA BOURGUIGNONNE

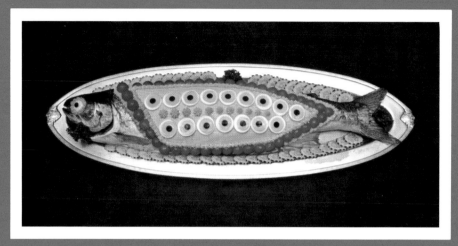

WHOLE BOILED SALMON DECORATED WITH CHERRY
TOMATOES, CUCUMBERS, EGG YOLKS AND SLICED
HARD-BOILED EGGS

MOUSSE OF COLD SALMON DECORATED WITH CUCUMBERS,
SLICED TOMATOES, RADISHES AND LEMON WEDGES

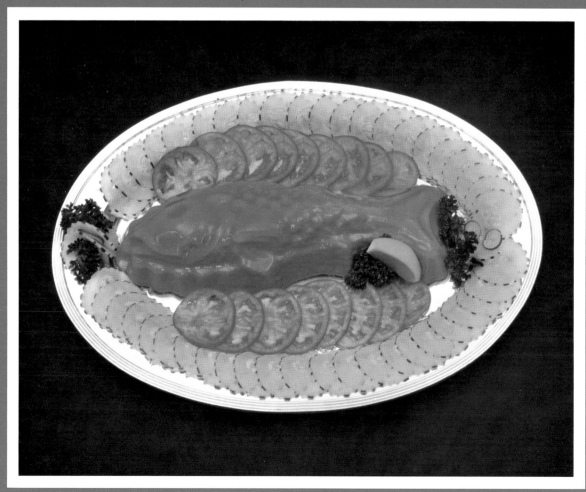

CHICKEN SAUTE
HUNGARIAN STYLE

*2 cut up broiler-fryers,
3 pounds each*

2 teaspoons salt

⅛ teaspoon freshly ground pepper

½ cup shortening or lard

2 large onions, minced

1 green pepper, minced

¼ pound fresh mushrooms, sliced

*2 tablespoons sweet
Hungarian paprika*

⅓ cup chili sauce

2 cups chicken stock or broth

1 tablespoon butter

1 tablespoon flour

½ cup dairy sour cream

Makes 6-8 servings

Sprinkle chicken with salt and pepper. In a heavy skillet with cover, heat shortening or lard. Brown chicken pieces on all sides, then remove. Add onions to fat remaining in skillet. Cook until golden. Add green pepper and mushrooms. Cook few minutes, or until soft. Stir in paprika, chili sauce and chicken stock. Simmer until blended.

Return chicken to skillet. Cover and simmer over low heat for 40 minutes. Blend butter and flour to a smooth paste. Drop this in small pieces over surface of mixture and stir in. Bring to a quick boil and remove from heat. Correct seasonings. Allow to cool for about 5 minutes, then stir in sour cream.

Serve with buttered poppy seed noodles—to applause! E.B.

GRAIN-FED CHICKEN EN
CASSEROLE

*2 cut up broiler-fryers,
2½ pounds each*

Seasoned flour

6 tablespoons Clarified Butter*

2 cups Chicken Stock*

1 cup heavy cream, scalded

Salt and pepper

Makes 6 servings

Have your butcher cut chicken into serving-size pieces. Dip in water and then roll in seasoned flour.

Heat clarified butter in heavy skillet. Brown chicken in butter, a few pieces at a time, until golden on all sides.

Transfer to baking dish and pour Chicken Stock over. Cover baking dish. Bake in moderate oven, 350°, for 45 minutes, or until chicken is tender. Add scalded cream and salt and pepper to taste.

SUPREME OF CHICKEN EUGENIE UNDER GLASS

2 whole chicken breasts, split

6 tablespoons Clarified Butter*

4 slices white toast

4 thin slices Virginia ham

1½ cups Sauce Suprème*

4 whole mushrooms

Makes 4 servings

Sauté chicken breasts in clarified butter in a heavy skillet until golden on all sides, about 25 minutes.

Top a slice of toast with a slice of Virginia ham and then place a chicken breast over ham. Spoon heated Sauce Suprème over chicken and top with a whole mushroom that has been sautéed in butter.

At the Plaza each serving is placed under a glass dome and brought quickly to the table. E.B.

BAKED STUFFED TOMATOES, BRESSANE, WITH BACON, SAUCE CHASSEUR

6 large ripe tomatoes

½ cup chopped onion

½ cup butter

1 whole raw chicken breast, boned, skinned and chopped

1 tablespoon chopped parsley

1 tablespoon flour

1 cup hot Chicken Broth*

⅓ cup heavy cream

Pinch of salt

Pinch of black pepper

1 egg, well beaten

½ cup bread crumbs

Sauce Chasseur (recipe follows)

Makes 6 servings

Cut a slice from top of tomatoes, scoop out the flesh and discard the seeds. Finely chop the meaty pulp.

Brown onions in ¼ cup butter in a heavy skillet. Add chopped chicken, tomato pulp and parsley. Simmer 5 minutes. Then sprinkle with flour and stir in until mixture thickens.

Stir in Chicken Broth with wire whip. Add cream and seasonings. Simmer over very low heat for 15 minutes.

Remove from heat and blend in egg. Return to heat and simmer for a few minutes, but do not let mixture boil. Remove skillet from heat and allow to cool.

Form chicken mixture into balls and stuff into tomato shells. Arrange filled tomatoes in baking dish and sprinkle tops with bread crumbs. Dot with remaining butter. Bake in moderate oven, 350°, for 20 minutes.

Serve with Sauce Chasseur.

SAUCE CHASSEUR

2 shallots, chopped

⅓ cup butter

6 large mushrooms, chopped

1 sprig parsley, chopped

1 sprig chervil, chopped

1 garlic clove, crushed

1 ripe tomato, peeled, cored
and chopped

⅓ cup dry white wine

1 cup Brown Gravy*

6 grilled bacon strips

Brown shallots in hot butter. Add mushrooms, parsley, chervil, garlic, tomato and wine. Simmer for 15 minutes.

Add Brown Gravy and cook over low heat for 3 to 4 minutes. Season to taste.

Pour over baked stuffed tomatoes and garnish with bacon strips.

OLD-FASHIONED CHICKEN POT PIE

3 cups cubed cooked chicken

1 cup cooked small white onions

1 cup cooked sliced carrots

1 cup cooked sliced mushrooms

1 cup cooked diced potatoes

¾ cup cooked peas

2 tablespoons finely diced
fried salt pork

3 cups Sauce Suprème*

Pie Crust* (⅓ of recipe)

Makes 4 servings

Combine chicken, onions, carrots, mushrooms, potatoes, peas and salt pork in a large bowl. Fold in Supreme Sauce. Divide mixture among 4 deep individual casseroles.

Divide Pie Crust into 4 portions and roll out each portion to an area 1 inch wider than casserole. Place over chicken mixture and flute edge. Make several slits for steam to escape.

Bake in a moderately hot oven, 375°, for 40 minutes, or until pastry is golden.

COQ AU VIN A LA BOURGUIGNONNE

⅓ cup finely diced salt pork

1 cut up broiler-fryer,
about 2½ pounds

Salt and pepper

8 small white onions, peeled

4 small potatoes, peeled

8 whole mushrooms

½ cup dry red Burgundy wine

⅓ cup Brown Sauce*

Parsley

Makes 2 servings

Render salt pork in a flameproof casserole. Remove salt pork pieces with a slotted spoon and reserve.

Season chicken pieces with salt and pepper and brown in fat in casserole. Remove and reserve. Brown onions and potatoes in same casserole until onions are golden. Pour off excess fat.

Return chicken and salt pork to casserole. Add mushrooms, wine and Brown Sauce. Heat to a boil. Cover casserole.

Bake in moderate oven, 350°, for 40 minutes, or until chicken is tender. Garnish with chopped parsley.

PORCUPINE OF BREAST OF CHICKEN AUX AMANDES

6-pound fowl

Bouquet garni

2 teaspoons salt

Seasoned flour

¼ cup milk

1 egg

¼ cup soft white bread crumbs

2 tablespoons flour

1 cup sliced blanched almonds

Orange-Lime Sauce (recipe follows)

Makes 2-3 servings

Boil the fowl with the bouquet garni and salt in water to cover. When the chicken is tender, let it cool in the broth.

Use a sharp knife to remove the breast, discarding the skin. (The remaining chicken can be used later in salad or croquettes.)

Cut each breast into 4 or 5 slices. Dredge the slices in seasoned flour and let dry while preparing batter.

Mix together milk, egg, soft crumbs and 2 tablespoons flour. Beat until smooth and thickened.

Dip the floured slices in the batter, then roll them in the sliced almonds. Place on waxed paper or foil and chill for 1 hour.

Fry the slices to a golden brown in deep fat. Serve hot with Orange-Lime Sauce (recipe follows).

ORANGE-LIME SAUCE

3 limes

⅓ cup orange marmalade

1 small piece green ginger, peeled

Makes about ½ cup sauce

Peel the limes with a vegetable peeler, and use scissors to shred the peel.

Cover shredded peel with cold water and boil for 5 minutes. Drain off water.

Add the juice of the limes, marmalade and minced ginger. Bring to a boil and cook 3 to 4 minutes. Serve hot with the chicken.

CHICKEN SAUTE CYNTHIA

2 cut up broiler-fryers, 2½ pounds each

Seasoned flour

½ cup Clarified Butter*

1 bottle (6½ ounces) Champagne

1 tablespoon lemon juice

2 tablespoons Curaçao

1 teaspoon Bovril (or use Glacé de Viande*)

½ cup sweet butter

1 cup powdered sugar

½ cup water

1 cup seedless white grapes

8 fresh peaches or pears, peeled and halved

3 tablespoons bar-le-duc (currant jelly)

2 navel oranges, peeled and sectioned

Makes 6 servings

Dredge chicken with seasoned flour. Brown quickly on all sides in hot clarified butter. Add ½ of the Champagne, cover and cook over low heat until tender, about 25 minutes. Remove from heat, place chicken on oven-proof serving platter and keep warm.

To the liquid in the skillet add the remaining Champagne, lemon juice, Curaçao, and Bovril or glacé. Simmer until reduced by about one half, then add half the sweet butter and stir in until melted. Strain and pour over chicken. Keep warm.

Heat remaining fresh butter. Add sugar and water and simmer over low heat until sugar dissolves. Add grapes. Simmer until heated through. Skim grapes from liquid with a slotted spoon and strew over chicken pieces. Repeat with peach or pear halves, turning them until tender. Lift out of syrup and arrange around the chicken pieces like a frame. Fill the hollow of each fruit half with bar-le-duc. Simmer orange sections in the remaining syrup until heated. Spoon overall and serve at once.

This is an elegant dish to set before company! E.B.

CHICKEN A LA CREN

1 broiler-fryer, 3–3½ pounds

3 chicken livers

½ teaspoon butter

3 shallots, coarsely chopped

3 mushrooms, coarsely chopped

3 cooked chicken gizzards, coarsely chopped

3 tablespoons white wine

4 chestnuts (canned or boiled), chopped

3 tablespoons celery leaves, chopped

1 hard-cooked egg, chopped

¾ cup cold Chicken Broth*

1½ cups fine white bread crumbs

½ teaspoon white pepper

Pinch of nutmeg

Salt

1 carrot, chopped

1 stalk celery, chopped

1 onion, chopped

1 cup strong Chicken Broth*

1 tablespoon sweet butter

Juice of ½ lemon

Makes 3-4 servings

Bone the chicken by cutting the skin down the back; then, while holding the skin with the left hand, insert the point of a small sharp knife between flesh and bones and scrape away as close as possible the meat from the carcass, then from the legs. When finished, lay the skin and meat flat on a wooden board. Pound the flesh with the edge of a heavy plate or the flat side of a cleaver, flattening it out to more or less cover the skin.

Sauté the livers in hot butter. Remove and chop coarsely. Brown the shallots and mushrooms in the same butter. Then add the gizzards and wine. Cook 4 or 5 minutes. Remove pan from heat and let cool before adding chestnuts, celery leaves, egg and chopped livers.

Add chicken broth to bread crumbs, mixing thoroughly. Combine the two mixtures, then add seasonings. Spoon the stuffing across the center of flattened chicken. Roll the chicken around the stuffing so that it is completely enclosed. Tuck in ends at same time to make a more shapely roll. Tie the rolled chicken with string or, if preferred, roll it tightly in a piece of greased foil.

Place in a greased roasting pan and surround with some of the chopped chicken bones. Place in moderate oven, 350°. After chicken has cooked for 30 minutes, add to roasting pan chopped carrot, celery and onion, plus 1 cup strong chicken broth. Cook another 30 minutes. To brown, carefully remove foil and raise oven temperature to 425° for 15 minutes.

Let chicken rest about 15 minutes, then slice it as you would a jelly roll. Put slices on a hot platter. Pour over it the strained cooking liquor into which has been stirred a tablespoon of sweet butter and the juice of half a lemon.

This dish has an affinity for leeks. When the weather is cold I serve it with braised leeks; hot, I serve it with Leeks Vinaigrette*. E.B.

PINK CHICKEN SAUTE

2 2-pound chickens, quartered

Seasoned flour

⅓ cup Clarified Butter*

1 small onion, finely chopped

1 tablespoon paprika

Salt and pepper

1 cup Chicken Broth*

1 cup heavy cream

1½ tablespoons fresh butter

½ teaspoon lemon juice

Chopped parsley

Makes 6 servings

Roll chicken pieces in seasoned flour. Heat clarified butter in a heavy covered skillet. Brown chicken pieces in hot fat. When chicken is golden brown, add onion, paprika and a generous sprinkling of salt and pepper. Cover, reduce heat to low and simmer for 15 minutes, or until chicken is tender.

Remove chicken pieces to a serving platter and keep warm. Pour broth into skillet and bring to a boil. Use a wire whip to stir in cream and butter. Bring to a quick boil and remove from heat. Blend in lemon juice and parsley. Pour over chicken and serve hot.

CHICKEN A LA REINE

½ pound fresh mushrooms, diced

2 tablespoons butter

1 tablespoon flour

½ cup Chicken Broth*

½ cup cream

Salt and pepper

1 cup cooked breast of chicken, diced

1 teaspoon truffles, diced

4 warm patty shells

Makes 4 servings

Sauté mushrooms in butter until soft. Sprinkle in the flour and blend over low heat, stirring constantly, for about 3 minutes. Add chicken broth gradually, stirring constantly until sauce is smooth.

Simmer for 5 minutes. Add cream and bring to a quick boil. Adjust seasoning, add diced chicken and truffles. Mix gently and serve hot in warm patty shells.

SUPREME OF CHICKEN PLAZA

4 whole chicken breasts, split

4 tablespoons butter

Salt and pepper

½ cup Chicken Stock*

Sauce Suprème*

Fluffy rice

Cherry tomatoes

Makes 4 servings

Bone the split chicken breasts and remove skin. Sauté chicken breasts in hot butter in heavy skillet until golden on all sides. Season with salt and pepper. Add Chicken Stock and cover skillet.

Simmer about 15 minutes, or until breasts are tender. Place 2 breasts in individual au gratin dishes. Cover with Sauce Suprème and serve with fluffy rice and sautéed cherry tomatoes.

Very elegant, yet very simple. I serve this often when chicken is a bargain at the supermarket. E.B.

SUPREME DE VOLAILLE AUX CHAMPIGNONS
Chicken and Mushrooms en Gelée

3 whole chicken breasts

½ pound small mushrooms

1 cup Chicken Stock*

1 envelope unflavored gelatin

½ cup heavy cream

2 cups hot chicken Velouté Sauce*

Sliced truffles

Tarragon leaves

Makes 6 servings

Poach chicken breasts and cool until easy enough to handle. Split breasts, remove skin and bones and trim into neat ovals.

Remove stems from mushrooms and save for soup stock. Poach mushroom caps in chicken stock just until soft. Drain.

Soften gelatin in heavy cream. Stir into chicken Velouté in saucepan and heat until gelatin dissolves. Chill until syrupy.

Arrange chicken ovals and mushrooms on a chilled platter. Spoon chilled gelatin over chicken breasts and mushrooms. Garnish with sliced truffles. Chill until ready to serve. Garnish with fresh tarragon leaves.

CHICKEN QUENELLES #1

½ cup fine dry crumbs

½ cup milk

2 tablespoons butter

1 egg white, beaten

½ raw chicken breast, diced

Salt

Cayenne

Nutmeg

Makes 2 servings

Mix crumbs and milk. Cook to a paste over low heat. Stir in butter and stiffly beaten egg white.

Puree the raw chicken in blender until it is a smooth paste. Blend this into the first mixture. Season lightly to taste.

When mixture is very smooth, chill for 30 minutes.

Shape the chicken mixture into small oval cakes with 2 tablespoons. Drop the ovals into boiling water, stock or chicken broth and cook about 4 minutes.

Serve as entree with a rich sauce.

These savory chicken ovals are often used as a garnish for soups. E.B.

CHICKEN QUENELLES #2

1 raw chicken breast

2 egg whites

Salt and pepper

Pinch of nutmeg

Heavy cream

Makes 2 servings

Puree chicken breast in blender until smooth. Or put through fine blade of food grinder, then pound in mortar until smooth.

Work in egg whites until mixture is thoroughly blended and smooth. Add seasonings.

Slowly add heavy cream, a little at a time, until mixture is right consistency for shaping.

Shape mixture into oval cakes with 2 tablespoons. Gently slide the ovals into boiling broth or water and cook 4 to 5 minutes.

CHICKEN TANDOORI

2 broilers, 2½ pounds each

12 red chilies (fresh if possible)

1 teaspoon peppercorns

2 pints yoghurt

Sauce (recipe follows)

Makes 4 servings

Split the broilers and flatten them with the side of a heavy cleaver. Remove the skin and use a sharp pointed knife to slit the flesh 6 or 8 times (this helps the chicken absorb flavor).

Put the chilies and peppercorns in the blender with a little cold water. Grind until almost smooth. Stir into yoghurt.

Dip the chicken pieces into the seasoned yoghurt until well coated. Let stand about 2 hours. Wipe the chicken pieces with a damp towel to remove as much of the coating as possible.

Broil on top rack closest to heat in preheated broiler, for about 15 minutes, turning once. Serve with sauce (recipe follows).

SAUCE

2 ripe tomatoes, peeled and chopped

¼ cup butter

8–10 green chilies (fresh if possible)

1 teaspoon peppercorns

1 piece cinnamon stick

1 teaspoon salt

Combine all ingredients in a saucepan and cook over moderate heat for about 15 minutes. Remove cinnamon stick and pour sauce in blender container. Chop medium fine. Reheat and pour over chicken.

BREADED CAPON LEG CUTLET

6 capon legs

6 thin slices prosciutto

4 tablespoons chopped pine nuts

4 tablespoons parsley

4 tablespoons melted butter

¾ cup soft white bread crumbs

½ cup seasoned flour

Sauce Suprème*

Makes 6 servings

Bone capon legs by cutting down on one side of leg and carefully scrapping meat away from bone. Pound meat between waxed paper until thin.

Spread prosciutto with a mixture of pine nuts and parsley. Roll up and place one roll on each capon fillet. Roll up and secure with food picks.

Dip capon rolls in butter and then a mixture of crumbs and seasoned flour. Place on cookie sheet. Drizzle butter over.

Bake in moderate oven, 350°, for 35 minutes, or until tender. Place on heated serving platter and serve with Sauce Suprème.

BREAST OF CAPON A LA BROCHE, ON HAM

2 capon breasts, about 2 pounds each

16 medium-size mushrooms

6 tablespoons butter

3 tablespoons dry Vermouth

1 teaspoon salt

Freshly ground pepper

8 slices broiled Virginia ham

Watercress

Cherry tomatoes

Makes 4-8 servings

Skin and bone capon breasts and cut into 1½-inch cubes. Thread capon cubes and mushrooms on 8 kebabs.

Combine butter, Vermouth, salt and pepper. Brush over kebabs on broiler pan.

Broil kebabs 4 inches from heat for 15 minutes, or until capon is golden. Turn and baste often.

Serve on slices of Virginia ham and garnish with watercress and cherry tomatoes.

GALANTINE OF DUCK

2 ducklings, about 4 pounds each

½ pound leg of veal

½ pound pork tenderloin

1½ pounds fat pork

¼ pound boiled ham

¼ pound cooked tongue
(lamb or beef)

2 teaspoons salt

½ teaspoon leaf thyme, crumbled

1 bay leaf

Few sprigs parsley

2 shallots, minced

¼ cup Sherry

2 eggs

3 quarts strong stock (made with
duck pieces, bones, etc.)

Pistachio nuts

Sliced truffles

Split one duckling down the back. Open it flat on a cutting board, skin side up. Remove the skin carefully by peeling and cutting it away from the flesh. The skin should be in one piece. Scrape away and discard fat.

Remove the breasts and boned thighs. Remove breasts and boned thighs from second duck.

Cut the duckling breasts and thighs into lengthwise strips, making about 12 or 14 in all.

Repeat this with one half the veal and pork, enough slices of the fat pork to make 12 strips, and all the tongue and ham.

Put the duck and meat strips in a bowl with 1 teaspoon salt, thyme, bay leaf, parsley, shallots and Sherry. Mix well, cover and refrigerate overnight.

Take all the remaining meat from the ducklings, removing fat and sinews. Combine this with the remaining veal, pork and fat pork and put all through food grinder twice.

Thoroughly mix the remaining salt, the eggs and the liquid drained from the marinated meat strips with the chopped mixture.

Lay a clean kitchen towel or a square of cotton cloth on a board and spread the duck skin on this flesh side up.

Spread one fourth the ground mixture evenly on the skin. On this place one third the meat strips, alternating them so a design will be formed when the galantine is cut. Repeat until there are 4 layers of ground mixture and 3 layers of meat strips.

Shape all the layers into a roll and wrap the roll firmly in the skin. Then roll all up tightly in the towel or cloth. Tie the ends tightly with string.

Lower the roll into boiling broth and cook at a simmer for about 2 hours.

GALANTINE OF DUCK (*continued*)

Remove the roll from the stock. Cool. Take off the towel and replace with another clean towel, again rolling and tying firmly.

Lay the roll on a platter. Place a flat pan on top and weigh it down with 2 or 3 heavy plates. The roll should be slightly flattened but not squeezed so that it loses moisture. Chill.

When galantine is cold remove towel. Glaze with aspic and garnish with pistachio nuts and sliced truffles.

This is complicated to prepare but well worth all the trouble. And what a marvelous conversation piece for a buffet party! E.B.

Makes 10–12 servings

DUCK WITH ONION STUFFING

1 5-pound duckling, cleaned and ready to cook

½ cup water

½ teaspoon salt

1 cup minced onions

¼ cup minced green pepper

1 egg, slightly beaten

3 cups diced white bread

⅓ cup melted butter

2 teaspoons poultry seasoning

Salt and pepper

Makes 4 servings

Rinse duckling and pat dry inside and out with paper towels.

Combine water, salt, onions and pepper in a saucepan and bring to a boil. Simmer 10 minutes. Remove from heat, add remaining ingredients and mix thoroughly. Stuff lightly into duck to allow for expansion.

Place duck on rack in roasting pan. Pour a little water in bottom of pan and baste while roasting. Roast in a hot oven, 400°, for 1 hour, or until bird is brown and crisp.

DUCKLING BIGARADE

1 cleaned and ready-to-cook duckling, about 5 pounds

½ cup diced carrots

½ cup diced onions

½ cup diced celery

2 tablespoons cider vinegar

2 cloves

10 peppercorns, crushed

2 oranges

2 tablespoons fresh lemon juice

1 cup Chicken Broth*

4 tablespoons currant jelly

1 tablespoon cornstarch

3 tablespoons Curaçao

Makes 2-3 servings

Place ducking on a rack in a shallow roasting pan. Roast in a hot oven, 400°, for about 1½ hours, or until duckling is brown and crisp.

About 15 minutes before the bird is completely cooked, drain all fat from the roasting pan, remove rack and set duckling directly in pan.

Add diced vegetables, vinegar and spices to pan. Complete cooking duckling. Remove from pan and keep warm until ready to serve.

Place roasting pan over direct heat, stir in ⅓ cup water and bring to a boil. Reduce heat to low and add juice of 1 orange (reserve skin), lemon juice, chicken broth and currant jelly. Simmer for 15 minutes. Strain through a sieve lined with a piece of cheesecloth into a clean saucepan.

Stir in slivered orange peel. Heat to a boil. Blend in cornstarch dissolved in a little cold water. Continue stirring over low heat until sauce is thickened to taste. Add the liquor.

Pour the sauce over the duckling and garnish with half slices of orange. Use a very sharp knife to peel the reserved orange skins from the white pulp. Cut peel in fine slivers and cover with water. Cook for 20 minutes, drain and hold for sauce. Serve with wild rice or wheat pilaff.

This excellent dish is served in a very dramatic fashion. The cooked duckling is presented to the guests, then the Captain cuts the bird into several pieces and places these on a sizzling hot sauté pan. He then spoons warmed Grand Marnier over the duckling and flames the dish in front of the guests. The hot sauce is served from a chafing dish. E.B.

DUCK A L'ORANGE

1 duckling, about 5½ pounds

Salt and pepper

1 orange, quartered

1 clove garlic, mashed

1 bay leaf

1 cup red wine

Duck liver

½ cup chopped onions

½ cup chopped mushrooms

3 tablespoons flour

2 teaspoons Meat Glaze*

1 cup stock or broth

1 tablespoon shredded orange rind

⅓ cup Brandy

1 cup fresh orange sections

Makes 4 servings

Rub the duck all over with salt and pepper. Stuff it with the orange, garlic and bay leaf. Place on a rack in a shallow pan and roast in a hot oven, 400°, for 1 hour, or until tender.

Baste with about ½ cup of the wine while roasting.

To make the sauce, spoon 3 or 4 tablespoons fat from the roasting pan into a heated skillet or saucepan. Sauté the duck liver, onions and mushrooms in this fat.

Remove the liver. Blend in the flour, meat glaze and stock or broth.

Stir the sauce over medium heat until it comes to a boil, then stir in remaining wine. Add the shredded rind and correct the seasonings. Keep at a simmer until the duck is ready to serve.

To serve, cut the duck into pieces and place on a hot serving dish. Skim the fat off the juices in the pan and add the Brandy. Bring to a boil and scrape all the browned bits adhering to the pan into the liquid until dissolved.

Strain the pan liquid into the sauce and blend well. Stir into orange segments.

Spoon a little of the hot sauce over the duck (serve the remainder from a gravy boat). Garnish with the sautéed liver. Serve with Wild Rice*.

LONG ISLAND DUCKLING
AU GRAND MARNIER

1 duckling, 4½–5 pounds

Salt and pepper

Pinch of powdered rosemary

1 bay leaf, crumbled

1 onion, chopped

1 carrot, chopped

1 cup consommé*

½ cup red wine

1 orange, sectioned

¼ cup Grand Marnier, warmed

Sauce (recipe follows)

Makes 2–3 servings

Rinse and dry the duck. Sprinkle the cavity with salt, pepper and rosemary. Add the bay leaf. Place duckling in roasting pan and roast in a hot oven, 425°, for about 40 minutes.

Drain off accumulated fat from pan. Add the chopped vegetables and turn duckling on one side. Return to hot oven for 25 minutes.

Drain off accumulated fat from pan. Turn duckling on other side and return to oven for 25 minutes. Remove duckling and keep warm. Drain accumulated fat from pan.

To the ingredients remaining in pan add consommé and wine. Mix well, scooping all the cooked-on bits from bottom and sides of pan. Bring to a boil and cook until liquid is reduced to half the original amount. Strain, cool and skim. Reserve for sauce.

Place the duck on serving platter and garnish with orange sections. Pour the Grand Marnier over the duckling and flame it. Baste the duck until the flames die out.

The duckling is served carved, with sauce in boat.

SAUCE

1 tablespoon sugar

2 teaspoons vinegar

Juice of 1 orange

Juice of ½ lemon

½ cup red wine

Reserved stock from pan

Consommé or broth

1 teaspoon cornstarch

Makes about 2 cups

Heat the sugar with a teaspoon of water until it caramelizes to a golden brown. Stir in vinegar and fruit juices.

Measure the reserved stock and add consommé or broth to bring amount to 1½ cups. Stir into other ingredients and bring to a boil. Cook 5 minutes, strain.

Dissolve cornstarch in 2 tablespoons cold water, add to strained sauce. Cook and stir until sauce is thickened. Correct the seasonings.

ROAST GOOSE

1 goose, 10-12 pounds

1 pound pitted soft prunes

6 apples, peeled, cored and sliced

1 lemon, quartered

½ cup Sherry

1 teaspoon salt

⅛ teaspoon pepper

Makes 10-12 servings

The goose should be drawn and ready for the pan. Remove the oil sac from tail and any disfiguring pin feathers.

Combine remaining ingredients and use to stuff goose. Close vent.

Place the goose on a rack in a deep roasting pan. Roast in a slow oven, 325°, for about 3 to 3½ hours, or until goose is crisply browned and tender.

If desired, the goose may be basted at intervals with pan drippings. Or baste with wine if preferred.

I like to serve a fine chestnut puree when duck or goose is the main dish. E.B.

ROAST MARYLAND BABY TURKEY FILLED WITH WHEAT PILAFF AND APPLES

2 small onions, chopped

¼ cup butter

2 cups uncooked wheat pilaff

4 cups water

1 teaspoon Ac'cent

2 teaspoons salt

⅛ teaspoon white pepper

1 bay leaf

3 tart apples, peeled and sliced

Juice of ½ lemon

1 turkey, 10-12 pounds

6 tablespoons butter, melted

Makes 10-12 servings

Sauté onions in butter heated in a heavy skillet with cover. Add wheat pilaff and stir until wheat is golden. Add water, seasonings and bay leaf. Cover and bring to a boil. Reduce heat and simmer 20 minutes.

Sprinkle apple slices with lemon juice and mix with the wheat pilaff.

Stuff turkey with apple-wheat pilaff mixture, brush with butter and roast in a low moderate oven, 325°, for approximately 2½ hours. Baste the turkey every half hour until browned and tender.

BREAST OF GUINEA HEN
UNDER GLASS

3 guinea hens, about 2 pounds each

Remove breasts from guinea hens and remove skin. Divide each whole breast in half. Season with salt and pepper.

Salt and pepper

4 tablespoons butter

Melt butter in a heavy skillet. Sauté breasts until golden on all sides. Lower heat and cook (shaking pan often) 20 minutes, or until breasts are tender.

6 toasted bread rounds

2 shallots, minced

Arrange a breast on each bread round and place on individual serving plates. Keep warm.

½ cup dry white wine

Sauté shallots until soft. Deglaze pan with dry white wine. Combine sour cream and flour until smooth.

1 cup sour cream

1 tablespoon flour

Blend into skillet and cook slowly for 2 minutes. Season with salt and pepper.

6 large mushroom caps, sautéed

Chopped truffles

Spoon sauce over breasts and garnish with a mushroom cap and chopped truffles. Cover each plate with a glass dome. Serve immediately.

Makes 6 servings

ROCK CORNISH HEN
AUX PRIMEURS

6 Rock Cornish game hens, 1 pound each

Wash out hens and sprinkle with salt and pepper inside and out.

Salt and pepper

3 cups cooked wild rice

Combine rice, shallots, 4 tablespoons melted butter and parsley. Stuff hens with dressing and truss. Place hens in a roasting pan. Combine 4 tablespoons butter and fines herbes in a small cup. Brush hens with mixture.

½ cup shallots, sautéed

8 tablespoons melted butter

Roast hens in hot oven, 425°, for 45 minutes, or until hens are tender. Baste often with pan drippings.

2 tablespoons chopped parsley

1 teaspoon fines herbes

Arrange hens on a heated platter with asparagus bundles, baby carrots and watercress.

Buttered asparagus bundles

Glazed baby carrots

Watercress

Makes 6 servings

ENTREE~FISH

COLORADO BROOK TROUT SAUTE BELLE
   MEUNIERE
COLD STRIPED BASS EN GELEE
STRIPED BASS PRINTANIERE
SUPREME OF HALIBUT IN WHITE
   WINE SAUCE
FILLETS OF MACKEREL, CHAMBERTIN
FILLET OF GRAY SOLE SAUTE
   MEUNIERE
STUFFED SMELTS
COULIBIAC DE SALMON
FILLET OF SOLE MARGUERY
CODFISH IN CREAM
ENGLISH SOLE VERONIQUE
MOUSSE DE TURBOT
HALIBUT STEAK A LA LADY DUVEEN
FRESH BAKED STRIPED BASS CREOLE
FLAKED FISH SALAD
PAUPIETTES OF DOVER SOLE
MOUSSE OF SOLE
FRIED SILVER SMELTS EN COLERE
SALMON PARISIENNE
SEA BASS PERSIAN
POACHED STRIPED BASS

COLORADO BROOK TROUT SAUTE BELLE MEUNIERE

4 cleaned brook trout, about 8 ounces each

⅓ cup milk

⅓ cup seasoned flour

⅓ cup vegetable oil

½ cup butter

1 lemon

2 medium-size tomatoes, halved and cored

Salt and pepper

4 large mushroom caps

Chopped parsley

Makes 4 servings

Dip trout into milk and then into flour seasoned with salt and pepper. Pat flour onto fish, firmly but gently. Heat oil in a heavy skillet with 2 tablespoons of the butter.

Place trout in hot fat. Cook over moderate heat until brown on one side. Turn to brown on other side. (Total cooking time should be not more than 15 minutes.)

Place trout on heated serving platter and drizzle with juice of ½ lemon. Keep warm.

Drain fat from skillet. Add 2 more tablespoons of butter and melt over moderate heat. Season tomatoes with salt and pepper. Cook with mushrooms in hot butter until mushrooms are well browned. Place a tomato half, topped with a mushroom cap, on each fish.

Heat remaining 4 tablespoons butter in skillet until hazelnut-brown, but do not allow to burn. Pour over fish. Garnish with lemon slices and chopped parsley.

COLD STRIPED BASS EN GELEE

Poached striped bass*

1 egg white, slightly beaten, and shell

2 envelopes unflavored gelatin

Sliced truffles

1 hard-cooked egg, sliced

Pimiento

Makes 6 servings

Prepare Poached Striped Bass and allow bass to cool in liquid. Chill thoroughly.

Strain fish liquid into a saucepan. Add egg white and egg shell. Boil for 2 minutes. Cool and strain through a double thickness of cheesecloth.

Soften gelatin in ½ cup cold water. Add to fish liquid and heat until gelatin dissolves. Chill until mixture begins to set.

Cover the bottom of a cold platter with thickened gelatin. Arrange bass on it. Spoon some of the gelatin mixture over bass and decorate with truffles, hard-cooked egg slices and pimiento cut into fancy shapes. Let set. Spoon more gelatin over garnish, chill until firm. Serve with mayonnaise.

STRIPED BASS PRINTANIERE

⅔ cup butter

1 striped bass, about 5 pounds,
    split and backbone removed

1 heart of celery, finely diced

6 mushrooms, finely diced

2 small carrots, finely diced

2 leeks, finely diced

1 small onion, finely diced

1 cup parsley sprigs, minced

⅔ cup dry white wine

Juice of 2 lemons

Salt and pepper

Makes 6 servings

Coat the bottom and sides of a large shallow baking dish with 2 tablespoons butter. Place the 2 pieces of fish in the dish.

Sprinkle vegetables evenly over fish. Pour wine and lemon juice over and season with salt and pepper. Dot with remaining butter.

Bake in a moderate oven, 350°, until liquid begins to boil, about 15 minutes. Reduce heat to 250° and bake 20 minutes longer, or until fish is done. (Be sure oven is slow enough to prevent liquid from evaporating. There should be about 1 cup of broth in pan when fish is cooked.)

SUPREME OF HALIBUT IN WHITE WINE SAUCE

4 halibut steaks, about 8 ounces each

Salt

Paprika

1½ cups heavy cream

Flour

6 tablespoons clarified butter*

1 cup dry white wine

Makes 4 servings

Skin and bone halibut steaks. Season with salt and paprika. Dip in ½ cup heavy cream and then coat with flour.

Brown halibut in clarified butter in a heavy skillet. Place in a shallow baking dish and pour pan juices over halibut.

Bake in a hot oven, 400°, for 15 minutes, or until fish flakes easily, basting several times with juices. Place halibut on heated serving platter and keep warm.

Sprinkle 4 tablespoons flour over pan juices and cook roux for 3 minutes. Stir in wine and simmer several minutes. Add remaining 1 cup cream and heat to boiling. Correct seasonings and strain sauce over fish.

FILLETS OF MACKEREL, CHAMBERTIN

4 mackerel fillets, 6-8 ounces each

½ cup Chambertin wine OR
Other dry red wine

½ cup water

Dash of salt

1 sprig of parsley

Sauce Chambertin (recipe follows)

Makes 4 servings

Place fillets skin side down in a shallow saucepan. Combine wine and water and pour over fillets. Add salt and parsley. Heat to boiling.

Cover pan and simmer for 10 minutes. Remove saucepan from heat and transfer fillets to a heated serving platter and keep warm. Strain fish liquid and reserve for sauce.

Prepare Sauce Chambertin. Pour over fish and serve.

SAUCE CHAMBERTIN

¼ salmon head OR
¼ other fish

¼ cup chopped carrots

¼ cup chopped celery

¼ cup chopped onion

¼ cup chopped mushrooms

12 sprigs of parsley

2 cups Chambertin wine OR
Other dry red wine

½ teaspoon salt

8-10 peppercorns

½ bay leaf

Remainder of fish liquid

1 tablespoon flour

1 tablespoon butter

Place fish head, vegetables, wine and seasonings in a saucepan. Bring to a boil, then lower heat and add remainder of fish liquid. Simmer until liquid is reduced to one third.

Strain liquid through a very fine sieve. Knead flour and butter together to make a thick paste. Crumble into pieces and drop into hot liquid. Beat with a wire whip over low heat until sauce is thick and smooth. Strain. Pour over fish fillet and serve hot.

FILLET OF GRAY SOLE
SAUTE MEUNIERE

4 fillets of gray sole, about 6 ounces each

⅓ cup milk

⅓ cup seasoned flour

⅓ cup vegetable oil

½ cup butter

1 lemon

Chopped parsley

Makes 4 servings

Dip fillets into milk and then into flour seasoned with salt and pepper, patting flour into fish, firmly but gently.

Heat oil in a heavy skillet with 2 tablespoons of the butter.

When fat is hot, place fillets in skillet. Cook over moderate heat until brown on one side. Turn carefully with a broad spatula and brown on other side.

Place fillets on heated serving platter. Drizzle juice of ½ lemon over fillets and keep warm.

Drain fat from skillet. Heat remaining butter in skillet until hazelnut-brown, but do not allow to burn.

Pour over fish. Garnish with lemon slices and parsley.

I use this same recipe for other fish fillets such as flounder, halibut and English sole. E.B.

STUFFED SMELTS

12 large smelts, cleaned

Salt and pepper

⅓ cup bread crumbs

2 tablespoons chopped mushrooms

1 teaspoon minced onion

1 teaspoon minced parsley

Hot milk

2 tablespoons lemon juice

1 cup buttered crumbs

Makes 2 servings

Wash smelts thoroughly in cold water. Sprinkle with salt and pepper.

Combine bread crumbs, mushrooms, onion and parsley. Add just enough hot milk to make stuffing with a not-too-wet consistency.

Stuff smelts with mixture and place side by side in a buttered shallow baking dish. Drizzle with lemon juice and cover dish with a piece of heavy foil.

Bake in a hot oven, 400°, for 10 minutes. Remove cover and sprinkle buttered crumbs over smelts. Bake 10 minutes longer, or until crumbs are brown.

The chef serves this dish with Hashed Brown Potatoes* and grilled tomatoes. E.B.

COULIBIAC DE SALMON
Russian Salmon Pie

3 ounces dried vesiga

Consommé*

1½ pounds salmon

1 cup butter

1 cup sliced raw mushrooms

½ cup diced onion

Brioche Dough*

1 cup long-grain rice, cooked

2 hard-cooked eggs, chopped

1 egg, beaten

½ cup fine dry bread crumbs

Makes 8 servings

Soak the vesiga in cold water for at least 4 hours. Drain. Place in a heavy saucepan, cover with Consommé and simmer for 3½ hours. Drain, finely chop and reserve.

Skin and bone salmon and cut into small pieces. Brown in 4 tablespoons butter in a heavy skillet. Reserve. Sauté mushrooms and onions in 3 tablespoons of the butter in the same skillet.

Divide Brioche Dough in half and roll out each portion into a rectangle 12 × 8 inches.

Sprinkle half the rice over a pastry rectangle. Layer salmon, prepared vesiga, chopped eggs, mushrooms, onion and remaining rice. Top with second pastry rectangle.

Moisten the pastry edges with beaten egg and pull edges of the top pastry down over filling layers to join bottom pastry layer. Press firmly together to seal well.

Invert "loaf" onto a greased cookie sheet, keeping edges well sealed. Place loaf in a warm place and allow it to rise for 25 minutes.

Brush loaf with 1 tablespoon melted butter and sprinkle with bread crumbs. Cut several slits in top pastry for the steam to escape.

Bake in a moderate oven, 375°, for 45 to 50 minutes. Melt remaining ½ cup butter and pour over pastry loaf before serving.

This is a classic Russian dish from the days of the Czars. Vesiga is the dried spine marrow of the sturgeon and is almost impossible to find in this country. If you make the recipe, just leave it out and no one will ever know! E.B.

FILLET OF SOLE MARGUERY

2 pounds fillet of sole

Salt

Cayenne pepper

3 cups dry white wine

3 cups Fish Velouté*

¾ cup whipped cream

½ pound tiny shrimp, shelled, cleaned and cooked

10 mussels or clams, cleaned and cooked

10 Fleurons

Makes 5 servings

Place fillets in a large shallow buttered baking dish. Season with salt and cayenne. Pour wine over fish and cover pan with buttered parchment paper or heavy foil.

Poach in a hot oven, 400°, for 20 to 25 minutes. Place fillets on a heated serving platter and keep warm.

Pour wine into a saucepan and boil until reduced to one half. Add Fish Velouté and boil for 5 minutes. Strain sauce through cheesecloth. Fold in whipped cream and correct seasonings.

Garnish fish platter with shrimps and mussels or claims. Spoon sauce over fish to cover.

Place in broiler to glaze. Serve with Fleurons.

Fleurons are baked, crisp crescent-shaped puff pastries. You can buy these in a good French bakery. If you wish to make them yourself, see Puff Pastry*. E.B.

CODFISH IN CREAM

4 codfish fillets, 6-8 ounces each

¼ teaspoon salt

⅓ cup heavy cream

1½ cups hot Béchamel Sauce*

⅓ cup Hollandaise Sauce*

Makes 4 servings

Place codfish fillets in a shallow pan. Add just enough water to cover. Season with salt. Heat to a boil, then reduce heat and simmer 10 minutes. Remove from heat and place on serving platter. Keep warm.

Blend heavy cream into Béchamel Sauce in a saucepan. Heat to boiling over moderate heat. Remove from heat.

Gently fold in Hollandaise Sauce. Pour over poached fish and serve at once.

A very elegant version of Grandmother's Sunday breakfast dish. E.B.

ENGLISH SOLE VERONIQUE

12 fillets of English sole
3 to 4 ounces each

Salt and pepper

1 small onion, chopped

2 tablespoons chopped parsley

Juice of ½ lemon

1 cup dry white wine

½ cup water

2 cups Fish Velouté Sauce*

5 tablespoons butter

¾ cup seedless grapes

Makes 6 servings

Fold the fillets in half and season with salt and pepper. Place in buttered flameproof baking dish. Add onion, parsley, lemon juice, wine and water.

Cover dish and heat to the boil. Lower heat and simmer 6 to 8 minutes, or just until fish flakes easily. Transfer fillets to a flameproof serving platter with a slotted pancake turner and keep warm.

Stir Fish Velouté Sauce into liquid in baking dish. Cook until mixture is reduced one-third. Stir in butter until butter melts.

Strain sauce through cheesecloth and spoon over fillets. Place platter under very hot broiler just until sauce turns golden.

Make a pyramid of heated seedless grapes in the center of platter and serve immediately.

MOUSSE DE TURBOT

1½ pounds fillet of turbot OR
Filet of sole

3 egg whites

¼ cup Cognac

Salt and cayenne

1½ cups heavy cream

3 tablespoons chopped truffles

Sauce Madeira (recipe follows)

Makes 6 servings

Put fillets through the finest blade of a food chopper. Then rub through a fine sieve into a mixing bowl. Gradually blend in egg whites, Cognac, salt and cayenne.

Place bowl over cracked ice and begin to chill mixture. Gradually blend in heavy cream with a wooden spoon until the mixture is smooth and creamy. Stir in truffles.

Butter a 5-cup ring mold and spoon in fish mixture. Place mold into a pan filled with hot water to a depth of 2 inches.

Bake in a moderate oven, 350°, for 30 minutes, or until mold is set. Unmold onto a heated platter and fill center with Sauce Madeira.

SAUCE MADEIRA

2 tablespoons sweet butter

2 tablespoons flour

½ teaspoon salt

¼ teaspoon curry powder

2 cups light cream

2 egg yolks

2 tablespoons Madeira

1 tablespoon chopped truffles

1 tablespoon chopped parsley

Makes about 2 cups

Melt butter in a heavy saucepan. Stir in flour, salt and curry powder. Cook, stirring constantly, for 2 minutes.

Blend in cream and cook, stirring constantly, until mixture boils. Beat egg yolks and gradually stir in 1 cup of hot mixture. Return to saucepan and cook over low heat for 2 minutes. Stir in Madeira, truffles and parsley.

This dish is a particular favorite for banquets and buffets. E.B.

HALIBUT STEAK A LA LADY DUVEEN
A Plaza Great

1 halibut steak, 1-inch thick

5 tablespoons butter

1 lemon

GARNITURE

1 cup cooked baby carrots

1 cup cooked green beans, julienne

1 cup cooked peas

1 cup cooked diced white turnip

Chopped parsley

Paprika

Makes 1 serving

Place halibut steak on broiler pan. Melt 2 tablespoons of the butter and add juice of half the lemon. Brush halibut with the mixture.

Broil about 7 inches from heat for 10 minutes. Turn and brush with remaining lemon butter. Broil 10 minutes longer, or until done.

Place in center of a heated serving platter. Arrange Garniture vegetables in attractive mounds around fish.

Heat remaining butter until golden brown. Pour over fish and Garniture. Serve at once.

FRESH BAKED STRIPED BASS CREOLE

1 tablespoon butter

1 tablespoon chopped shallots

6 fillets of striped bass, about 6 ounces each

Salt and pepper

⅓ cup dry white wine

1 quart Sauce Creole*

Chopped parsley

Makes 6 servings

Coat the bottom of a shallow heat-proof casserole with butter. Scatter with chopped shallots. Place fish, skin side down, in casserole. Season with salt and pepper. Pour wine over fish. Cover fish with buttered wax paper cut to fit the top diameter of the casserole.

Place the casserole over moderate heat and bring to a boil. Then simmer until liquid is reduced to one third, about 15 minutes.

Remove casserole from heat and add Sauce Creole.

Bake in a slow-moderate oven, 325°, for 15 minutes, or until fish is done. Garnish with parsley.

FLAKED FISH SALAD

2 fish steaks, about 12 ounces each (any large firm-fleshed fish such as salmon, halibut, cod, tuna, can be used)

1 cup water

½ cup dry white wine

Dash of salt

1 sprig of parsley

Leaf lettuce

3 hard-cooked eggs, shelled

2 ripe tomatoes, cut in wedges

12 artichoke hearts

Russian Dressing (recipe follows)

Makes 6 servings

Place steaks in a skillet. Combine water and wine and pour over steaks. Add salt and parsley. Heat to boiling.

Cover skillet and simmer 10 minutes. Remove skillet from heat and allow steaks to cool in broth. Skin, bone and flake fish. Chill at least 2 hours.

Line 6 chilled plates with lettuce. Pile flaked fish in center. Surround with slices of egg, tomato wedges and artichoke hearts. Serve with Russian Dressing.

RUSSIAN DRESSING

1 cup freshly made Mayonnaise*

3 tablespoons chili sauce

*1 tablespoon finely chopped
sweet red pepper*

1 teaspoon finely chopped shallot

Makes about 1¼ cups

Combine all ingredients and allow flavors to blend for
at least 1 hour.

PAUPIETTES OF DOVER SOLE

*½ pound fresh mushrooms,
finely chopped*

½ cup butter

1 medium-size onion, finely chopped

½ cup finely chopped chives

½ cup finely chopped parsley

8 fillets of Dover sole

Salt and white pepper

¾ cup milk

1 cup fine dry bread crumbs

3 tablespoons flour

1 cup dry white wine

1 cup light cream

Freshly grated Parmesan cheese

Makes 8 servings

Sauté mushrooms in ¼ cup butter in a skillet. Add
onion, chives and parsley and cook until vegetables
are tender.

Season fillets with salt and pepper. Divide mushroom
mixture among fillets and spread to coat evenly.
Roll up each fillet and secure with a wooden food
pick.

Dip fillet rolls into milk and then into bread crumbs.
Allow to dry for 15 minutes.

Melt remaining ¼ cup butter in a skillet. Brown fish
fillets on all sides in butter. Transfer to a heat-proof
serving dish.

Stir flour into pan and cook roux 3 minutes, stirring
constantly. Add wine and simmer 2 minutes. Add
cream and heat to boiling. Pour over fish fillets and
sprinkle with Parmesan cheese.

Broil just until sauce is golden. Serve with watercress
and lemon wedges, if you wish.

MOUSSE OF SOLE

1 pound boned sole

Cut the boned sole in small pieces and chop in blender to a smooth paste.

1 egg white

1 teaspoon salt

Blend in egg white and seasonings. Turn the fish mixture into a bowl set over ice.

Dash of white pepper

Dash of ground nutmeg

Use a wooden spoon to gradually fold the heavy cream into the fish. Work the mixture together until it is thoroughly blended and begins to thicken.

1½ cups heavy cream

Correct the seasonings and turn mixture into a mold decorated with thin slices of truffle.

1 large truffle, thinly sliced

Cover the mold and place it in a pan filled with hot water to a depth of about 3 inches.

Makes 5–6 servings

Bake in a slow oven, 325°, for 25 minutes.

FRIED SILVER SMELTS EN COLERE

2 pounds silver smelts, cleaned and boned

Wash smelts and pat dry. Dip first into beaten eggs and then into seasoned crumbs.

2 eggs, beaten

Deep fat fry a few at a time at 360° until smelts are a golden brown. Drain on paper towels.

1 cup seasoned bread crumbs

Fat for frying

Arrange on a heated platter and spoon Tomato Sauce over. Garnish platter with parsley and lemon wedges.

2 cups Tomato Sauce*

Parsley

Lemon wedges

Makes 6 servings

SALMON PARISIENNE

2 cups dry white wine

2 cups water

1 onion, peeled and stuck with 2 cloves

1 carrot, sliced

1 stalk green celery, sliced

1 clove garlic, sliced

½ teaspoon leaf thyme, crumbled

1 bay leaf

Salt and pepper

1 whole cleaned salmon, about 4 pounds OR *salmon steaks, 2 inches thick*

1 slightly beaten egg white, and shell

2 envelopes unflavored gelatin

Sliced truffles

Tarragon leaves

Parisienne Garniture†

Makes 8 servings

† Parisienne Garniture consists of crisp lettuce hearts, sliced hard-cooked eggs and marinated vegetables such as peas, beets, carrots, etc.

Combine liquids, vegetables and seasonings in fish poacher or large shallow baking pan. Simmer for 10 minutes.

Place whole salmon or salmon steaks into hot court bouillon. Cook 10 minutes, turning salmon steaks once. Allow whole salmon to cool in liquid. Remove salmon steaks at once.

Chill whole salmon or salmon steaks.

Strain court bouillon into a saucepan. Add egg white and shell. Boil for 2 minutes. Cool and strain through a double thickness of cheesecloth.

Soften gelatin in ½ cup cold water. Add to court bouillon and heat until gelatin dissolves. Chill until mixture begins to set.

Cover the bottom of a cold platter with thickened gelatin. Arrange salmon on it. Spoon some of the gelatin mixture over salmon and garnish with sliced truffles and fresh tarragon leaves. Let set. Spoon more gelatin over garnish, chill until firm. Pour remaining gelatin into a shallow pan and chill until firmly set.

Garnish platter with Parisienne Garniture. Cut gelatin in pan into diamonds and arrange around platter. Serve with mayonnaise.

SEA BASS PERSIAN

1 fresh sea bass, split, boned and skinned, about 1¼ pounds

2 tablespoons chopped shallots

½ cup sliced mushrooms

2 teaspoons chopped parsley

½ teaspoon salt

¼ teaspoon pepper

1 cup dry white wine

1 tablespoon flour

2 tablespoons butter

2 tablespoons heavy cream

1 tablespoon Lobster Butter*

Fines herbes

Oyster crabs

Makes 1 serving

Wash fish and pat dry. Butter a shallow baking pan and scatter shallots, mushrooms and parsley over bottom. Place fish over vegetables and season with salt and pepper. Pour wine over fish. Cover baking pan (use heavy foil if necessary).

Simmer over low heat until fish is done, about 15 minutes. Remove fish to heated serving dish and keep warm.

Return baking pan to heat and simmer to reduce liquid to half. Knead flour and butter together and drop pieces into hot liquid. Stir with wire whip until thick and smooth.

Strain liquid through a fine sieve or cheesecloth. Stir in cream and Lobster Butter. Heat.

Spoon sauce over fish, and sprinkle with fines herbes (minced tarragon, chervil, chives and parsley). Top with oyster crabs fried in butter.

Oyster crabs are hard to find, so omit them if you wish. E.B.

POACHED STRIPED BASS

1 small leek, cut in 1-inch pieces

1 small carrot, coarsely chopped

1 small onion, coarsely chopped

1 clove garlic, peeled

3 cups water

1 cup dry white wine

2 teaspoons peppercorns

1 sprig fresh thyme OR
½ teaspoon dried

1 sprig fresh tarragon OR
½ teaspoon dried

1 bay leaf

Salt

1 cleaned striped bass, 3-4 pounds

Makes 4 servings

Combine vegetables, liquids and seasonings in a fish poacher or other pan large enough to hold fish. Simmer for 10 minutes.

Place fish on rack of fish poacher or improvise with a cheesecloth sling.

Lower fish into court bouillon and simmer for 20 minutes. Remove pan from heat and allow fish to stand in liquid until ready to serve.

When ready to serve, carefully transfer fish to a board or heated platter. Discard the garlic, thyme and tarragon sprigs. Garnish with vegetables. Serve sauce separately to be added to taste.

A simple but very delicious way with fish. Try same recipe using red snapper. E.B.

ENTREE~SHELLFISH AND SEAFOOD

HOW TO COOK SHRIMP

3 pounds raw shrimp

Water

2 tablespoons white vinegar

Salt

1 stalk celery, chopped

Makes 2 pounds cooked, shelled shrimp

Put shrimp in a kettle. Cover with water. Add vinegar, salt and celery.

Bring to a boil and simmer for 10 minutes. Remove kettle from heat and cool shrimp in stock.

Drain shrimp. Shell and devein.

GRILLED SCAMPI FRA DIAVOLO

¾ cup cider vinegar

½ cup chopped onion

¼ cup chopped leeks

¼ cup chopped celery

1 clove garlic, minced

1 cup Sauce Espagnole*

1 can (6-ounces) tomato puree

¼ cup chili sauce

1 tablespoon dry mustard

1 tablespoon French mustard

1 bay leaf

1 teaspoon leaf tarragon, crumbled

Dash of pepper

2 tablespoons chopped parsley

2 pounds large shrimp, cleaned and shelled

¼ cup olive oil

Makes 6 servings

Pour vinegar into a heavy saucepan. Add onion, leeks, celery and garlic. Cook until vegetables are tender.

Stir in Sauce Espagnole, tomato puree, chili sauce, both mustards, bay leaf, tarragon and pepper. Simmer 15 minutes. Add parsley.

While sauce simmers, arrange shrimp in a broiler and brush with olive oil.

Broil shrimp 5 minutes. Turn, brush with olive oil and broil 3 minutes longer.

Place shrimp in au gratin dish and spoon sauce over. Serve immediately.

A wonderful way with shrimp! And you can use the sauce with any favorite fish dish. E.B.

CASSEROLETTE OF SHRIMP AU XERES

½ cup butter

2 pounds cooked shell shrimp
(see How to Cook Shrimp*)

⅓ cup dry Sherry

½ cup finely chopped onion

3-4 teaspoons paprika

3 tablespoons flour

4 cups hot milk

Salt and pepper

Makes 4 servings

Melt ¼ cup butter in large saucepan over moderate heat. Add shrimp and Sherry. Simmer until liquid is reduced to one third. Pour into heated serving dish and keep warm.

Smother onions in remaining butter in a second saucepan for 2 minutes. Add paprika and blend well.

Blend in flour and stir constantly for 3 minutes until mixture bubbles and thickens. Remove from heat. Add hot milk gradually, mixing with a wire whip until blended and smooth.

Return saucepan to low heat and cook, beating briskly with a wire whip until sauce comes to a boil. Reduce heat and add seasonings. Simmer 12 to 15 minutes, stirring occasionally.

Correct seasonings and strain through a fine sieve or cheesecloth. Pour over shrimp and serve.

CURRIED SHRIMP

1 tablespoon butter

1 teaspoon onion juice

2 tablespoons flour

1 tablespoon curry powder

2 cups milk

1 pound cooked shelled shrimp
(½ recipe, How to Cook Shrimp*)

4 cups hot cooked rice

Major Grey Chutney

Bombay Duck (optional)

Makes 4 servings

Melt butter in heavy saucepan. When butter begins to bubble, add onion juice, then flour and curry powder blended together. Stir until thoroughly blended, about 4 minutes.

Remove saucepan from heat and gradually beat in milk, stirring briskly until blended and smooth.

Return saucepan to heat and cook over low heat, stirring all the time, until sauce is just below the boiling point.

Reduce heat and add shrimp. Simmer just long enough to heat shrimp through. Correct seasoning. Serve on rice with Major Grey Chutney and bits of Bombay Duck.

Bombay Duck is a salt fish, usually cod, that is shredded, put in the oven and browned. It is served with curried dishes and may be purchased in specialty food shops. E.B.

SHRIMP JAMBALAYA

⅓ cup butter

1 cup sliced onion

1 large green pepper, cleaned and
cut in strips

1 cup sliced fresh mushrooms

2 ripe tomatoes, peeled and chopped

⅓ cup tomato paste

½ pound boiled ham, cut in slivers

2 cups Chicken Broth*

2 cups dry white wine

1½ pounds fresh shrimp,
shelled and cleaned

1 can (about 1 pound) cut okra, drained

Salt and pepper

Freshly cooked seasoned rice

Makes 4 servings

Heat butter in a large heavy skillet with cover.
Lightly sauté onion, green pepper and mushrooms.

Stir in chopped tomatoes and tomato paste. Cover and
smother 4 to 5 minutes.

Stir in ham, broth and wine. Bring to a boil. Reduce
heat and cook about 20 minutes, stirring often,
until liquid is reduced.

Add shrimp. Cook 10 minutes, or until tender.
Stir in okra and heat through. Correct seasonings.

Serve over hot fluffy freshly boiled rice.

SHRIMP CREOLE

2 tablespoons butter

2 pounds cooked shelled shrimp
(see *How to Cook Shrimp**)

¼ cup white wine

Salt and pepper

1 quart Sauce Creole (recipe follows)

Chopped parsley

Makes 4-5 servings

Heat butter in a large saucepan. Add shrimp and
cook for about 1 minute. Add wine, salt and pepper.
Bring to a boil over moderate heat, then simmer to
reduce liquid to one third.

Pour Sauce Creole over shrimp. Mix well and return
to the boil. Simmer for 10 minutes. Correct seasonings and garnish with chopped parsley.

I usually serve this dish with fluffy hot rice, green
salad, hot biscuits and Champagne. E.B.

CREOLE SAUCE

½ cup vegetable oil

1 medium-size onion, sliced

3 small green peppers, cleaned
and sliced

½ cup dry white wine

8–10 mushroom caps, sliced

2 ripe tomatoes, peeled and chopped

1 clove garlic

¾ cup tomato puree

1 bay leaf

1 teaspoon salt

⅛ teaspoon freshly ground
black pepper

1½ cups water or stock

Makes about 4 cups

Use a heavy covered skillet to heat oil. Add onion
and green peppers. Cook 3 to 4 minutes. Add wine,
mushrooms, tomatoes and garlic. Cover and simmer
over low heat for about 4 minutes, or until liquid is
slightly reduced. Add remaining ingredients and
bring to a rapid boil, stirring constantly.

Reduce heat to low. Cover and simmer until sauce
is thick and rich, or consistency desired. Stir
occasionally during cooking to prevent scorching.
Adjust seasonings. Garnish with chopped parsley to
serve.

My favorite sauce with shrimp and rice. E.B.

CLAM PIE

2 cans (8 ounces each)
Doxsee minced clams

4 slices bacon

1 small white onion, chopped

1 unbaked 9-inch pie shell

4 eggs

Heavy cream

Salt and pepper

Makes 4 servings

Drain the clams and reserve the liquid.

Fry the bacon until crisp, then drain and crumble.
Sauté the onion in the bacon fat.

Sprinkle the crisp crumbled bacon in the pie shell.
Add the sautéed onion. Spread the minced clams in
a layer over the onion.

Beat the eggs and clam liquor together and beat in
enough cream to make 1½ cups liquid. Add
seasonings to taste and pour over clams.

Bake in a hot oven, 450°, for 10 minutes. Reduce
temperature to 350° and bake until done.

SHRIMP AND SCALLOPS POULETTE

2 tablespoons butter

2 tablespoons flour

1 cup heavy cream

1 cup milk

Salt and cayenne pepper

2 egg yolks, beaten

1 cup cooked shrimp

1 cup cooked scallops

Buttered bread crumbs,
slightly browned

Makes 2 servings

Melt butter over low heat in heavy saucepan. Blend in flour and cook over low heat for 3 minutes, stirring constantly. Remove saucepan from heat.

Gradually add cream and milk. Return to low heat and beat vigorously with a wire whip until sauce begins to boil. Add seasonings.

Use whip to blend in beaten egg yolks. Add shrimp and scallops. Reduce heat to very low and cook just until seafood is hot. *Do not allow to boil.*

Spoon mixture into 4 scallop shells and sprinkle with buttered crumbs. Serve at once.

This is not the classic Poulette, but one that can be more easily followed at home and tastes almost as good. E.B.

CASSEROLETTE OF SCAMPI AU PERNOD

4 pounds medium-size shrimp

½ cup butter

1 tablespoon minced shallots

¾ cup Pernod

Dill Cream Sauce (recipe follows)

4 branches dill, chopped

Juice of 1 lemon

Makes 5-6 servings

Peel and clean shrimp, leaving tail intact. Slit the backs of the shrimp half-way through.

Melt the butter in a skillet over moderate heat. Add the shrimp and cook 5 minutes. Add the shallots and Pernod. Reduce heat to low and simmer for 8 to 9 minutes.

Pour the sauce over shrimp, add the chopped dill leaves and bring to a boil.

Stir in lemon juice, correct seasoning and turn into a casserole for serving.

DILL CREAM SAUCE

¼ cup butter

4 tablespoons flour

4 cups hot milk

1 onion stuck with 2 cloves

1 bay leaf

4 branches dill

Salt and pepper

1 cup cream

Makes about 4 cups sauce

Melt the butter in a heavy saucepan over low heat. Stir in flour and blend to a paste.

Use a wire whip to blend hot milk into roux. Bring to a boil, stirring all the time. Reduce heat to low.

Add onion, bay leaf and dill *stems*–chop and reserve the dill leaves. Simmer for 15 minutes.

Correct seasoning and stir in cream. Strain.

Accompany this with a dish of Saffron Rice*. E.B.

SCALLOPS VENTIMILLE

½ pound thin spaghetti

1 cup sliced fresh mushrooms

1 cup julienne strips ham

½ cup butter

1 cup hot broth or stock

2 pounds scallops

2 tablespoons lemon juice

1 teaspoon salt

¼ teaspoon pepper

Chopped parsley

Makes 4-6 servings

Cook spaghetti in rapidly boiling salted water for 15 minutes. Drain and place in shallow baking dish. Keep warm.

Sauté mushrooms and ham for about 10 minutes in 2 tablespoons butter heated in a heavy skillet. Add to spaghetti with hot broth and toss until well mixed. Keep warm.

Simmer scallops in their own liquor for 3 to 4 minutes. Drain. Sauté for 5 minutes or so in remaining butter heated in same skillet.

Spoon scallops and browned butter over spaghetti. Sprinkle with lemon juice, seasonings and parsley.

Heat in a hot oven, 400°, for 10 minutes. Serve at once.

OYSTER BAR CLAM STEW

1 pint cherrystone clams

2 cups light cream

1 cup clam juice

2 tablespoons butter

1 teaspoon Worcestershire sauce

½ teaspoon salt

Dash of celery salt

Dash of paprika

Chopped parsley

Makes 2 servings

Heat clams, cream, clam juice and butter slowly to a boil in a heavy saucepan.

Add Worcestershire sauce, salt, celery salt and paprika. Simmer several minutes.

Ladle into heated soup bowls and garnish with chopped parsley.

OYSTERS REMICK

24–30 raw oysters

2 cups mayonnaise

½ cup chili sauce

1 teaspoon English dry mustard

½ teaspoon paprika

Dash of Tabasco sauce

4–5 slices bacon, cut in 1-inch pieces

1 cup buttered bread crumbs

Makes 6 servings

Heat oysters in their own liquor until plump. Drain.

Combine mayonnaise with chili sauce, mustard, paprika and Tabasco.

Dip oysters into seasoned mayonnaise until thoroughly coated. Return oysters to their shells. Top each oyster with a square of bacon and buttered bread crumbs.

Place under broiler for 2 to 3 minutes to cook bacon and brown crumbs.

Serve on a large platter with a garnish of a lemon basket filled with Tartar Sauce, if you wish.

This is a specialty of Joseph Boggia, Chef de Cuisine at the Plaza. E.B.

HOW TO COOK LOBSTER

5 cups water

1 cup dry white wine

1 stalk celery, sliced

1 onion, sliced

1 carrot, sliced

1 sprig parsley

1 teaspoon salt

10 peppercorns

1 bay leaf

1 live lobster, about 2 pounds

Combine water and wine, vegetables and seasonings in a large kettle with a cover.

Bring to a boil, then simmer for 10 minutes. Plunge lobster into court bouillon. Cover kettle and simmer for 18 minutes.

Remove kettle from heat. Lift lobster from court bouillon and let cool.

LOBSTER STEW
A LA OAK ROOM

¾ pound fresh lobster meat

1 cup clam juice

1 cup heavy cream

2 tablespoons butter

Dash of celery salt

Dash of Worcestershire sauce

Dash of paprika

Chopped parsley

Makes 2 servings

Heat lobster meat, clam juice, cream and butter slowly to a boil in a heavy saucepan.

Add celery salt, Worcestershire sauce and paprika. Simmer several minutes.

Ladle into heated soup bowls and garnish with chopped parsley.

STUFFED BAKED LOBSTER

4 lobsters, about 1 pound each

1 pound lump crabmeat

1 cup Béchamel Sauce*

1 tablespoon English mustard

2 teaspoons French mustard

2 teaspoons chopped parsley

Juice of 1 lemon

Salt and pepper

¼ cup fine dry bread crumbs

¼ cup grated Parmesan cheese

2 tablespoons sweet butter

Dash of paprika

Makes 4 servings

Cook lobster and prepare lobster meat, following directions in Lobster Thermidor*.

Combine lobster meat, crabmeat, Béchamel Sauce, mustards, parsley, lemon juice, salt and pepper and mix gently. Spoon mixture into reserved lobster shells.

Combine bread crumbs, Parmesan cheese, butter and paprika. Sprinkle over filled lobster shells.

Broil about 4 inches from the heat until topping is golden brown.

OYSTER BAR LOBSTER STEW

8 cups milk OR
8 cups half and half

1 pound raw lobster meat,
cut in medium chunks

4 tablespoons butter

4 slices white bread, toasted or baked

Paprika

Makes 4 servings

Combine milk or half and half, lobster meat and butter in a large saucepan. Heat to boiling and simmer 5 minutes, or until lobster meat is tender. Remove half of the lobster and reserve.

Ladle stew into 4 serving bowls and float a piece of toast on each bowl. Top with reserved lobster and sprinkle with paprika. Serve very hot, immediately.

At the Oyster Bar this is freshly prepared one serving at a time on order. E.B.

LOBSTER THERMIDOR

1 live lobster, about 2 pounds, cooked (see *How to Cook Lobster**)

¼ teaspoon English dry mustard

2 egg yolks

1 tablespoon whipped cream

¼ teaspoon salt

Dash of cayenne pepper

1 cup diced fresh mushrooms

3 tablespoons butter

Juice of ½ lemon

¼ cup Cognac

1 cup Béchamel Sauce*

1 tablespoon grated Parmesan cheese

Makes 2 servings

Split the cooked lobster in half lengthwise with a sharp knife. (Do this carefully. You'll use the shells for the lobster filling.) Discard sand sack (just below head) and intestinal tube (it runs through the tail).

Remove the coral and the liver (green substance) and rub through a fine sieve into mixing bowl. Blend in dry mustard, 1 egg yolk, whipped cream, salt and cayenne. Beat with a small wire whip until mixture is smooth and evenly colored. Set aside.

Remove meat from lobster tail and claws and cut into ¼-inch cubes.

Simmer mushrooms for 5 minutes in 1 tablespoon butter heated with the lemon juice. Remove from heat and set aside.

Melt remaining butter in heavy skillet over moderate heat. Add cubed lobster and stir for 2 to 3 minutes.

Add Cognac and cook for a minute or two to reduce liquid to half.

Add sautéed mushrooms and ½ cup Béchamel Sauce. Simmer for a few minutes, stirring constantly. Add prepared coral mixture and stir until well blended. Correct seasonings and remove from heat.

Arrange split lobster shells in a shallow oven-proof serving dish. Spoon lobster mixture into shells. Cover with remaining Béchamel Sauce blended with remaining egg yolk. Sprinkle with Parmesan cheese and dot with butter.

Bake in a hot oven, 450°, for 10 minutes, or until tops are golden brown. Serve immediately.
Rich, delicious and fattening–but worth it. E.B.

CRABMEAT REMICK
A Plaza Great

½ teaspoon English dry mustard

½ teaspoon paprika

Pinch of celery salt

Dash of Tabasco sauce

Dash of Worcestershire sauce

2 cups mayonnaise

½ cup chili sauce

Dash of tarragon vinegar

3 cups cooked flaked crabmeat (about 1 pound)

6 slices bacon, cut in 1-inch pieces

Makes 6 servings

In a bowl blend together mustard, paprika, celery salt, Tabasco and Worcestershire sauce. Stir in mayonnaise, chili sauce and tarragon vinegar.

Divide flaked crabmeat among 30 to 36 small scrubbed clam shells. Heat filled shells in a moderate oven, 350°, for 10 minutes.

Spoon sauce over crabmeat and top each with a piece of bacon. Place shells under broiler until sauce browns and bacon crisps.

When you live too far from the sea for fresh crabmeat, you may find it convenient to use canned crabmeat. Frozen Alaska Crab is good, too, but nothing surpasses fresh crabmeat. E.B.

SOFT-SHELL CRABS
SAUCE MEUNIERE

16 soft-shell crabs, thoroughly cleaned, rinsed and drained

½ cup milk

½ cup seasoned flour

⅓ cup vegetable oil

½ cup butter

1 lemon

Chopped parsley

Makes 4 servings

Dip crabs into milk and then into flour seasoned with salt and pepper. Pat flour into crabs, firmly but gently.

Heat oil in heavy skillet with 2 tablespoons of the butter. When fat is very hot, place crabs, stomach side down, in skillet. Cook until brown on one side, turn to brown other side. Place on heated serving dish and drizzle with juice of ½ lemon. Keep warm.

Drain fat from skillet. Add remaining butter to skillet and heat until it is hazelnut-brown, but do not allow to burn. Pour over crabs. Garnish with lemon slices and chopped parsley. Serve at once.

FLORIDA CRABMEAT RISOLE ON SPINACH, CROUSTADE

*Puff Pastry**

1 egg, beaten

6 tablespoons butter

3 cups cooked lump crabmeat

½ cup slivered blanched almonds

*2 cups Mornay Sauce**

Salt and pepper

2 cups well-drained chopped cooked spinach

Makes 8 servings

Divide Puff Pastry in half and roll out each half to a 7-inch square. Place one square, top side down, on a large cookie sheet. Brush with beaten egg.

Cut a 6-inch square from center of second pastry square. Place the 1-inch rim over solid pastry square and brush with egg. Place 6-inch square on second cookie sheet and brush with egg. Chill 1 hour.

Bake pastry in a very hot oven, 450°, for 10 minutes. Then reduce oven to 375° and bake 30 minutes longer, or until pastry is golden.

While pastry bakes, melt butter in a skillet and add crabmeat and almonds. Cook, stirring often, until heated through. Stir in heated Mornay Sauce and mix well. Season with salt and pepper.

Transfer pastry shell to serving platter. Line with cooked spinach and spoon crabmeat mixture over. Top with separately baked pastry square. Serve immediately.

WHITEBAIT AND OYSTER CRABS

1 whitebait fillet (about 6 ounces)

½ cup oyster crabs

Milk

Seasoned flour

Fat for frying

Tartar sauce

Lemon wedges

Parsley

Makes 1 serving

Dip whitebait and oyster crabs into milk to moisten and then into seasoned flour to coat well.

Fry until golden in deep fat. If you use a thermometer it should indicate 350°. Drain well on paper towels.

Serve on a heated plate with tarter sauce, lemon wedges and parsley.

MARYLAND CRAB CAKES

4 slices white bread, crusts removed

¼ cup light cream

2 pounds Maryland crabmeat, flaked

2 eggs, beaten

2 tablespoons baking powder

2 tablespoons chopped parsley

1 teaspoon salt

½ teaspoon fines herbes

Freshly ground pepper

4 tablespoons clarified butter*

3 tablespoons salad oil

Watercress

Lemon wedges

Fish Velouté Sauce*

Makes 4 servings

Break bread into crumbs and combine in bowl with cream. Whip with a spoon until well blended.

Add flaked crabmeat, eggs, baking powder, parsley, salt, fines herbes and pepper. Shape into 8 cakes. Chill at least 1 hour.

Heat butter and salad oil in a large skillet. Brown crab cakes on both sides. Place on a heated serving platter. Garnish with watercress and lemon wedges. Serve with Fish Velouté Sauce.

CRABMEAT LORENZO GRATINE

1¼ pounds lump crabmeat

¼ cup dry Sherry

Sauce Lorenzo (recipe follows)

2 tablespoons grated Parmesan cheese

Butter

Makes 4 servings

Combine crabmeat and Sherry in a heavy saucepan over very low heat. Simmer mixture to reduce Sherry to one half. Do not stir or handle roughly in order to avoid breaking crabmeat lumps. Remove saucepan from heat. Add prepared sauce and mix very gently using a folding motion.

Carefully spoon into an oven-proof serving dish. Sprinkle with Parmesan cheese and dot with butter. Broil just until cheese browns.

SAUCE

3 tablespoons butter

¼ cup minced onion

3 tablespoons flour

3½ cups hot milk

1 teaspoon salt

Dash of pepper

Dash of grated nutmeg

⅓ cup heavy cream

½ teaspoon English dry mustard

2 teaspoons lukewarm water

Makes about 3½ cups

Heat butter in a heavy saucepan. Add onion and smother for 1 to 2 minutes. Add flour. Stir constantly to make a roux, about 2 minutes. Remove from heat.

Add hot milk gradually, mixing with a wire whip until blended. Add seasonings.

Cook over low heat, beating all the time with a wire whip. When sauce boils, reduce heat to very low and simmer 15 minutes, stirring occasionally.

Strain sauce through cheesecloth and pour back into saucepan. Stir in heavy cream and mustard (mixed smooth in lukewarm water.)

Simmer slowly to boiling. Remove from heat and correct seasonings. Pour over crabmeat.

QUICHE OF KING CRAB

4 eggs

2 egg yolks

2 cups heavy cream

½ cup freshly grated Parmesan cheese

Salt and pepper

1 9-inch unbaked pastry shell (see Pie Crust*)

1 egg white, unbeaten

1 pound fresh king crab

Makes 8 servings

Beat the 4 whole eggs and the 2 egg yolks with the cream until smooth. Stir in cheese, salt and pepper.

Brush the pastry shell with the egg white. Reserve the largest pieces of crab for the top. Place the remaining crab in the pastry shell. Pour the egg mixture into and over the crab, then place the reserved large crab pieces on top.

Bake in a moderate oven, 375°, for 35 minutes, or until the custard is set and the top is light brown.

SEAFOOD A LA KING WITH WHEATCAKES

2 tablespoons butter

1 small onion, chopped

1 green pepper, diced

2 tablespoons flour

1 cup milk

1 cup cream

2½ cups mixed cooked seafood
(scallops, crabmeat, lobster,
shrimp, etc.)

Salt

Few drops Tabasco sauce

3 tablespoons chopped pimiento

2 egg yolks, beaten

Small Wheatcakes*

Makes 3-4 servings

Heat butter in heavy saucepan over low heat. Add onion and green pepper. Simmer for 5 minutes, but do not allow to color.

Add flour and stir over low heat for 3 minutes. Do not allow to color. Remove saucepan from heat and stir in milk and cream, a little at a time, until well blended.

Simmer over low heat, stirring constantly with a wire whip, until mixture boils.

Reduce heat. Add seafood, seasonings and pimiento. Heat through. Let cool about 5 minutes. Stir in well-beaten egg yolks.

Serve at once over hot buttered Wheatcakes.

Chef René adds oyster crabs to this dish when they are available. E.B.

CRABMEAT RAVIGOTE

¾ pound cooked lump crabmeat

1 cup thinly sliced celery

4 anchovy fillets, diced

Ravigote Sauce (recipe follows)

8 lettuce leaves

Green stuffed olives, sliced

Lemon wedges

Makes 4 servings

Combine crabmeat, celery, anchovies, and Ravigote Sauce in a bowl. Cover and chill at least 1 hour to blend flavors.

Line 4 chilled luncheon plates with lettuce leaves. Mound crab mixture on lettuce leaves and garnish salads with sliced stuffed olives and lemon wedges.

RAVIGOTE SAUCE

5 tablespoons olive oil

2 tablespoons tarragon vinegar

2 tablespoons finely chopped onion

1 tablespoon prepared mustard

1 hard-cooked egg, finely chopped

1 teaspoon chopped parsley

1 teaspoon chopped chervil

Salt and pepper

Makes about ¾ cup

Blend together olive oil, tarragon, onion and prepared mustard to make a smooth mixture. Blend in remaining ingredients.

MUSSELS MARINIERE

36 large mussels

½ cup dry white wine

1 tablespoon chopped shallots

1 cup heavy cream

¼ teaspoon salt

Dash of pepper

1 teaspoon chopped chives

Makes 2 servings

Place cleaned mussels in a large saucepan with wine and shallots. Heat to boiling. Reduce heat and simmer 6 to 8 minutes, or until mussels open up, separating from shells.

Remove mussels from liquid with a slotted spoon. Discard upper shells. Arrange mussels in lower shells side by side on warm serving platter.

Strain cooking liquid through cheesecloth. Pour into saucepan and simmer until liquid is reduced to one third.

Blend in cream and heat to boiling. Simmer. When liquid is reduced to half, season with salt and pepper and pour over mussels. Sprinkle with chopped chives and serve.

Chef André stresses, emphatically, the importance of thoroughly cleaning mussels before cooking. Scrub them vigorously with a stiff brush to remove sand and shell particles. Remove beards with small sharp knife. Rinse cleaned mussels several times in cold running water. E.B.

MINCED SWEETBREADS AND SHAD ROE, CALCUTTA

3 pounds sweetbreads

2 pair shad roe

½ cup chopped onion

½ cup butter

1 tart apple, peeled, cored and diced

1 tablespoon finely shredded fresh coconut

4 tablespoons curry powder

1 teaspoon flour

4 cups Chicken Broth*

2 cups light cream or half and half

Salt and pepper

1½ cups white rice for Rice Pilaff (recipe follows)

Makes 6 servings

Place the sweetbreads in a colander and set the colander in a deep bowl to fit. Let cold water run over sweetbreads for about 2 hours. Drain and put in saucepan with boiling salted water to cover. Poach 10 minutes. Drain and cool.

Poach the shad roe in boiling salted water to cover for 10 minutes. Drain and cool.

Carefully trim the sweetbreads, cutting away all tubing, membrane, and so on. Do the same with the roe. Use a very sharp knife to mince (finely dice) both.

Sauté the onion in the butter until golden brown. Stir in apple, coconut, curry powder and flour. Mix over low heat for 2 to 3 minutes to mellow curry powder and cook flour.

Gradually add 1 cup chicken broth and the cream, stirring all the while. Simmer over low heat 15 to 20 minutes, stirring often.

Add the minced sweetbreads and shad roe. Taste the sauce and correct the seasoning with salt and pepper. Simmer for another 15 minutes, stirring 2 or 3 times.

Serve hot with Rice Pilaff.

This is a good pungent curry. You might want to start with less curry powder and work your way up. E.B.

RICE PILAFF

Sauté ¼ cup onions in 4 tablespoons butter. When onions are a golden brown, stir in 1½ cups white rice and simmer 2 to 3 minutes. Add remaining 3 cups chicken broth plus 1 cup water. Season with salt and pepper. Cover and cook over low heat until rice is tender and liquid absorbed.

VOL-AU-VENT OF SEAFOOD

Puff Pastry (recipe follows)

1 egg, beaten

1 pound sea scallops,
cooked and halved

1 pound cooked cleaned shrimp

½ cup cooked lobster meat

2 cans (6 ounces each)
button mushrooms

3 cups Béchamel Sauce*

Makes 8 servings

Divide Puff Pastry into thirds and roll out each piece to ¼-inch thick. Cut pastry into 8-inch rounds. Make a second cut 1 inch from the rim of 2 rounds. Place solid round on a large cookie sheet. Brush rim with beaten egg. Remove center from 1 round and lay rim over first pastry layer. Brush rim with beaten egg and top with final pastry round, using rim and center (cut but unseparated). Chill 1 hour.

Bake in a very hot oven, 450°, for 10 minutes. Then reduce heat and bake in a moderate oven, 375°, for 25 minutes longer, or until vol-au-vent is golden.

While vol-au-vent bakes, combine scallops, shrimp, lobster meat, mushrooms and Béchamel Sauce in a heavy saucepan. Heat slowly until warmed through.

Place vol-au-vent on heated serving platter. Carefully remove the indented center of the pastry and fill with seafood mixture. Top with pastry lid and serve immediately.

PUFF PASTRY

1 pound sweet butter

4 cups sifted all-purpose flour

1 teaspoon salt

1 cup ice cold water

Makes 1 8-inch vol-au-vent

Knead sweet butter in a large bowl filled with ice-cold water until it is smooth and waxy-firm, but not soft. Squeeze out excess water and chill.

Combine flour and salt in a large bowl. Cut in 2 tablespoons of the prepared butter until crumbly. Work in cold water, using your hands, until dough is firm but not hard.

Roll out dough on a lightly floured board to a rectangle, 18 × 12. Dot butter over pastry. Fold pastry into thirds, widthwise and then lengthwise, to make a packet. Chill 30 minutes. Roll out pastry on floured board to a rectangle 18 × 12 and repeat folding. Chill, roll and fold pastry at least two more times. Chill at least 1 hour before using.

SEAFOOD POT PIES

½ pound sea scallops, halved

½ pound cleaned and shelled shrimp

½ pound cooked lobster meat

2 cans (6 ounces each) button mushrooms

2 cups Béchamel Sauce*

1 cup heavy cream

½ cup white wine

2 tablespoons sweet butter

½ teaspoon salt

Dash of white pepper

Dash of lemon juice

Dash of Worcestershire sauce

2 cups freshly cooked rice

Pastry (⅓ Pie Crust* recipe)

Makes 4 servings

In a bowl combine seafood and mushrooms with liquid from cans.

Combine Béchamel Sauce with cream, wine, butter, salt, pepper, lemon juice and Worcestershire sauce in a heavy saucepan. Heat to a simmer and pour over seafood.

Divide cooked rice among 4 individual casseroles or baking dishes. Add seafood mixture with sauce, measuring an equal amount into each baker. Divide the pastry into 4 equal portions and roll each one to a size slightly larger than top area of baking dish. Place pastry on top of seafood. Flute edge and cut several slits for steam to escape.

Bake in a moderate oven, 375°, for 40 minutes, or until pastry is golden.

FINNAN HADDIE A LA KITCHEN

2 pounds boneless finnan haddie

2 cups milk

1 bay leaf

1 teaspoon peppercorns

1 small onion stuck with 2 cloves

¼ cup butter

¼ cup flour

¼ cup light cream

2 hard-cooked eggs, chopped

Dash of cayenne pepper

4 freshly boiled potatoes

Paprika

Makes 4 servings

Soak the smoked fish in the milk with bay leaf, peppercorns and onion stuck with 2 cloves for about 1 hour.

Place over low heat and simmer gently for about 10 minutes, or until fish is tender and easily pierced with a fork. Skim out fish with a slotted spoon and keep warm. Strain liquid.

Melt butter and stir in flour. Cook a minute or two until bubbly, but do not allow to brown. Add strained milk.

Cook over low heat, stirring all the time, until sauce is thick and smooth. Stir in cream, chopped eggs and cayenne. Correct seasonings and add flaked fish.

Serve with sliced hot boiled potatoes. (Good, too, with baked potato, buttered toast or boiled rice.)

This recipe has been revised for home preparation, but all the good flavor is there. Be sure to use real imported finnan haddie! E.B.

TERRAPIN MARYLAND

1 live cow terrapin

Water

Cut off the head of the terrapin and plunge into ice-cold water. Wash and scrub the shell and flesh, changing the water several times.

¼ cup butter

2 egg yolks

Place terrapin with head in a large kettle. Cover with water and heat quickly to boiling. Simmer until head and feet turn white.

Salt and cayenne

Dry Sherry

Drain. Cover with fresh water. Cook until feet are tender and the shells part easily. Remove terrapin from kettle and cool on its back.

Pry the flesh from the shell. Remove the liver and gall bladder, being careful not to break the gall bladder. Cut the liver into thin slices and reserve eggs, if any. Save the liquid in the upper shell. Cut the meat into ½-inch pieces.

Place terrapin meat in the top of a double boiler. Add liquid from shell and enough water to cover. Place over boiling water and cook 1½ hours, or until meat is tender.

Heat butter in a chafing dish. Add terrapin meat and reserved terrapin eggs. Cook several minutes. Beat egg yolks in a bowl and gradually add 1 cup of the terrapin liquid. Add to chafing dish and cook until sauce thickens slightly. Season to taste with salt, cayenne and Sherry.

Makes 4 servings

You can buy prepared terrapin meat and start this recipe at the chafing dish stage. E.B.

FROGS LEGS SAUTE PROVENÇALE

20 pairs frogs legs

½ cup milk

½ cup seasoned flour

¼ cup vegetable oil

½ cup butter

1 lemon

2 cloves garlic, chopped

Chopped parsley

Makes 4 servings

Rinse the frogs legs and wipe dry. Dip into milk and then into flour seasoned with salt and pepper. Pat flour into frogs legs, firmly but gently.

Mix oil with 2 tablespoons butter in a heavy skillet and heat. Place frogs legs in skillet and brown, turning often, until cooked, about 10 minutes.

Place legs on heated serving platter and drizzle with the juice of ½ lemon. Keep warm.

Drain fat from skillet. Heat remaining butter in same skillet and add garlic. Cook, stirring constantly, until butter turns hazelnut-brown, but do not allow to burn.

Pour sauce over frogs legs and garnish with lemon slices and chopped parsley.

Add ½ cup stewed fresh tomatoes to the butter sauce for a pleasant variation. E.B.

LOBSTER BUTTER

½ cup cooked lobster

½ cup sweet butter, melted

Makes about ½ cup

Rinse the blender container several times with very hot water. When container is heated, shake dry. Immediately add the lobster and the hot butter. Process at highest speed.

As soon as the butter stiffens, pour the mixture from container into a saucepan. Heat gently until butter melts. Return to container and process again.

Repeat this action as many times as necessary to achieve a smooth paste. Season with salt and pepper to taste.

VEGETABLES

ARTICHOKE SUPREME

ASPARAGUS WITH HOLLANDAISE

BRAISED BELGIAN ENDIVES

ONION AND CHEESE PIE

STUFFED PEPPERS, ARABIAN STYLE

POTATOES ANNA

ASPARAGUS POLONAISE

POMMES SOUFFLES

RATATOUILLE

TIMBALES OF SWEET POTATOES

POTATOES BRENTONNE

BELGIAN ENDIVES WITH DANISH HAM
   AU PORTO

DOUBLE SQUASH AND MUSHROOM
   CASSEROLE

CHESTNUT PUREE

CARROTS WITH ROSEMARY

GREEN BEANS ORIENTAL

QUICK CHESTNUT PUREE

CHINESE PEAPODS

GRILLED TOMATOES

PARSNIP SOUFFLE

HASHED BROWN POTATOES

SPINACH RING

HEART OF ARTICHOKE WITH GREEN
   PEA PUREE

CREOLE LIMA BEANS

DELMONICO POTATOES

DUCHESS POTATOES

BROCCOLI AMANDINE

PERSIAN CABBAGE DOLMA

GLAZED BELGIAN BABY CARROTS

FRENCH PEAS

CARROTS A LA BOURGUIGONNE

ARTICHOKE SUPREME

12 large artichokes

Water

Trim artichokes and cover with water in a large kettle. Heat to boiling and simmer 20 minutes, or until tender.

¼ pound mushrooms, chopped

2 tablespoons butter

Drain and allow to cool slightly. Remove all stems and leaves. Scrape out prickly chokes with a spoon, leaving on the bottoms. Arrange on a baking dish.

Salt and pepper

1½ cups Mousseline Sauce*

Sauté mushrooms in butter until soft. Season with salt and pepper. Blend in ½ cup Mousseline Sauce. Divide mushroom mixture among artichoke bottoms. Spoon remaining Mousseline Sauce over mushrooms.

Makes 6 servings

Bake in moderate oven, 350°, for 15 minutes, or until tops are golden.

ASPARAGUS WITH HOLLANDAISE

2 pounds asparagus spears

Water

Break off coarse stems from asparagus. Soak asparagus in warm salted water several minutes and drain well.

Salt and pepper

Hollandaise Sauce*

Stand stalks up in an asparagus steamer or the bottom of a double boiler. Add salted hot water to a depth of 2 inches. Cover steamer, or top with inverted top of double boiler.

Makes 6 servings

Steam asparagus 10 minutes, or just until crisply tender. Place on heated serving platter and spoon Hollandaise Sauce over. Serve immediately.

BRAISED BELGIAN ENDIVES

6 Belgian endives

Salt and pepper

Endives usually need little more than a quick rinse in cold water. However, if there seem to be bits of dark soil present, it is best to slightly separate the outside leaves and rinse under running water.

⅓ cup butter

⅓ cup dry white wine

Lay the endives in a baking dish and sprinkle with salt and pepper. Dot with butter.

½ tablespoon lemon juice

Makes 6 servings

Add the wine and lemon juice. Cover and bake in a slow oven, 300°, for 1 hour.

ONION AND CHEESE PIE

2 large onions, chopped

4 tablespoons butter

Pastry shell (⅓ Pie Crust* recipe)

1½ cups diced Swiss cheese

4 eggs

2 cups heavy cream

Salt

Cayenne pepper

Dash of nutmeg

Makes 6 servings

Sauté onions in butter in skillet until very soft. Spoon into the bottom of prepared pastry shell. Top with diced Swiss cheese.

Beat eggs until light. Stir in cream, salt, cayenne and nutmeg. Pour into pastry shell.

Bake in moderate oven, 375°, for 45 minutes, or until custard is set and top is golden. Cool on wire rack 15 minutes before serving.

STUFFED PEPPERS, ARABIAN STYLE

8 large green peppers

½ cup white rice

¾ cup chopped onion

3 tablespoons vegetable oil

1 pound ground beef

1 small tomato, peeled and chopped

3 tablespoons chopped parsley

2½ teaspoons salt

¾ teaspoon freshly ground black pepper

1 can (8 ounces) tomato sauce

½ cup water

Makes 4-8 servings

Wash peppers and cut a thin slice off the stem end. Scoop out the seeds and rinse the shells.

Cook rice in salted boiling water for 5 minutes. Drain.

Sauté onion in oil for 10 minutes. Combine with parboiled rice, ground beef, chopped tomato, parsley, 1½ teaspoons salt and ½ teaspoon pepper to make a smooth mixture.

Stuff peppers with prepared mixture and arrange in baking dish. Combine tomato sauce, water and remaining salt and pepper. Pour over peppers.

Cover baking dish and bake in a moderate oven, 350°, for 30 minutes. Remove cover and baste peppers with sauce from dish. Cook 30 minutes longer, or until peppers are tender and stuffing is brown. Baste several times with sauce.

POTATOES ANNA

8 medium-size potatoes,
about 3 pounds

Salt and pepper

¼ cup clarified butter

Peel, trim and slice potatoes to the size and thickness of a silver dollar. Sprinkle slices with salt and pepper.

Heat clarified butter in a heavy skillet until smoking hot. Pour butter into a measuring cup. With the hot skillet over moderate heat, lay in the first layer of potatoes, letting them slightly overlap. Pour on part of the hot butter. Repeat the process until all potatoes are layered in pan.

After a few minutes, remove skillet from heat and cover.

Bake in a moderate oven, 350°, for 40 to 45 minutes. When done, press down on the potatoes with a spatula and pour off any excess butter.

Let potatoes stand in skillet for 10 to 15 minutes, then invert skillet onto serving dish. Lift off, leaving a round cake. Cut into 10 wedges. Serve at once.

To clarify butter, melt 1 cup butter in the top of a double boiler over hot water. Put double boiler over low heat, just until the butter melts. Let stand until the milky sediment has separated from the melted fat. Carefully pour off the clear yellow fat–this is the clarified butter. The milky sediment on the bottom is the whey, and is discarded. E.B.

Makes 10 servings

ASPARAGUS POLONAISE

2 pounds asparagus, cooked

1 cup soft white bread crumbs,
toasted

4 tablespoons butter

1 tablespoon chopped parsley

Salt and pepper

1 hard-cooked egg, sieved

Makes 6 servings

Arrange asparagus on heated serving platter and keep warm.

Toss toast crumbs with butter and parsley. Season with salt and pepper. Spoon over asparagus. Top with sieved egg.

POMMES SOUFFLES

8 long white potatoes

Fat for frying

Salt

Peel potatoes and trim to make potatoes very even. Cut potatoes into ⅛-inch thick slices. Soak in ice cold water 15 minutes. Drain thoroughly on paper towels.

Fill 2 large deep saucepans one-half full of fat for frying. Heat fat in one saucepan to 350°. Heat fat in second saucepan to 400°.

Plunge potatoes into 350° fat and remove saucepan from heat. Allow to stand until fat lowers to 250°, about 10 minutes. Stir occasionally.

Remove potatoes from fat and plunge into 400° fat. Potatoes will begin to puff at once. Cook, stirring often, until golden brown.

Makes 6 servings

Drain on paper towels. Place on heated serving platter and sprinkle with salt.

RATATOUILLE

1 large onion, sliced

2 cloves garlic, sliced

½ cup olive oil

3 zucchini, sliced

1 small eggplant, peeled and diced

1 green pepper, cut in strips

1 red pepper, cut in strips

4 ripe tomatoes, peeled and diced

1 teaspoon leaf thyme, crumbled

Salt and pepper

Freshly grated Parmesan cheese

Makes 8 servings

In large skillet sauté onion and garlic in olive oil until soft.

Add zucchini, eggplant and pepper. Stir until well coated. Cover skillet and simmer 30 minutes, stirring occasionally.

Add tomatoes, thyme, salt and pepper. Uncover skillet and simmer 10 minutes, or until mixture is thick. Serve with freshly grated Parmesan cheese.

TIMBALES OF SWEET POTATOES

6 large sweet potatoes, about 4 pounds

Place unpeeled potatoes in large kettle. Add water to cover. Cook until potatoes are fork tender, about 25 minutes.

6 egg yolks

¼ cup sweet butter

1 teaspoon salt

1 teaspoon granulated sugar

Drain potatoes and peel while still hot. Mash in kettle. Return kettle to heat until excess moisture disappears and potatoes look dry and fluffy. Add egg yolks, butter, salt and granulated sugar. Beat until light and smooth. Remove from heat and allow potato mixture to cool to room temperature.

1 tablespoon brown sugar, sieved

Fill a buttered timbale case with the sweet potato mixture, or spoon mixture into a buttered 6-cup baking dish. Place in a shallow pan with ½ inch hot water.

Bake in a moderate oven, 350°, for 25 minutes. Remove from oven and allow to set for 10 minutes.

Makes 8 servings

Unmold onto a broiler-proof serving plate. Sprinkle with brown sugar and broil until golden.

POTATOES BRENTONNE

2 large potatoes

Peel potatoes and dice into ½-inch cubes.

2 cups Meat Stock* OR Consommé*

Cook in saucepan with Meat Stock *or* consommé, onion and garlic until almost done. Drain off most of the liquid and reserve for other uses.

1 small Spanish onion, chopped

½ clove garlic, crushed

Add tomato, butter, salt and pepper and complete cooking. Correct seasonings. Serve hot.

1 large ripe tomato, peeled, seeded and diced

I use two large baking potatoes in this recipe and find it makes four adequate servings. E.B.

2 tablespoons butter

Salt and pepper

Makes 4 servings

BELGIAN ENDIVES WITH DANISH HAM AU PORTO

8 endives, halved

6 tablespoons butter

1 cup Chicken Stock*

1 tablespoon Port wine

Salt and pepper

1 cup slivered Danish ham

2 tablespoons flour

¼ cup cold water

Makes 8 servings

Crisp endives by soaking in ice water for 30 minutes. Drain on paper towels.

Heat butter in large skillet. Arrange endives on butter and brown 2 minutes. Add Chicken Stock, Port, salt and pepper. Cover skillet.

Cook over low heat 10 minutes, or until crisply tender. Remove endives with slotted spoon to shallow baking dish and sprinkle with ham.

Blend flour and water together to make a smooth paste. Stir into boiling liquid in skillet and cook 2 minutes. Pour sauce over endives.

Bake in slow oven, 325°, for 15 minutes.

DOUBLE SQUASH AND MUSHROOM CASSEROLE

3 zucchini, about 1 pound

3 yellow squash, about 1 pound

3 tablespoons butter

1 clove garlic, minced

2 cups sliced mushrooms

½ cup Chicken Stock*

2 teaspoons chopped dill

2 tablespoons flour

1 cup sour cream

Makes 6 servings

Cut zucchini and yellow squash into thin slices. Sauté slices in butter with garlic in large skillet until transparent.

Add mushrooms and cook 2 minutes. Stir in Chicken Stock and dill. Cover skillet and simmer 5 minutes, or until vegetables are crisply tender.

Stir flour into sour cream in a small bowl. Blend sour cream into skillet and cook slowly, just until heated through.

CHESTNUT PUREE

1½ pounds Italian chestnuts

2 teaspoons vegetable oil

1 onion, studded with 4 cloves

1 tablespoon lemon juice

2 tablespoons butter

¼ cup heavy cream

Salt and pepper

Makes 6 servings

Make a cross on flat side of each chestnut.

Heat oil in baking pan in moderate oven, 350°, for 10 minutes. Toss nuts in oil and return pan to oven. Heat 15 minutes, or until shells and skins are easily removed.

Place shelled chestnuts in saucepan and cover with water. Add onion studded with cloves and lemon juice. Heat to boiling and simmer 20 minutes, or until chestnuts are tender. Drain and remove onion.

Mash chestnuts in saucepan and beat in butter, cream, salt and pepper. Spoon into heated serving dish.

CARROTS WITH ROSEMARY

2 pounds carrots

1 medium-size onion, chopped

4 tablespoons butter

Salt and pepper

½ teaspoon rosemary, crumbled

2 teaspoons lemon juice

2 tablespoons chopped parsley

Makes 6 servings

Peel carrots and cut into thin slices. In a small amount of salted boiling water in a saucepan, cook carrots 15 minutes, or until tender. Drain and keep warm.

In large skillet sauté onion in butter until soft. Add carrots and toss to coat well. Season with salt, pepper, rosemary and lemon juice. Spoon into heated vegetable dish and garnish with chopped parsley.

GREEN BEANS ORIENTAL

2 pounds fresh green beans

½ cup sliced water chestnuts

4 tablespoons butter

1 tablespoon soy sauce

Makes 6 servings

Tip green beans and cut French-style. Cook in a small amount boiling salted water for 5 minutes, or just until tender. Drain and place in heated vegetable dish. Keep warm.

Sauté water chestnuts in butter until lightly browned. Stir in soy sauce and simmer 1 minute. Pour over green beans and serve immediately.

QUICK CHESTNUT PUREE

2 large cans unsweetened chestnuts

½ cup butter

½ teaspoon salt

Pinch of nutmeg

3-4 tablespoons heavy cream

Makes 6 servings

Drain and rinse chestnuts. Puree them in blender. Heat the butter and stir in chestnut puree. Stir over very low heat until heated through. Season with salt and nutmeg.

With saucepan still on low heat, stir in cream a tablespoon at a time. Serve at once.

CHINESE PEAPODS

1 pound fresh edible peapods

3 tablespoons vegetable oil

1 pound fresh white mushrooms, sliced

Soy sauce

Makes 5-6 servings

Rinse and trim peapods. Put them in a bowl with a generous quantity of ice cubes and let them stand for about 30 minutes. Drain and refrigerate until needed.

Heat oil in a large skillet. Add mushrooms and fry for about 3 minutes, stirring all the time. Add whole peapods and continue to fry. Toss and stir for an additional 2 to 3 minutes. Add soy sauce to taste (not more than 1 tablespoon), and other seasoning if desired.

You must use the edible or Chinese peapods in this dish. And the whole mixture must be crisp-crisp-crisp! E.B.

GRILLED TOMATOES

6 medium-size tomatoes

Salt and pepper

3 tablespoons butter, melted

½ cup fine dry bread crumbs

¼ cup freshly grated Parmesan cheese

2 tablespoons chopped parsley

Makes 6 servings

Halve and core tomatoes. Season cut sides with salt and pepper and arrange on broiler pan.

Brush tomatoes with butter and top with a mixture of bread crumbs, Parmesan cheese and parsley.

Broil 4 inches from heat for 3 minutes, or until tomatoes are tender and topping is golden.

PARSNIP SOUFFLE

4 medium-size parsnips

1 teaspoon salt

1 teaspoon sugar

Dash of pepper

3 tablespoons butter

2 tablespoons flour

1 cup milk

2 egg yolks, well beaten

2 egg whites, stiffly beaten

Makes 6 servings

Cook parsnips in boiling water until tender, about 20 minutes. Peel while hot and rub through a sieve. Add seasonings and 1 tablespoon butter. Mix until blended.

Melt remaining 2 tablespoons butter in a saucepan over low heat. Blend in flour until it forms a roux, about 2 to 3 minutes. Gradually add milk and beat with a wire whip until sauce boils.

Remove from heat and blend in egg yolks. Pour over seasoned parsnips and blend thoroughly. Gently fold in stiffly beaten egg whites.

Spoon into a 4-cup buttered baking dish. Bake in a moderate oven, 350°, for 25 minutes. Serve immediately.

Parsnips were never a favorite vegetable of mine, but prepared this way they are delicious. E.B.

HASHED BROWN POTATOES

4 large potatoes, cooked and peeled

1 small white onion, minced

1 tablespoon flour

1 teaspoon salt

Dash of freshly ground black pepper

½ cup light cream

5 tablespoons butter

Parsley

Makes 5-6 servings

Chop the potatoes. Add onion, flour, salt and pepper. Toss together until well mixed. Add the cream and mix very well.

Heat the butter in a large shallow skillet. Add the potato mixture. Use a spatula to press the mixture firmly into the hot fat. At the same time, shape the potatoes into a round, pulling them in from the sides of the skillet.

Fry over moderately high heat for about 15 minutes, or until crisp and brown on the underside.

Use the spatula to make a line down the center and fold over as you would an omelette. Slide from pan and garnish with parsley.

Some cooks leave out the onion, but I say it is not the real thing if you do! E.B.

SPINACH RING

2 pounds fresh spinach, washed and stemmed

2 teaspoons prepared horseradish

½ teaspoon salt

Dash of white pepper

2 tablespoons butter

Cooked diced beets

Makes 4-6 servings

Cook spinach until tender. Drain well. Chop very fine. Add seasonings and pack into a well-buttered 4-cup ring mold.

Place mold in a pan of hot water. Bake in a slow-moderate oven, 325°, for 30 minutes, or until set.

Unmold onto heated serving platter and fill center with hot buttered diced beets, seasoned with lemon juice.

A colorful and delicious vegetable combination. E.B.

HEART OF ARTICHOKE WITH GREEN PEA PUREE

Artichoke Bottoms

2 pounds fresh peas, shelled

½ cup water

2 tablespoons butter

Dash of sugar

Makes 8 servings

Prepare Artichoke Bottoms as in recipe for Artichoke Suprème*.

Combine peas, water, butter and salt in heavy saucepan. Cover with tight-fitting lid.

Cook until peas are tender, about 10 minutes. Drain peas and press through a feed mill or process in an electric blender.

Return puree to saucepan and correct seasonings. Heat slowly until hot, and spoon into prepared artichokes. Garnish with watercress.

CREOLE LIMA BEANS

2 pounds fresh lima beans

2 slices bacon

1 medium-size onion, chopped

2 cups Sauce Espagnole*

Makes 6 servings

Shell lima beans and cook in a small amount salted boiling water 20 minutes, or just until tender. Drain and keep warm.

Dice bacon and fry until crisp in skillet. Remove bacon and sauté onion and pepper in bacon fat, just until tender. Stir in Sauce Espagnole. Heat slowly until heated through.

Combine lima beans and sauce and spoon into heated serving dish. Garnish with crisp bacon.

DELMONICO POTATOES

3½ cups hot diced cooked potatoes

1½ cups Béchamel Sauce*

½ teaspoon celery salt

¼ cup buttered crumbs

¼ cup grated cheese

Makes 4 servings

Mix the potatoes with the Béchamel Sauce and celery salt. Turn into a buttered casserole.

Combine crumbs and cheese. Sprinkle over potatoes.

Bake in a moderate oven, 350°, for about 35 minutes, or until top is browned and crusty.

This recipe is based on the original dish as served at the famous Delmonico restaurant in old New York. E.B.

DUCHESS POTATOES

6 medium-size potatoes

3 eggs

3 tablespoons butter

Salt and pepper

Dash of nutmeg

Makes 6 servings

Peel potatoes and cook in salted boiling water in heavy saucepan until soft but firm.

Drain and return to saucepan. Heat over low heat several minutes to dry out potatoes. Put through food mill in large bowl.

Beat in remaining ingredients until light and fluffy.

These are the potatoes that can be shaped through a pastry tube and used as a garnish on planked dishes or on top of casseroles. Broil for a few minutes and they turn brown. E.B.

BROCCOLI AMANDINE

1 bunch broccoli, about 2 pounds

Water

½ cup butter, melted

2 tablespoons lemon juice

Salt and pepper

¼ cup freshly roasted slivered almonds

Makes 6 servings

Soak broccoli in salted warm water 5 minutes. Drain and cut off coarse outer leaves. Trim lower parts of the stalk. Cut stalks lengthwise in quarters.

Stand broccoli stalks in large saucepan. Fill skillet to a depth of 1 inch with hot salted boiling water. Cover and steam 15 minutes, or just until stalks are tender. Drain and place on heated serving platter.

Combine butter, lemon juice, salt and pepper. Pour over broccoli and sprinkle with almonds. Serve immediately.

PERSIAN CABBAGE DOLMA

1 large head cabbage

½ cup dried split peas, soaked overnight

1 pound ground lamb or beef

1 cup chopped onions

½ cup chopped parsley

¼ teaspoon cinnamon

2 teaspoons salt

½ teaspoon freshly ground pepper

1 can (14 ounces) beef broth

¼ cup sugar

½ cup lemon juice

Rinse cabbage and place in a large kettle. Add cold water to cover. Bring to a boil and simmer 15 minutes, or until cabbage is crisp tender. Turn cabbage into a colander, drain and cool. Carefully separate cabbage into leaves.

Cook dried peas in boiling salted water until tender, about 1 hour. Drain.

Combine cooked peas, ground meat, onions, parsley, cinnamon, 1 teaspoon of the salt and ¼ teaspoon of the pepper. Mix very well.

Divide the mixture as evenly as possible among the 24 largest cabbage leaves. Place mixture in the center of each leaf, then fold in the ends and roll up to look like a sausage.

Line the bottom of a deep heavy skillet or chicken fryer with cabbage leaves and arrange a layer of cabbage rolls in it. Then make a second layer of leaves and rolls.

Combine beef broth and remaining 1 teaspoon salt and ¼ teaspoon pepper. Pour into skillet. Top with remaining cabbage leaves.

Cover skillet and simmer 30 minutes. Stir sugar into lemon juice and add to skillet. Cover and cook another 30 minutes. Correct seasonings. Serve the rolls with some of the pan liquid.

I do not discard the plain cabbage leaves. I chop them with cooked potatoes and onions for my version of Colcannon. E.B.

Makes 6-8 servings

GLAZED BELGIAN BABY CARROTS

½ cup butter

½ cup sugar

2 cans (1 pound each) Belgian baby carrots, drained

Melt butter in a large heavy skillet. Stir in sugar and cook until sugar caramelizes (mixture should be a light golden brown).

Add drained carrots. Cook and stir over low heat until carrots are heated through and evenly coated.

Makes 6 servings

FRENCH PEAS

2 large lettuce leaves

2 pounds fresh peas, shelled

1 small white onion, thinly sliced

1 tablespoon chopped parsley

½ teaspoon salt

Pinch of sugar

2 tablespoons butter

3 tablespoons water

Makes 4 servings

Line heavy saucepan with 1 large lettuce leaf. Place peas on lettuce (you should have about 2 cups shelled peas). Top with remaining ingredients. Cover with second lettuce leaf.

Cover saucepan and cook slowly over medium heat until vegetables steam for 10 minutes. Remove lettuce leaves and garnish with additional chopped parsley.

CARROTS A LA BOURGUIGONNE

12 medium-size carrots

Salt

1 teaspoon sugar

1 tablespoon butter

1 cup finely chopped onion

1 tablespoon flour

Salt and pepper

1 cup Meat Stock*

Makes 6 servings

Peel and cut carrots into 2-inch lengths. In salted boiling water to which sugar has been added, cook carrots until tender. Drain.

Melt butter in heavy saucepan. Sauté onions in butter until golden brown. Add drained carrots and dust with flour, salt and pepper. Stir to mix well.

Add the stock and simmer over low heat for 10 minutes. Serve immediately.

STUFFINGS

PLAZA TURKEY STUFFING

OYSTER STUFFING

APPLE STUFFING

CHESTNUT STUFFING

FRENCH CHESTNUT STUFFING

FRUIT STUFFING FOR DUCK OR GOOSE

PLAZA TURKEY STUFFING

¼ cup butter

3 large onions, chopped

1 stalk celery, finely chopped

1 pound bulk sausage meat

6 cups white bread cubes

1 cup milk

3 eggs, beaten

1 teaspoon celery salt

¼ teaspoon pepper

2 tablespoons chopped parsley

1 teaspoon leaf thyme, crumbled

½ teaspoon powdered sage

2 cups seeded white grapes

Makes enough for a 10- to 12-pound turkey

Melt the butter in a skillet and sauté onions and celery. Reduce the heat and add sausage. Crumble the sausage with a fork as it cooks.

Mix the bread cubes with the milk and let stand 10 minutes. Press out the milk and put the squeezed bread into a bowl with the eggs and seasonings. Mix well.

Stir in the sautéed mixture and the grapes. Mix lightly but well.

OYSTER STUFFING

3 cups finely diced white bread

1 teaspoon salt

⅛ teaspoon pepper

1 tablespoon chopped parsley

2 dozen raw oysters

¼ cup oyster liquor

¼ cup butter

Makes enough stuffing for a 10-pound turkey

Combine diced bread, salt, pepper and parsley. Mix well. Add oysters.
Pour oyster liquor into saucepan. Add butter. Simmer over low heat until butter melts. Add other ingredients and mix well.

APPLE STUFFING

4 cups soft white bread crumbs

2 cups cider

1 small onion, chopped

2 tablespoons minced parsley

*¼ pound bulk sausage,
cooked and crumbled*

2 teaspoons salt

¼ teaspoon pepper

¼ teaspoon leaf thyme

Dash of nutmeg

Dash of cloves

2 eggs, beaten

*Makes enough for a 10-pound
suckling pig*

Put the bread crumbs in a colander and pour the cider all over and through them. Squeeze the crumbs dry, rubbing them through your hands to lighten and fluff them.

Combine all the ingredients and mix very well.

CHESTNUT STUFFING

3 cups soft white bread crumbs

1 teaspoon salt

¼ teaspoon pepper

1 tablespoon fresh chopped parsley

*2 cups hot boiled chestnuts,
chopped or mashed*

¼ cup butter

¼ cup hot milk

*Makes enough stuffing for a
10-pound turkey*

Mix bread crumbs, salt, pepper and parsley. Add the chestnuts, mixing them in well with other ingredients. Melt the butter in the hot milk. Add to bread mixture and mix well.

FRENCH CHESTNUT STUFFING

1 quart large French chestnuts

½ pound bulk sausage meat, cooked and crumbled

3 cups diced French bread

1 teaspoon salt

2 tablespoons butter

Turkey stock

Makes enough stuffing for a 16-pound turkey

Shell chestnuts and put into large kettle. Add hot water to cover and cook until skins are softened, about 10 minutes. Drain and peel chestnuts.

Put the peeled chestnuts back into kettle of boiling water and cook until soft and tender (about 30 minutes). Remove a few at a time with a slotted spoon and put through a potato ricer while they are still hot.

Mix the riced chestnuts with crumbled sausage meat, diced bread, salt and butter. Moisten lightly with turkey stock. Thoroughly combine ingredients.

FRUIT STUFFING FOR DUCK OR GOOSE

4 large apples, peeled, cored and chopped

2 cups coarse dry bread crumbs

1 teaspoon powdered sage

1 teaspoon salt

1 teaspoon paprika

Grated rind of 1 lemon

Pineapple juice

Makes enough stuffing for 2 ducks OR a large goose

Mix apples with bread crumbs, seasonings and lemon rind. Add just enough pineapple juice to moisten ingredients.

PASTA, RISOTTO AND PILAFF

SPAGHETTI AL PESTO

RAVIOLI IN CHEESE SAUCE

WILD RICE

SPAGHETTI ADOLF

WHEAT PILAFF

SAFFRON RICE

RICE WITH SOUR CREAM AND CHIVES

NOODLES ALFREDO

RICE PILAFF

SPAGHETTI BOLOGNAISE

SESAME NOODLES

SPAGHETTI AL PESTO

1 pound spaghetti

2 cloves garlic

*½ cup firmly packed fresh
basil leaves*

⅓ cup minced parsley

1 teaspoon salt

1 cup grated Parmesan cheese

¼ cup olive oil

Makes 4 servings

Follow package directions and cook spaghetti
al dente.

Combine remaining ingredients in blender. Grind to
a smooth paste. If too thick, add additional olive oil,
a teaspoon at a time, until desired consistency is
achieved.

Spoon or pour sauce over hot spaghetti. Toss lightly
until well mixed. Serve at once.

RAVIOLI IN CHEESE SAUCE

3 cups sifted flour

2 teaspoons salt

3 eggs

3 tablespoons olive oil

Cornstarch

¼ cup ice cold water

1 cup ricotta cheese

*¾ cup freshly grated
Parmesan cheese*

1 egg, beaten

*3 tablespoons chopped
Italian Parsley*

Cheese Sauce (recipe follows)

Makes 8 servings

Combine flour and salt in large bowl. Make a well
and add 3 eggs, olive oil and water. Blend with
hands until a stiff dough is formed.

Knead dough on board sprinkled with cornstarch
until dough is smooth and elastic. Cover with transparent wrap and let stand 1 hour.

Combine ricotta cheese, Parmesan cheese, egg and
parsley in a bowl until smooth.

Roll out one-fourth of pasta dough to a rectangle
12 × 9. Place 12 spoonfuls of cheese mixture, evenly
spaced, on half of strip, and fold second half of
strip over cheese filling. Cut between mounds of
filling with a fluted pastry wheel. Repeat with
remaining ingredients.

Cook in a large kettle of salted boiling water, a
dozen at a time, 10 minutes. Remove with a
slotted spoon.

Place in heated serving platter and top with
Cheese Sauce.

CHEESE SAUCE

¼ cup butter

¼ cup flour

Salt and pepper

English mustard to taste

2½ cups scalded milk

2 cups grated sharp Cheddar cheese

Melt butter in a heavy saucepan. Stir in flour. Cook roux 3 minutes, but do not allow to brown. Stir in salt, pepper and mustard.

Blend in milk and cook, stirring constantly, until sauce thickens and boils 1 minute. Simmer over very low heat 10 minutes. Stir in cheese just until blended.

 # WILD RICE

2 cups wild rice

½ cup raisins

¼ cup white wine

6 slices bacon, diced

1 small onion, chopped

1 clove garlic, mashed

4 cups stock or broth†

2 bay leaves

2 tablespoons chopped chives

½ cup melted butter

½ cup toasted slivered almonds

Salt and pepper

† Use duck or chicken broth if available.

Makes 6 servings

Rinse the wild rice very well under running cold water, then cover with fresh cold water. Let stand overnight. Drain.

Soak the raisins in the wine. Sauté the diced bacon until crisp, then skim out the bacon bits and reserve. Sauté the onion and garlic in the bacon fat.

Add the drained rice, stock or broth, bay leaves, drained raisins, sautéed onion and garlic, and chives to a deep kettle with a tight fitting cover. Mix well. Cover tightly and place in a moderate oven, 375°, for about 1 hour, or until the rice is tender.

Remove bay leaves. Add the butter, almonds and reserved bacon. Use 2 forks to toss and turn the rice until it is fluffed and mixed. Correct the seasonings. Serve hot.

Wild Rice prepared this way makes a good accompaniment for duck and game dishes. E.B.

SPAGHETTI ADOLF

8 large mushrooms, sliced

6 shallots, minced

½ clove garlic, crushed

⅓ cup butter

6 large ripe tomatoes, peeled, seeded and chopped

⅓ cup dry white wine

½ cup Brown Sauce*

Few leaves fresh tarragon

Few leaves fresh chervil

Salt and pepper

2 pounds spaghetti

1 cup grated Parmesan cheese

Makes 6-8 servings

Simmer mushrooms, shallots and garlic in 3 tablespoons hot butter for 4 to 5 minutes.

Stir in tomatoes, wine, Brown Sauce and herbs. Simmer for 15 minutes, stirring often.

Correct seasonings and swirl in remaining butter. Cook spaghetti (*al dente* is preferred). Drain and toss with ⅓ cup cheese. Turn into a large casserole or baking dish.

Pour the hot sauce over the spaghetti. Sprinkle with the remaining grated cheese. Brown under broiler and serve at once.

A great party dish, with a different fresh tomato taste. E.B.

WHEAT PILAFF

1 cup wheat pilaff (1 packet)

½ small onion, chopped

1 tablespoon butter or cooking oil

1¼ cups water

½ packet spices (included with wheat)

Makes 4 servings

Sauté pilaff and onion in butter or oil until pilaff is golden and onions clear. Add water and spices (½ packet).

Cover and bring to boil. Reduce heat and simmer 20 minutes.

Serve with shish kebab, curries and poultry dishes.

SAFFRON RICE

1 medium-sized onion, chopped

3 tablespoons butter

2 cups long-grain rice

4 cups boiling Chicken Stock*

1 teaspoon salt

½ teaspoon leaf saffron, crumbled

¼ cup freshly grated Parmesan cheese

Makes 8 servings

Sauté onion in butter in heavy saucepan until golden. Add rice and stir until grains glisten.

Stir in Chicken Stock, salt and saffron. Cover and simmer 15 minutes, or until grains are tender. If mixture becomes too dry before grains are tender, add ½ cup more boiling Chicken Stock.

Spoon rice into heated serving bowl and sprinkle with Parmesan cheese.

RICE WITH SOUR CREAM AND CHIVES
A Chef André Special

1 small onion, chopped

½ clove garlic, mashed

3 tablespoons vegetable oil

1½ cups raw rice

½ bay leaf

1 tablespoon lemon juice

1 teaspoon salt

¼ teaspoon pepper

2 egg yolks

1 teaspoon chopped chives

1 cup sour cream

Makes 6 servings

Sauté the onion and garlic in hot vegetable oil. Add the rice. Stir over low heat for a few minutes.

Add the seasonings and enough boiling water or stock to cover rice.

Bring to a boil and cover tightly. Place covered saucepan in a moderate oven, 350°, for about 25 minutes, or until all the liquid is absorbed.

Remove the bay leaf and turn the rice into a casserole or heat-proof serving dish.

Beat the egg yolks until fluffy. Fold in chives and sour cream. Spread this mixture over the rice and broil for a minute or two to color topping.

A very special prize-winning recipe from Chef André. Very popular with fish dishes. E.B.

NOODLES ALFREDO

1 package (8-ounces) broad noodles

¼ cup butter

¼ cup grated Parmesan cheese

¼ cup grated Gruyère cheese

½ cup heavy cream

½ teaspoon freshly ground black pepper

Makes 4-6 servings

Cook the noodles following package directions. Drain thoroughly and return to pan.

Add the remaining ingredients and toss with 2 forks until thoroughly mixed.

RICE PILAFF

2 cups white rice

1 cup finely chopped onion

1 tablespoon olive oil

¼ bay leaf

Salt and pepper

1 quart Chicken Broth*

¼ cup pine nuts OR

⅓ cup parboiled currants

Makes 6 servings

Sprinkle rice into a large kettle of boiling salted water. Cook for 5 minutes. Drain rice in colander and wash thoroughly under cold running water until water runs clear. Spread rice on tray and allow to dry until all grains separate easily.

Sauté onion in olive oil in large deep saucepan until golden brown. Add rice, seasonings and Chicken Broth. Mix well.

Cover saucepan and bake in a preheated moderate oven, 350°, for 20 to 25 minutes, or until all liquid is absorbed.

Remove bay leaf. Add nuts or currants and stir in with fork. Serve at once.

SPAGHETTI BOLOGNAISE

1 cup dried mushrooms

2 tablespoons olive oil

2 tablespoons butter

¾ cup chopped onions

1 pound ground beef

4 thin slices prosciutto, slivered

4 cups canned plum tomatoes
with juice

1 can (6 ounces) tomato paste

1 pound spaghetti

Makes about 4 cups sauce AND
6 servings spaghetti

Rinse the dried mushrooms and soak in warm water until soft. Drain and chop.

Heat the oil and butter in a good-size skillet. Sauté onions until golden. Add the beef, slivered prosciutto and mushrooms. Cook and stir over medium heat until the meat is cooked through, about 5 minutes.

Add the tomatoes and tomato paste. Simmer over low heat, stirring occasionally to prevent sticking.

Cook sauce about 2 hours, or until very thick.

Cook the spaghetti following package directions. Drain and keep warm.

Add some of sauce to spaghetti and use 2 forks to toss and turn until well mixed. Serve hot with extra sauce on the side.

SESAME NOODLES

1 package (8 ounces) wide noodles

1 tablespoon salt

⅓ cup melted butter

3 tablespoons toasted sesame seeds

Makes 5-6 servings

Add the noodles to 3 quarts boiling salted water. Bring back to a boil.

Cook until just tender, about 8 minutes. Do not allow to overcook. Stir often with a long fork or wooden spoon to prevent sticking. Drain in a colander.

Return noodles to cooking pot. Add melted butter and sesame seeds. Use 2 long-handled forks to toss and turn noodles until thoroughly mixed. Serve hot.

DESSERTS

WEDDING CAKE

EASY DANISH-TYPE PASTRY

APPLE RICE PUDDING

SPONGE CAKE

VILLAGE CUSTARD

SCHWARZWAELDER KIRSCHTORTE

BRANDIED STRAWBERRIES

OEUFS A LA NEIGE AUX FRUITS

CREAM RICE MERINGUE

POTS DE CREME AU CHOCOLAT

APRICOT MACAROON CAKE

SAUCE BRAZILIAN

SABOYON SAUCE

CREPES SUZETTES

MACEDOINE A MA FAÇON

KIRSCH APRICOT PUDDING

APRICOT SOUFFLE

CUP CUSTARD

CHRISTMAS FRUITCAKE

CHRISTMAS LOG

COFFEE PIE

BLUEBERRY PUDDING

STRAWBERRY TART

FRENCH ICE CREAM

TRIFLE

MONTMORENCY PUDDING

VANILLA SAUCE

SACHER TORTE

ORANGE RICE PUDDING

GOLD DESSERT

FRUIT AND NUT PUDDING

RICE PUDDING

CHERRIES JUBILEE

REAL CHRISTMAS PLUM PUDDING

BEIGNETS SOUFFLES

FLAKY SWAN DESSERT

FRESH PINEAPPLE ICE

PINEAPPLE CREAM SHERBET

PATE A CHOUX

PEAR TART

PECAN BALLS

CREPES SNOW MAIDEN

CREME RENVERSEE AU CARAMEL
    OR CREME CARAMEL

PASSOVER WALNUT CAKE

PIE CRUST

SAUCE AU CHOCOLAT

BUTTER CREAM FROSTING

PARFAIT PLAZA

STRAWBERRY CHIFFON PIE

CASSATA A L'ITALIENNE

CREME DIPLOMATE

AVOCADO MOUSSE

FROZEN SOUFFLE FRAMBOISE

BOMBE GLACE ANDRE

PLAZA CHEESECAKE

DOUBLE FRUIT MOLD

COUPE NEILSON

PINEAPPLE PARADISE

BRANDIED BING CHERRY SAUCE

WEDDING CAKE
Nixon-Eisenhower Wedding

2 cups butter

Let the butter stand at room temperature until it is slightly softened. Use the large bowl of electric mixer to beat the butter and sugar together until creamy and smooth.

2½ cups sugar

12 eggs

Beat in the eggs, one at a time. Add the lemon rind and vanilla. Continue to beat until mixture is very light and fluffy.

Grated rind of 1 large lemon

1 teaspoon vanilla

2 cups sifted all-purpose flour

Stir the 2 flours together and add a little at a time to butter mixture. Blend in each addition on low speed. When flour is all added, continue mixing for a minute or two to assure a smooth thick batter.

2 cups sifted cake flour

Lemon Cream Frosting (recipe follows)

Turn the batter into 2 deep greased and floured 9-inch cake pans. Bake in a slow oven, 275°, for about 2 hours, or until tops are golden brown and spring back to the touch.

Let stand in pans for 10 minutes, then turn out on racks and cool. Cakes must be cold before filling and frosting.

Makes one 9-inch layer cake

Fill and frost cakes with Lemon Cream.

LEMON CREAM

2 cups water

Bring the water to a boil in a large heavy saucepan. Stir in 1½ cups sugar until dissolved. Bring to a boil.

2 cups granulated sugar

½ cup cornstarch

Mix the remaining sugar and the cornstarch. Blend into a paste with the lemon juice and rind. Add hot liquid from the syrup in saucepan to the paste until it is smooth and soft.

Juice of 3 lemons

Grated rind of 2 lemons

Add the soft paste to the syrup in saucepan, stirring all the time. When paste is completely blended in, bring mixture to a boil and keep at a full rolling boil for about 1 minute.

Yolks of 4 eggs, beaten

Pinch of salt

Beat egg yolks and salt in a bowl. Stir in 1 cup hot mixture. Return to saucepan and cook 2 minutes, stirring constantly.

Makes enough to fill two 9-inch layers

Remove from heat and immediately place saucepan in a large pan filled with cold water. Let cool, folding mixture with a wire whip frequently until it is cold.

EASY DANISH-TYPE PASTRY
Truman Capote

1 envelope active dry yeast

¼ cup very warm water

¼ cup sugar

1 teaspoon salt

1 cup milk

3 eggs

1 teaspoon vanilla

4½ cups flour (approx.)

½ pound cold butter

1 egg yolk

3 tablespoons cream

Sliced, blanched almonds (optional)

Dissolve yeast in water in large bowl. Mix in sugar, salt, milk, eggs, vanilla and enough flour to make a dough that is soft but still firm enough to be kneaded. Knead until very smooth and pliable. Cover and refrigerate for ½ hour.

Roll out chilled dough on a floured cloth to make a rectangle about 15 inches by 5 inches. Make a line with the back of a knife at 5-inch intervals to divide into three sections. Dot the center section with two thirds of the butter. Fold the ends of the rectangle over butter so that they meet in the middle. Press edges together all around.

Dot one side of dough fold with remaining butter, fold other side over to cover butter. Press edges together all around. Wrap and chill ½ hour.

Place dough on floured cloth. With short end toward you, roll again into rectangle, fold, press and chill as before.

Repeat this rolling, folding, chilling procedure five times in all (this includes the first time when butter was used).

After fifth repeat, chill dough about 3 hours. Roll out thin on floured cloth, shape pastries and chill 30 minutes for small, 45 minutes for large.

Place chilled pastries on buttered baking sheets. Brush with egg yolk beaten with 1 tablespoon cream and 1 teaspoon water. Sprinkle with sugar and/or sliced blanched almonds.

Bake small pastries in a hot oven, 425°, for 10 minutes. Reduce heat to 350° and continue to bake about 15 minutes, or until golden brown.

Bake large pastries in a hot oven, 450°, for 15 minutes. Reduce heat to 350° and continue baking 35 to 40 minutes, or until golden brown.

Makes about 3½ dozen small pastries

This recipe may seem complicated but it is really much more simple than the true "Danish" technique. Very good pastries, too. E.B.

APPLE RICE PUDDING

Rice Pudding*

Prepare Rice Pudding up to cooling pudding in a shallow pan.

1 large Rome Beauty apple

Peel and core apple. Cut into ½-inch thick slices. Heat water and sugar to boiling in a small skillet until sugar dissolves.

1 cup water

½ cup sugar

½ cup heavy cream, whipped

Poach apple slices in syrup until slices are tender. Arrange cooled slices on top of pudding and top with stiffly beaten cream.

Makes 8-10 servings

Sprinkle with sugar and glaze quickly under pre-heated broiler. Chill before serving.

SPONGE CAKE

6 eggs, separated

Beat the egg whites and salt until soft peaks form. Gradually beat in sugar, about 2 tablespoons at a time. When it is all incorporated, continue to beat until whites are very stiff.

Dash of salt

1 cup fine granulated sugar

1 tablespoon lemon juice

Combine egg yolks with lemon juice and vanilla. Mix well. Fold about one fourth of the beaten whites into the yolks. Mix lightly but thoroughly.

1 teaspoon vanilla

1 cup sifted flour

Pour this egg mixture over the remaining egg whites and sprinkle the flour over the top.

Lightly mix all together (an electric hand mixer on the lowest speed is suggested for this) only until all the whites disappear. Stop at this point–*do not overmix*. The batter should be fluffy.

Pour the batter into two 9-inch cake pans greased and floured on the bottoms only.

Bake in a moderate oven, 350°, for 35 minutes, or until golden brown and springy to the touch.

Cool in pan. Loosen sides and remove from pan when cold.

Makes 2 layers

This is an excellent basic cake you can use in many desserts. E.B.

VILLAGE CUSTARD

1 package (3 ounces) ladyfingers

Kirschwasser

Fruit in season (such as pears, peaches or apples), peeled

1 cup powdered sugar

8 whole eggs

4 egg yolks

3½ cups milk

Makes 6-8 servings

Spread the ladyfingers on a baking sheet and toast in a slow oven, 300°, for 10–12 minutes. Allow to become cold and firm. Saturate the ladyfingers with Kirschwasser and arrange them in a deep casserole with alternating layers of thinly sliced fruit.

Mix the powdered sugar, whole eggs, egg yolks and milk. Beat until well blended, then pour over contents of casserole.

Place casserole in pan filled with hot water to depth of 2 inches. Bake in a slow-moderate oven, 325°, for about 25 to 30 minutes. Serve warm or cold.

SCHWARZWAELDER KIRSCHTORTE

⅓ cup butter

¼ cup shortening

1¼ cups sugar

4 whole eggs

2 squares unsweetened chocolate

1 cup buttermilk

2 cups cake flour, sifted

½ teaspoon baking powder

2 cups heavy cream, whipped and sweetened

¾ cup sweet-sour cherries, drained

¼ cup Kirschwasser

Makes 2 cakes, 12–14 servings

Use an electric mixer to beat butter, shortening, sugar and eggs together at medium speed until fluffy. Melt chocolate over hot water, let cool to room temperature. Beat into batter. Sift flour with baking powder, fold it with the buttermilk into the mixture.

Grease and flour two 7-inch by 3-inch round cake pans. Divide the batter between them. Bake in a preheated moderate oven, 375°, for 35 minutes. When done, turn out on a wire rack to cool.

When cooled, cut horizontally through the center of each cake to make 4 round layers; this will give you 2 double-layer cakes. Cover bottom layers with about 2 inches of whipped cream and divide the cherries between them. Cover with a top layer and sprinkle with Kirschwasser.

Frost the top and sides of cakes with remaining whipped cream and sprinkle chocolate shavings over the top. Let stand several hours before cutting.

Standard 8-inch by 2-inch cake pans will do nicely if size indicated is not available. E.B.

BRANDIED STRAWBERRIES

2 quarts ripe strawberries

Select fine, ripe, shapely berries. Rinse and hull them, then pat off excess moisture between paper towels.

Lemon juice

Sugar

Heap the berries in individual crystal bowls and sprinkle very lightly with fresh lemon juice and sugar. Chill.

Grand Marnier

When ready to serve, pour about ¼ cup Grand Marnier over each serving.

Makes 6-8 servings

Add whipped vanilla ice cream to this for a really supreme dessert. E.B.

OEUFS A LA NEIGE AUX FRUITS
Floating Island with Fruits

4 eggs, separated

1¼ cups sugar

Beat egg whites until foamy. Very slowly add ¾ cup of the sugar, beating until a stiff meringue forms. Beat in vanilla.

1 teaspoon vanilla

3 cups milk

Bring milk to a simmer in a large heavy skillet. Shape meringue into ovals using 2 dessert spoons and poach about 4 minutes in milk. Remove with slotted spoon and allow to dry on paper towels.

2 cups fresh fruits (hulled strawberries, quartered apricots, sliced peaches, pitted sweet cherries OR orange sections)

When all meringue ovals are poached, strain milk into a 2-cup measure (add more milk, if necessary, to make 2 cups).

1 tablespoon Apricot Brandy

Toasted slivered almonds

Beat egg yolks until light and lemon-colored. Beat in remaining ½ cup sugar and milk. Pour into a heavy saucepan.

Cook over low heat, stirring constantly, until mixture coats a metal spoon. Strain mixture immediately into a bowl, and stir in Apricot Brandy. Chill until very cold, at least 4 hours.

When ready to serve, pour chilled soft custard into a crystal bowl and add prepared fruits. Lay meringues on top and sprinkle with toasted slivered almonds.

Makes 8 servings

A simple dessert, but a delightful one. Very impressive for buffet-type service. E.B.

CREAM RICE MERINGUE

½ cup uncooked rice

3 cups milk

½ cup sugar

½ teaspoon salt

½ vanilla bean

Grated rind of 1 orange

2 tablespoons fresh orange juice

½ cup chopped dates

2 egg yolks, slightly beaten

½ cup light cream

2 egg whites

4 tablespoons powdered sugar

¼ teaspoon vanilla

Makes 8–10 servings

Prepare the rice as directed in Rice Pudding* recipe, using milk, sugar, salt and vanilla bean. After baking 25 minutes, remove from oven. Stir in orange rind and juice, chopped dates, beaten egg yolks and ½ cup light cream. Let stand until cool, stirring once or twice as mixture thickens.

Beat egg whites until frothy, then add powdered sugar and vanilla. Whip until meringue stands in stiff peaks. Drop small spoonfuls onto a baking sheet covered with waxed paper. Bake 20 minutes in a slow oven, 300°. When firm use a small spatula to lift meringue to top of rice pudding before serving.

POTS DE CREME AU CHOCOLATE

4 egg yolks

½ cup sugar

1 cup milk

1 cup light cream

½ vanilla bean

2 ounces sweet chocolate, grated

Makes 4 servings

Beat yolks with sugar until well mixed.

Heat milk, cream and vanilla bean to a simmer. Stir in chocolate and continue to cook until mixture is smooth and blended.

Add chocolate mixture to yolks, beating lightly all the time. Strain into custard cups or individual molds.

Place molds in a baking pan and add boiling water to fill pan about 2 inches deep. Cover each cup with a small square of foil (this retains shine on top). Bake in a preheated low-moderate oven, 325°, for 20 minutes. Cool. Serve in cups or molds.

APRICOT MACAROON CAKE

2½ dozen soft almond macaroons

4 cups dried apricots

2 envelopes unflavored gelatin

1½ cups sweet butter

3 cups confectioners' sugar

6 eggs, separated

Rind and juice of 1 lemon

½ cup granulated sugar

Whipped cream

Chopped pistachio nuts

Makes 10–12 servings

Crumble the macaroons and press enough on the bottom of a 9-inch spring form to make a crust about ½-inch thick.

Cook the apricots in water to cover until they are very soft and water is absorbed.

Soften the gelatin in ½ cup cold water, then stir into hot apricots until dissolved. Cool and puree in blender.

Cream the butter and confectioners' sugar until fluffy. Beat in egg yolks, one at a time.
Beat in apricots, lemon rind and juice.

Whip egg whites until foamy. Add granulated sugar and whip until soft peaks form. Fold into apricot mixture.

Pour about ¼ apricot mixture into prepared pan. Add a layer of crumbled macaroons. Continue alternating layers until all are used. Chill 24 hours.

Garnish with sweetened whipped cream put through a pastry tube. Sprinkle with chopped nuts.

SAUCE BRAZILIAN

5 squares semisweet chocolate

1 square unsweetened chocolate

1 tablespoon butter

⅓ cup light corn syrup

¼ cup light cream

1 tablespoon instant coffee

¼ cup dark Rum

Makes about 1 cup

Melt both chocolate and butter in top of double boiler over hot water.

Stir in corn syrup and cream. Use a wire whip to mix smooth.

Stir in instant coffee until dissolved. (Use an espresso blend for stronger coffee flavor.)

Warm the Rum in a small saucepan. Flame it and pour into the chocolate sauce.

When flame dies down, smooth sauce with wire whip. Serve hot over ice cream or other dessert.

SABOYON SAUCE

4 egg yolks

4 tablespoons powdered sugar

4 tablespoons white wine

Put ingredients into top part of double boiler. Beat vigorously with wire whip until blended and foamy. Place over gently boiling water and whip constantly until sauce has thickened to the consistency of whipped cream.

Spoon into sherbet glasses lined with ladyfingers and top with a cherry.

This easy-to-make sauce is a richly smooth topping for all kinds of plain cakes, but goes especially well with ladyfingers or sponge cake. Feather light, it is an ideal dessert to serve at the end of a hearty meal. It may be served either hot or cold on ice cream or fresh berries, and is wonderful mixed into cold rice pudding. E.B.

Makes 4 servings

CREPES SUZETTE

1 egg

1 teaspoon sugar

¼ cup flour

¼ teaspoon vanilla extract

Finely grated rind of ½ orange

½ cup light cream

2 tablespoons butter, melted

½ cup orange juice

7 lumps of sugar

1 lemon

1 orange

½ cup Cointreau or Curaçao

Grand Marnier or Brandy

Makes 5-6 servings

To make the crêpes, use a wire whip to combine the egg, sugar, flour, vanilla and orange rind. Whisk until ingredients are blended and very smooth. Add the cream gradually. When well mixed, stir in the melted butter. Let stand 1 hour to slightly thicken batter, then fry the cakes in a crêpe pan. Keep warm.

Place a shallow pan or chafing dish over moderate heat and pour in orange juice. Rub the lumps of sugar over the lemon and orange rinds until they have become impregnated with the zests (citrus oils), then put them into the pan with the hot orange juice and dissolve. Let the liquid in the pan reduce to about one half. Fold the crêpes into quarters, place them in the pan and spoon up some of the sauce to moisten the tops. Pour the Cointreau over them and add some Grand Marnier or good Brandy.

As soon as the liquid is very hot (this is essential), light it with a match. While the sauce is flaming, move the crêpes around in the liquid and get them hot and flaming. Use a long-handled fork to serve the flaming crêpes on hot dessert plates with a little of the sauce spooned over.

MACEDOINE A MA FAÇON

¾ cup sugar

Juice of 1 lemon

1 pear, peeled and sliced

¼ cup seedless grapes

¼ cup red grapes, pitted

1 large banana, sliced

2 large peaches, peeled and sliced

1 plum, sliced

1 large apple, peeled and sliced

2 seedless oranges, peeled and
cut into wedges

¼ pint fresh strawberries, hulled

¼ cup peach jam

1 tablespoon water

1½ teaspoons Kirsch or Cognac

Makes 4-5 servings

Mix together ½ cup sugar, lemon juice and prepared fruits. Place in a large bowl or crock (do not use metal).

Combine remaining sugar with jam and water. Cook and stir over low heat until very thick. Stir in Kirsch or Cognac.

Cool, then process in blender a second or two until smooth. Stir into prepared fruits. Serve very cold.

KIRSCH APRICOT PUDDING

6 sponge shells

3 tablespoons Kirschwasser

6 whole pitted apricots

3 eggs

⅓ cup sugar

2 cups milk, scalded

Makes 6 servings

Line 6 custard cups or individual soufflé dishes with sponge shells. Drizzle with Kirschwasser. Place an apricot in each dish.

Beat eggs until light and fluffy. Gradually beat in sugar, then milk. Pour into prepared cups.

Place cups in a pan filled to a depth of 1 inch with hot water. Bake in a moderate oven, 350°, for 20 minutes, or until custard is set.

Cool quickly and chill, if desired.

APRICOT SOUFFLE

4 cups sweetened stewed dried apricots

While preparing recipe, drain the apricots in a strainer set over a bowl.

3 tablespoons butter

4 tablespoons flour

Melt butter in a saucepan over low heat, but do not allow it to discolor. Stir in flour and continue stirring until blended and smooth.

1 cup milk

Slowly pour in milk, stirring constantly. Bring to a boil, stirring constantly to prevent scorching.

4 eggs, separated

⅓ cup sugar

¼ teaspoon salt

Combine egg yolks, sugar, salt and vanilla. Beat until thick and light. Slowly pour the hot sauce into egg yolk mixture, mixing all the time. Cool the mixture to room temperature.

½ teaspoon vanilla

Meanwhile line a buttered baking dish or soufflé dish with the drained apricots halved or quartered.

Beat egg whites until stiff and dry, then fold into cooled yolk mixture. Pour the mixture into prepared dish.

Bake in a slow oven, 325°, for 40 minutes.

Makes 6 servings

Serve immediately with the syrup drained from the cooked apricots and whipped cream or soft vanilla ice cream.

CUP CUSTARD

3 eggs

Grease 6 custard cups with butter.

⅓ cup sugar

2 cups light cream, scalded

Beat eggs until light and fluffy. Gradually beat in sugar, and then cream, vanilla and salt. Pour into prepared custard cups.

1 teaspoon vanilla

Dash of salt

Place cups in a pan filled with hot water to a depth of 1 inch. Bake in a moderate oven, 350°, for 20 minutes, or until custard is set.

Strawberry Sauce*

Makes 6 servings

Cool quickly and chill completely. Run a thin-bladed knife around edge of custard cups and unmold custards onto dessert dishes. Serve with Strawberry Sauce.

CHRISTMAS FRUITCAKE

½ cup mixed, diced glacéed fruit

½ cup diced candied orange peel

½ cup raisins

¼ cup chopped glacéed cherries

1 teaspoon grated lemon rind

⅓ cup Brandy

5 eggs

⅓ cup sugar

⅔ cup butter

½ cup almond paste

1 cup flour

½ cup cornstarch

Blanched almonds, sliced

Makes 12-15 servings

Mix the fruits, lemon rind and Brandy. Let stand about ½ hour, then drain.

Mix 4 eggs with the sugar in a large bowl and set this over a pan of hot water (an electric fry pan is very convenient for this). Keep the water hot and stir eggs often until they are about lukewarm. When eggs are warm, beat rapidly until they cool and become very thick and much increased in volume.

Cream butter and almond paste together until smooth. Beat in 5th egg.

Fold about ¼ of beaten eggs into creamed mixture. Mix this with drained fruit.

Pour fruit mixture into the remaining egg mixture. Sprinkle with mixed flour and cornstarch and fold all together until ingredients are combined and flour disappears.

Pour batter into a 9-inch tube pan or cake mold that has been greased, floured and sprinkled with sliced blanched almonds.

Bake in a low-moderate oven, 325°, for about 1 hour, or until top of cake is golden brown and sides pull away from pan.

This delicious cake is well worth the trouble! E.B.

CHRISTMAS LOG

1 pint heavy cream (2 cups)

1 cup granulated sugar

½ cup candied fruits, finely chopped

1 cup crushed walnuts

† If this form is not available, use an ice cube tray or a small loaf pan, and freeze as indicated.

Makes 4 servings

Whip heavy cream in a chilled bowl until it is thick but not stiff. Stir in sugar and continue to whip until stiff. Fold in candied fruits. Pack into a log-shape form† and freeze until firm.

To serve, unmold and roll in crushed walnuts. Decorate with holly sprigs (Angelica "leaves," candied cherry "berries"). Slice and serve with Saboyon Sauce*.

A delightfully easy dessert for small holiday dinners. E.B.

ASSORTED CHEESES, ACCOMPANIED
BY FRESH FRUITS

COFFEE PIE

2 envelopes unflavored gelatin

½ cup cold water

2 cups extra-strong hot coffee

2 eggs, separated

⅔ cup sugar (divided)

Pinch of salt

1 teaspoon vanilla

1 cup heavy cream, whipped

8- or 9-inch baked pastry shell

Makes 8- or 9-inch pie OR
8 small tarts

Soften gelatin in cold water. Stir the softened gelatin into the freshly brewed hot coffee until dissolved.

In the top section of a double boiler over hot water, mix the egg yolks with ⅓ cup sugar. Beat with a whisk until yolks begin to thicken. Then beat in coffee mixture. Cook and stir over hot water until mixture thickens. Remove from heat, stir in salt and vanilla, cool.

When filling is cold enough to begin to thicken and soft-set, whip rapidly with a rotary beater until light and foamy. Whip egg whites until frothy, then whip in remaining ⅓ cup sugar, a spoonful at a time, until whites stand in soft peaks. Whip cream until stiff.

Fold egg whites into filling, then fold in cream. Spoon into baked pie shell and chill until set.

BLUEBERRY PUDDING

1½ cups blueberries

2 cups flour

2 teaspoons cream of tartar

1 teaspoon baking soda

1 teaspoon salt

2 eggs

1 cup sugar

⅓ cup soft butter

½ cup milk

2 tablespoons molasses

Makes 6 servings

Rinse and drain berries. Sprinkle with 2 tablespoons flour. Combine and sift together remaining flour, cream of tartar, baking soda and salt. Set aside.

Beat eggs until light. Beat in sugar and softened butter. Add milk and molasses and mix well.

Stir the two mixtures together. When well blended, fold in berries very gently. Turn into a buttered and floured shallow pudding dish or baking pan. Bake for 30 minutes in a moderate oven, 375°. Serve with sugar and cream.

STRAWBERRY TART

¼ cup cornstarch

¾ cup sugar

¼ teaspoon salt

2½ cups light cream, scalded

3 egg yolks, slightly beaten

1 tablespoon butter

1 teaspoon Rum extract

Baked tart shell

1 pint (2 cups) strawberries

¾ cup strawberry jelly

Toasted sliced almonds

Makes 8 servings

Combine cornstarch, sugar and salt in a heavy saucepan. Gradually stir in scalded cream.

Cook over medium heat, stirring constantly, until mixture thickens and boils 1 minute. Gradually add part of the hot mixture to egg yolks. Then pour egg yolks into mixture remaining in saucepan. Cook for 2 minutes, stirring constantly. Stir in butter and flavoring.

Pour into tart shell and chill until filling is firm.

Wash, hull and halve berries. Arrange in a pretty pattern over pie.

Melt strawberry jelly in a small saucepan. Spoon over berries and garnish with toasted almonds. Chill until serving time.

FRENCH ICE CREAM

1 pint milk (2 cups)

6 egg yolks

1 cup sugar

1 pint heavy cream (2 cups)

Vanilla (to taste)

Makes 1 quart

Scald milk in a double boiler.

In a mixing bowl, beat the egg yolks and sugar together until light and thick. Add scalded milk to egg yolk mixture very slowly, stirring constantly. Pour mixture into top of double boiler over hot water and stir constantly until it thickens enough to coat spoon. Remove from heat at once.

Add the cream and flavoring and stir gently until partly cooled. Allow to cool completely to room temperature before freezing. When cold, freeze in the usual manner.

This makes a delicious solid, fine-grained cream that can be used as the foundation for any number of fancy desserts. Different flavorings can also be used to give variety to the recipe.

TRIFLE

1 package (3 ounces) ladyfingers

¼ cup sweet Sherry

1 package (3 ounces) strawberry-flavored gelatin

2 cups hot water

3 egg yolks

⅓ cup sugar

2 cups light cream

1 teaspoon vanilla

Sweetened whipped cream

Pistachio nuts, finely chopped

Makes 6 servings

Split ladyfingers and arrange on cookie sheet. Drizzle Sherry over them and allow to stand.

Dissolve gelatin in hot water in a bowl and chill until syrupy.

Arrange half the ladyfingers in bottom of a 6-cup crystal bowl. Pour gelatin syrup over and chill until gelatin is firm.

Beat egg yolks in a heavy saucepan until light. Add sugar gradually, beating all the while until mixture is light and lemon-colored. Stir in cream and vanilla.

Cook, stirring constantly, over very low heat or over simmering water, until mixture coats a metal spoon. Pour sauce immediately into a chilled bowl and cover surface with transparent wrap. Chill thoroughly.

Arrange remaining ladyfingers in the bowl on top of set gelatin and pour chilled custard over. Chill until serving time. Garnish with puff of sweetened whipped cream and finely chopped pistachio nuts.

MONTMORENCY PUDDING

6 sponge shells

1 can (16 ounces) Bing cherries, drained

3 eggs

⅓ cup sugar

2 cups milk, scalded

1 teaspoon vanilla

Dash of salt

Makes 6 servings

Line 6 custard cups or individual soufflé dishes with sponge shells. Divide cherries among cups.

Beat eggs until light and fluffy. Gradually beat in sugar and then milk, vanilla and salt. Pour into prepared cups.

Place cups in a pan filled to a depth of 1 inch with hot water. Bake in a moderate oven, 350°, for 20 minutes, or until custard is set.

Cool quickly and chill, if desired.

VANILLA SAUCE

2 cups light cream

1 3-inch piece vanilla bean†

5 egg yolks

½ cup sugar

½ cup whipped cream

Makes about 3 cups

Scald cream with vanilla bean in a heavy saucepan. Remove vanilla bean.

Beat egg yolks and sugar until very light. Blend in scalded cream. Return to saucepan.

Cook over *very low heat*, stirring constantly, until mixture is thick enough to coat a spoon. Strain into a bowl and chill. Just before serving, fold in whipped cream.

MOKA SAUCE

Add 2 teaspoons instant coffee powder to cream before scalding.

RUM COFFEE SAUCE

† Or 1 teaspoon vanilla.

Add 2 tablespoons dark Rum to Moka Sauce.

SACHER TORTE

½ cup butter

½ cup sugar

5 eggs, separated

4 squares (1 ounce each) sweet chocolate, melted

1 cup all-purpose flour

½ cup rice flour

1 cup apricot preserve

1½ cups Chocolate Fondant (recipe follows)

Makes two 8-inch layers or 12 servings

Use an electric mixer at medium speed to beat butter, sugar and egg yolks until light and fluffy. Add cooled melted chocolate. Blend.

Sift flours together and whip egg whites until stiff but not dry. Stir flour into chocolate mixture, then fold in egg whites.

Divide batter between two 8-inch round greased and floured cake pans.

Bake in slow oven, 325°, for 35 minutes. Turn cakes out on wire rack and let cool. When cakes are cool, spread with apricot preserve. Heat the Chocolate Fondant and pour over.

FONDANT

2 cups granulated sugar

⅔ cup water

1 tablespoon white corn syrup

Combine ingredients in a heavy saucepan. Bring to a boil. Cook quickly until syrup reaches the soft ball stage (238°F. on candy thermometer).

Pour the syrup at once onto an oiled baking sheet. Allow to cool until it is just barely warm and will not stick to greased fingers when touched.

Cream the mixture by working it with a spatula. Use a stiff spatula to scrape the mixture from one side of the baking sheet to the other folding it over and pulling in the edges.

As the mixture is worked it will become white and firm, almost like fudge in texture.

As soon as the fondant "sets up," place it in a bowl and cover with a damp cloth. Allow to stand (ripen) for 2 days before using.

CHOCOLATE FONDANT

Warm 1 cup fondant in a heavy saucepan. Blend in 3 to 4 squares melted unsweetened chocolate. Mix until smooth and creamy.

ORANGE RICE PUDDING

⅔ cup freshly cooked rice

1 cup orange juice

½ cup seedless raisins (or chopped dates)

1 teaspoon grated orange rind

½ cup sugar

2 eggs, separated

1 cup light cream

Makes 4-5 servings

Combine rice, orange juice, raisins and orange rind and mix well.

Beat sugar with egg yolks until light and thick. Add to rice mixture. Stir in light cream. Beat egg whites until stiff and fold carefully into mixture.

Pour into a buttered baking dish or casserole and bake in moderate oven, 350°, for 30 minutes. When the top is golden brown, remove from oven. Serve warm or cold with cream or a simple dessert sauce.

GOLD DESSERT
Orange Custard

½ cup sugar

¼ cup cornstarch

1 cup milk

1 cup orange juice

2 tablespoons butter

Orange slices

4 strawberries

Makes 4 servings

Mix sugar and cornstarch together in top of double boiler. Use a whip to gradually stir in milk and orange juice. Mix until thoroughly blended. Cook and stir over boiling water until thickened and smooth.

Remove from heat and add butter. Stir gently until butter melts and mixes in.

Pour into individual molds. Cool, then chill.

To serve, unmold and surround each custard with half slices of orange. Top each with a fresh strawberry. Serve plain or with a simple sauce.

FRUIT AND NUT PUDDING

1 cup peeled, cored and finely diced apples

1 cup peeled, seeded and diced oranges

½ cup seedless raisins

½ cup broken walnuts or pecans

6 tablespoons bread crumbs

¼ cup sugar

½ teaspoon ground cinnamon

¼–½ cup orange juice, depending on juiciness of apples

Butter

Makes 4 servings

Mix all ingredients, except butter, in a bowl. Pile lightly into a buttered baking dish, dot with butter and cover.

Bake in a moderate oven, 350°, about 25 minutes, or until apples are tender. Remove cover and brown quickly under broiler. Serve plain or with a lemon-butter sauce.

RICE PUDDING

¼	1 cup uncooked rice
1 c	1 quart (4 cups) milk, heated
	Pinch of salt
2 T	½ cup sugar
½ tsp	1 vanilla bean†
1 egg yolk	3 egg yolks, beaten
¾ c	3 cups light cream
2 T	½ cup heavy cream, whipped
½ T	2 tablespoons sugar
	Raisins (optional)

Makes 8-10 servings

† *Two teaspoons vanilla may replace vanilla bean. If extract is used, stir in with cream and egg yolks.*

Put the rice in a strainer or small colander and rinse under running cold water until water runs clear. (Rubbing the rice grains between the fingertips will hasten this process.) Turn the rice into a large saucepan, cover with cold water and bring to a rapid boil. Immediately pour into strainer and drain. Rinse with cold water.

Return rice to saucepan. Stir in hot milk, salt, sugar and vanilla bean. Bring to a slow boil over moderate heat.

Cover saucepan and place in preheated low-moderate oven, 325°, for 25 minutes. Do not disturb the rice in any way during this baking time.

Take saucepan from oven. Remove vanilla bean. Stir a little hot rice mixture into beaten egg yolks, then stir yolks into rice. Add light cream, one cup at a time, stirring well after each addition.

Turn the pudding into a shallow baking dish. Let cool to room temperature. Spread stiffly whipped cream in even layer over top and sprinkle with sugar. Glaze quickly under preheated broiler. Chill before serving.

RICE PUDDING WITH RAISINS

2 T

Soak ½ cup raisins for 1 hour in water to cover. Bring to a boil in same water. Simmer a few minutes until plump and soft. Drain. Stir into pudding with eggs and cream. (Use golden raisins for a delicious change.)

CHERRIES JUBILEE

1 can (1-pound, 13-ounces) pitted black Bing cherries

2 tablespoons sugar

1 tablespoon cornstarch

¼ cup Cognac

Makes about 2 cups, 4-5 servings

Drain the cherries and reserve 1 cup of juice from can. Blend the sugar and cornstarch together. Stir in juice and use a wire whip to mix smooth.

Cook over low heat, stirring constantly until clear and thickened. Stir in the cherries.

In a small separate pan, warm the Cognac and flame it. While flaming, pour it over the cherry sauce. Serve the sauce warm or cold over vanilla ice cream.

REAL CHRISTMAS PLUM PUDDING
As served at the Lion in Winter *reception*

1 16-ounce jar candied mixed fruits

1 15-ounce package golden raisins

1 8-ounce package pitted dates, cut up

1 cup chopped dried apricots

1 cup chopped English walnuts

½ cup dark Rum

4 eggs

1 cup firmly packed brown sugar

½ cup light corn syrup

1½ cups ground suet

1½ cups dry bread crumbs

1 cup sifted all-purpose flour

2 teaspoons apple-pie spice

½ teaspoon salt

Rum Saboyon (recipe follows)

Makes 8 servings

Butter and sugar a 6-cup steamed pudding mold.

Combine fruits, nuts and Rum. Beat eggs in large bowl until fluffy light. Gradually beat in sugar. Stir in corn syrup, suet and dry bread crumbs. Sift flour, apple-pie spice and salt over egg mixture. Pour over fruit-nut mixture and mix thoroughly.

Fill mold ¾ full and cover (use aluminum foil, if your mold does not have a cover).

Steam for 6 hours on rack in large kettle half-filled with boiling water. As necessary, add more water to kettle during steaming.

Let pudding stand in mold 10 minutes, then unmold. Serve warm with Rum Saboyon.

When cold, pudding can be wrapped in aluminum foil or transparent wrap and stored in a dry place. To reheat for serving, steam in top of double boiler. E.B.

RUM SABOYON

3 egg yolks

Beat egg yolks until light in the top of a heavy double boiler (copper-lined is best).

¼ cup sugar

¼ cup dark Rum

Gradually beat in sugar and then Rum until mixture is light and fluffy.

Place over simmering water and beat vigorously with a wire whip until custard foams and begins to thicken. Serve warm over Real Christmas Plum Pudding.

Makes 6-8 servings

BEIGNETS SOUFFLES

1 cup water

Combine water, butter, sugar and salt in a heavy saucepan. Heat to boiling. When butter melts, add flour. Beat with a wooden spoon over medium heat just until mixture pulls away from side of pan.

½ cup butter

1 teaspoon sugar

Pinch of salt

Remove saucepan from heat and beat in eggs, one at a time, until batter is smooth. Beat in vanilla.

1 cup sifted all-purpose flour

4 eggs

Heat fat in a heavy skillet to 375°. Drop batter by teaspoonfuls into hot fat. Brown on both sides. Remove with slotted spoon and drain on paper towels. Keep warm. Serve with Apricot Sauce.

1 teaspoon vanilla

Fat for frying

Apricot Sauce (recipe follows)

Makes 8 servings

APRICOT SAUCE

1½ cups apricot preserves

Mix apricot preserves, water and sugar in a heavy saucepan.

½ cup water

Heat to boiling and simmer 5 minutes, stirring often. Press sauce through a sieve and add Brandy. Serve warm or cold.

2 tablespoons sugar

2 tablespoons Apricot Brandy

Makes about 2 cups

FLAKY SWAN DESSERT

1 package (3 ounces) lemon-flavored gelatin

2 cups boiling water

1 pint fresh strawberries, hulled, washed and halved

1 cup moist flaked coconut

Whipped cream

6 macaroons

Makes 6 servings

Dissolve gelatin in boiling water and pour half the liquid into a mold. Chill. When gelatin begins to set, press half of the strawberries into it and cover with ½ cup coconut. Chill again. When firm, fill the mold with remaining gelatin and chill. When almost set, add remaining fruit (except 6 strawberry halves) and coconut as in first layer, and chill until firm.

To serve, unmold on a serving dish and garnish base with mounds of whipped cream. Press a strawberry half and a tiny macaroon into each cream mound.

FRESH PINEAPPLE ICE

1 large ripe pineapple

1 cup sugar

2 cups water

Juice of 2 lemons

1 tablespoon grated lemon rind

1 quart fresh strawberries (optional)

Cut off top of pineapple 2-3 inches below the leafy crown and reserve. Use a very sharp knife to cut out the edible flesh, leaving a shell about ½-inch thick. Be careful not to puncture the shell as the fruit ice is to be served from it. Chill.

Cut out the tough core and puree the pineapple flesh in the blender. It should be very smooth and almost liquid (about 2 cups).

Boil the sugar and water together for 10 to 12 minutes. Stir in pineapple puree and lemon juice and rind. Allow to cool to room temperature.

Add 1 cup ice water to pineapple mixture. Mix well and turn into refrigerator trays or pan. Freeze 5 to 6 hours.

To serve, scrape pineapple ice into a chilled bowl and beat until mushy (an electric mixer is fine for this). Pack the pineapple ice into the prepared chilled shell and replace top.

Place the filled shell in a bowl of crushed ice and allow guests to serve themselves.

If berries are used, rinse, hull and crush roughly. Sweeten to taste and pass with ice.

Makes 6-8 servings

PINEAPPLE CREAM SHERBET

Follow recipe for Pineapple Ice, but omit lemon juice and rind. When ice is beaten to a mush, stir in 1½ cups heavy cream slightly sweetened, whipped and flavored with 2 tablespoons Rum. Proceed as with ice.

PATE A CHOUX
Chef André René's Prize-Winning Recipe

1 cup water	Combine water, butter, sugar and salt in a heavy saucepan. Heat to boiling, stirring often. Remove saucepan from heat and blend in flour.
½ cup butter, cut into pieces	
2 teaspoons sugar	Return saucepan to heat and beat with a wooden spoon over low heat until mixture does not stick to the side of the saucepan. Remove from heat and beat in eggs, one at a time, until well blended. Cool.
Dash of salt	
1 cup sifted all-purpose flour	
4 eggs	Soak raisins in lukewarm water for 30 minutes. Drain on paper towels. Mix into choux until well blended.
1 cup California seedless raisins	Fill a deep saucepan to a depth of 3 inches with fat for frying. Heat to 375° on a deep-fat thermometer.
Fat for frying	
Confectioner's sugar	Fit pastry bag with a large star tip. Fill bag with choux. Drop puffs of choux into hot fat. Cook until puffs are golden brown. Remove with slotted spoon and drain on paper towels. Keep warm.
Makes 8 servings	Sprinkle with confectioner's sugar before serving.

PEAR TART

*Strawberry Tart Filling**	Prepare Strawberry Tart Filling and pour into tart shell. Chill until filling is firm.
*Tart shell**	
3 ripe pears	Pare, quarter and core pears. Arrange in a pretty pattern over filling.
¾ cup red currant jelly	Melt red currant jelly in a small saucepan. Spoon over pears and chill until serving time. Garnish with whipped cream.
Whipped cream	
Makes 8 servings	

PECAN BALLS

1 cup sweet butter

½ cup granulated sugar

2 teaspoons vanilla

2 cups finely ground pecans

2 cups flour

Confectioner's sugar

Vanilla sugar (recipe follows)

Makes 3 dozen

Cream butter and granulated sugar until smooth. Add vanilla, ground nuts and flour. Mix until smooth and blended (mixture should hold together when pressed between fingers). Mold heaping spoonfuls into balls the size of a large walnut.

Bake in a slow oven at 300° for 20 minutes. While hot, roll in confectioner's sugar. When cool, dust with vanilla sugar.

VANILLA SUGAR

2 vanilla beans

1 pound superfine sugar

Split vanilla beans and cut pieces in half. Add to sugar. Store in covered jar or bowl until ready to use.

CREPES SNOW MAIDEN

1 cup sifted flour

1 whole egg

2 egg yolks

Pinch of salt

1 tablespoon sugar

Grated rind of 1 lemon

2 cups milk

1 cup heavy cream

1 tablespoon butter

Makes 8 servings

Use a good-size bowl to combine the flour, egg, egg yolks, salt, sugar and lemon rind. Mix until smooth, then gradually add the mixed milk and cream. When thoroughly blended, strain batter through a fine sieve. Heat butter to a golden brown and stir into batter.

Fry spoonfuls of the batter in an iron crêpe pan, making thin French pancakes a little larger than a Crêpe Suzette. Keep warm while preparing filling (recipe follows).

FILLING

1 quart burnt almond OR
vanilla ice cream

Powdered sugar

4 ripe peaches, peeled and diced

½ cup Kirschwasser or Cognac

3 macaroons, crumbled

Fill warm crêpes with ice cream. Roll up and dust with powdered sugar. Arrange on a heat-proof serving dish. Work quickly–ice cream melts fast!

Put peaches into a shallow pan over low heat. Add Cognac or Brandy and spoon together until the liquor is hot. Pour peaches and liquor over pancakes and ignite. Serve immediately on warm dessert plates.

CREME RENVERSEE AU CARAMEL OR CREME CARAMEL

½ cup granulated sugar

3 whole eggs

4 egg yolks

1 quart milk (4 cups)

½ vanilla bean OR
1 teaspoon vanilla

Caramel (recipe follows)

Use a wire whip to beat the sugar, eggs and egg yolks until well mixed. Add 1 cup milk and continue to beat until blended.

Heat remaining milk in a saucepan with vanilla bean. Bring to a quick boil and remove from heat immediately. Very gradually add it to the mixture of sugar, eggs and milk, beating vigorously and constantly. Strain.

Have ready a mold lined with a film of caramel. Pour custard into prepared mold. Place mold in shallow baking pan and add boiling water to about half the depth of the mold. Bake in a slow moderate oven, 325°, for 40 to 45 minutes. Remove from oven, let cool, then chill in refrigerator.

When ready to serve, run a small pointed knife around rim to separate custard from mold; invert mold on serving dish and lift it off. Serve just as it is, or top with whipped cream (Crème Renversée Chantilly), or surround with fruit compote (Crème Renversée Beau Rivage).

Makes 6-8 servings

CARAMEL

¾ cup granulated sugar

¼ cup water

Cook sugar and water together over moderate heat until the syrup caramelizes. Then line the mold with a film of caramel. Let caramel set before using.

PASSOVER WALNUT CAKE

9 eggs, separated

1 cup superfine sugar

2 tablespoons cake meal

Pinch of salt

1 cup finely ground walnut meats

Makes one cake, 10–12 servings

Use a whip to beat egg yolks and sugar together in a large bowl until thick and lemon-colored. Combine cake meal, salt and nuts. Fold into egg yolks until dry ingredients completely disappear.

Beat egg whites until they form soft moist peaks. Carefully fold into nut mixture.

Turn mixture into a greased paper-lined 9 × 9 × 2-inch pan, or into a greased 9-inch tube pan.

Bake in a preheated moderate oven, 350°, for 45 minutes (square pan) or one hour (tube pan). Let stand in pan for 5 minutes. Turn out on wire rack and peel off paper, if used. Cool.

PIE CRUST

6 cups all-purpose flour

¾ teaspoon salt

5 tablespoons granulated sugar†

¾ cup butter

¾ cup vegetable shortening

1½ cups cold water

Mix dry ingredients in a large mixing bowl. "Break in" butter and shortening with a fork. Rub together with your hand until so well blended that mixture has a flaky look.

Add water, ½ cup at a time, mixing with fingers or a fork. Quickly gather together the dough and shape into a ball. *Do not work or mix any more*–the ball should hold together but should not be sticky.

Place dough ball on a floured pastry board or cloth (wherever you plan to do the final rolling out). Work the dough with the heel of your hand, away from you, using heavy firm strokes to finish the blending. Wrap dough in wax paper or put into plastic bag. Place in refrigerator for 1 hour or more before rolling out.

Divide the dough in thirds. Pat each third into a ball and then flatten into a circle. Sprinkle with a little flour and roll out as quickly as possible on a lightly floured surface with a rolling pin, applying pressure as you roll forward and back. Lift and turn the rounds as you roll. Sprinkle flour when necessary to prevent sticking.

† *Sugar should be omitted in pastry for appetizer or entree recipes.*

(*continued*)

PIE CRUST (*continued*)

Roll each round into a circle about ⅛-inch thick and 2 inches larger than circumference of pan.

Brush the pan with soft butter. Fold the rolled-out dough in half to make it easier to place in pie pan, or roll it around rolling pin and unroll it over pie pan. Press dough very lightly onto bottom and sides of pan, then cut off excess dough. With fingers or the back of a knife, flute the edges. Prick bottom of dough with a fork.

Cut a piece of waxed paper a few inches larger than pie pan, place it in the unbaked pastry shell and fill it with dry beans. The weight of the beans will keep the shell in shape while baking.

Bake in a preheated moderate oven, 375°, for 20 minutes. When shells start to color and shrink from sides of pans, remove from oven and let cool. Remove beans and paper and place shells on wire rack to cool.

Makes 3 12-inch shells

Our pastry chef prefers a wooden or marble surface for rolling. Says it makes for a more flaky pastry. E.B.

SAUCE AU CHOCOLAT

1 package (6 ounces) semisweet chocolate pieces

Combine both chocolates and butter in top of a double boiler. Melt over simmering water.

4 squares unsweetened chocolate

Blend in remaining ingredients. Cook, stirring constantly, until thick and smooth. Serve hot or cold.

2 tablespoons butter

2 tablespoons light corn syrup

½ cup sugar

1 cup milk

Dash of salt

Makes 2 cups

BUTTER CREAM FROSTING

½ cup sugar

¼ cup water

⅛ teaspoon cream of tartar

5 egg yolks

1¼ cups softened sweet butter

1 tablespoon Apricot Brandy

*Makes enough to frost two
9-inch layers*

Combine sugar, water and cream of tartar in a saucepan until sugar dissolves.

Cook until syrup reaches 230°, or until it spins a thread.

Beat egg yolks until light and lemon colored. Gradually beat in syrup until mixture is stiff and almost white.

Cut butter into small pieces and gradually beat into egg mixture until frosting is smooth and creamy. Flavor with Apricot Brandy. Chill until mixture is firm enough to spread.

PARFAIT PLAZA

Strawberry Sauce (recipe follows)

1 quart vanilla ice cream

1 cup heavy cream

2 tablespoons sugar

½ teaspoon vanilla extract

6 fresh strawberries

Makes 6 servings

Spoon Strawberry Sauce to a depth of 1 inch in bottom of 6 parfait glasses.

Alternate vanilla ice cream and Strawberry Sauce to fill parfait glasses.

Beat cream until stiff with sugar and vanilla. Swirl on top of parfait. Garnish each parfait with a fresh strawberry.

STRAWBERRY SAUCE

1 pint (2 cups) strawberries

¼ cup sugar

1 tablespoon cornstarch

½ cup red currant jelly

Red food coloring

¼ cup Brandy

Makes about 2 cups

Wash and hull strawberries. Slice into a heavy saucepan and mash berries.

Combine sugar and cornstarch until blended. Stir into berries. Add red currant jelly.

Cook, stirring constantly, until mixture thickens and boils for 1 minute. Tint sauce a bright pink with red food coloring.

Warm Brandy in a metal cup and set on fire. Stir flaming Brandy into sauce. Serve hot or cold.

STRAWBERRY CHIFFON PIE

2 envelopes unflavored gelatin

¾ cup sugar

Dash of salt

1¼ cups milk, scalded

3 eggs, separated

1 teaspoon vanilla

1 pint (2 cups) strawberries

1 cup heavy cream, whipped

1 9-inch baked pastry shell

Makes 8 servings

Combine gelatin, ¼ cup sugar and salt in a heavy saucepan. Stir in scalded milk.

Cook over low heat, stirring constantly, until gelatin dissolves. Beat egg yolks in a small bowl. Gradually pour part of the hot mixture into egg yolks and then pour contents of bowl into saucepan. Cook until mixture thickens slightly. Stir in vanilla. Pour into a bowl and chill thoroughly.

Beat egg whites until double in volume. Gradually add remaining ½ cup sugar until a meringue forms. Beat cream in a second bowl.

Wash and hull strawberries. Reserve the prettiest berries for garnish and slice remaining berries.

Fold meringue and 1 cup of the whipped cream into chilled gelatin mixture. Fold in sliced berries and spoon into baked pie shell. Garnish with remaining cream and berries.

CASSATA A L'ITALIENNE
Ice Cream Cake

1½ pounds ricotta cheese

½ cup sugar

1 teaspoon vanilla

2 tablespoons Brandy

1 tablespoon finely chopped candied orange peel

1 square semisweet baking chocolate, grated

¼ teaspoon salt

Sponge Cake*

Powdered sugar

Makes 8 servings

Mix the cheese, sugar and flavorings until smooth and creamy. Stir in peel, chocolate and salt.

Split the cake into 4 layers and put together again with the cheese filling. Cover cake loosely with wax paper or plastic wrap and chill in refrigerator for 4 to 5 hours.

To serve, dust with powdered sugar and cut in wedges.

CREME DIPLOMATE
Cabinet Pudding

¼ cup seedless raisins

¾ cup diced mixed glazed fruits:
apricots, melons, cherries,
pineapple and orange

50 ladyfingers (approximately)

¼ cup water

¼ cup Rum

⅓ cup apricot preserve, sieved

Custard (use recipe for
Crème Caramel*)

Makes 8–10 servings

Soften raisins by covering with boiling water and letting them soak up liquid for a few minutes. When they have plumped up, strain, combine with diced fruits and toss gently to mix. Let stand until ready to use.

Cover bottom of a deep, round mold with buttered wax paper. Dip ladyfingers in mixed Rum and water and arrange like spokes in bottom of mold, then line side of mold with ladyfingers. Pour some custard over bottom layer of ladyfingers, sprinkle with some of the fruit mixture and spread with some of the apricot preserve. Add a layer of ladyfingers, then custard, fruit and preserves. Continue in this way until ingredients are used up.

Place mold in baking pan and add boiling water until it reaches half the height of the mold. Bake in a preheated slow oven, 325°, for 40 to 45 minutes. Remove from oven, allow to cool and then chill in refrigerator. To serve, invert mold on serving dish and gently lift it off. Cut into wedge-shape portions.

AVOCADO MOUSSE
Green Tulip Specialty

1 ripe avocado

3 tablespoons superfine sugar

1 teaspoon fresh lemon juice

¼ teaspoon vanilla

2 tablespoons Brandy

Pinch salt

Pinch nutmeg

1 teaspoon unflavored gelatine

2 tablespoons milk

½ cup heavy cream, whipped

Thinly sliced avocado

Makes 4 servings

Peel avocado and remove pit. Cut in pieces.

Put avocado, sugar, liquids, and seasonings in blender container. Puree until smooth. Pour into a bowl.

Soften the gelatine in 2 tablespoons cold water, then dissolve in cold milk over low heat. Cool slightly.

Beat heavy cream, adding the cooled gelatine in a thin stream while whipping.

Fold the avocado mixture and the whipped cream together.

Pile the mixture into parfait glasses. Top with whipped cream and garnish with a thin slice of avocado.

FROZEN SOUFFLE FRAMBOISE

1 quart (4 cups) strawberries

1 cup sugar

2 tablespoons lemon juice

2 envelopes unflavored gelatin

4 egg whites

2 cups heavy cream

2 tablespoons Grand Marnier

Makes 8 servings

Make an aluminum foil collar around rim of a 4-cup soufflé dish.

Wash, hull and slice strawberries into a large saucepan. Stir in ½ cup sugar. Mash with a fork or potato masher, then stir in lemon juice.

Sprinkle gelatin over strawberries and mix well. Heat, stirring constantly, over low heat until gelatin dissolves. Chill just until mixture begins to mound.

Beat egg whites until foamy and double in volume in large bowl. Gradually beat in remaining ½ cup sugar until a soft meringue forms.

Beat cream until stiff in a second bowl.

Fold egg whites into strawberry mixture, then cream and Grand Marnier. Spoon into prepared soufflé dish.

Refrigerate at least 4 hours. Remove foil collar before garnishing with whipped cream and fresh straw-berries.

BOMBE GLACE ANDRE

1 quart raspberry sherbet

1 quart strawberry sherbet

Fresh strawberries

Makes 8-10 servings

Thoroughly chill a 2-quart bombe mold. If possible, place the chilled mold in a bowl of crushed ice before you start to fill it.

Put the raspberry sherbet in by spoonfuls, spreading it as evenly as possible until you have a lining layer about ½-inch thick.

Spoon the strawberry sherbet into the center, overflowing the mold.

Cover the surface with a piece of plastic wrap, pressing it flat. Cover tightly and place in freezer for 2 hours or more.

To serve, unmold and garnish with whole straw-berries.

PLAZA CHEESECAKE
CRUST

1 cup flour

¼ cup sugar

1 tablespoon grated lemon rind

1 egg yolk

*½ cup sweet butter
(at room temperature)*

For the crust, mix the flour and sugar. Add the remaining ingredients and mix well. Use your hands to achieve a smooth pliable dough. Chill.

Roll out about one third of dough to cover the bottom of a 9- or 10-inch spring-form pan. Bake in a hot oven, 400°, for 10 minutes.

Butter the sides of the pan and insert the bottom with baked crust inside it. Allow to cool.

Divide the remaining dough in half and roll each portion into a strip about 3 inches wide and 14 inches long. Press strips to sides of pan so they join the bottom crust and each other. Press edges firmly together.

FILLING

3 pounds cream cheese

1¾ cups fine sugar

½ teaspoon salt

3 tablespoons lemon juice

1 teaspoon vanilla

6 eggs

*Makes one 9- or 10-inch cake
(10–12 servings)*

To prepare filling, beat the softened cheese until it is very smooth and creamy. Beat in remaining ingredients in order given.

When the mixture is thoroughly blended, pour it into the prepared crust. Bake in a hot oven, 450°, for 10 minutes. Reduce heat to 325° and continue baking for 1 hour.

Let cake stand in the oven for 20 minutes with the heat off and the door partially open. Remove from oven and cool.

Don't even glance at this delectable delight if you tend to gain weight! E.B.

DOUBLE FRUIT MOLD

1 package (6 ounces)
strawberry flavor gelatin

3 cups hot water

1 cup ginger ale

1 tablespoon lemon juice

1 quart (4 cups) strawberries

Galax leaves

Makes 8 servings

Dissolve gelatin in hot water. Stir in ginger ale and lemon juice. Chill until syrupy.

Wash, hull and slice strawberries. Fold into syrupy gelatin. Pour into an 8-cup mold. Chill until firm, at least 4 hours.

Unmold onto silver platter and garnish with galax leaves.

You can use other fruit-flavored gelatin and fresh fruits in season, such as seedless grapes, melon balls, peaches, nectarines or canned pineapple chunks. E.B.

COUPE NEILSON

1 pint strawberries

2 tablespoons Kirsch

1 pint lemon sherbet

1 pint strawberry ice cream

Sweetened whipped cream

Crystallized cherries

Makes 6 servings

Wash, hull and slice strawberries. Drizzle Kirsch over strawberries in a bowl and let stand at room temperature 1 hour.

Line 6 chilled Champagne glasses with lemon sherbet and strawberry ice cream. Fill center with strawberries. Swirl whipped cream over and garnish with crystallized cherries.

PINEAPPLE PARADISE

1 package (3 ounces)
lemon-flavored gelatin dessert

1 cup boiling water

1 cup canned unsweetened
pineapple juice

½ teaspoon salt

1 cup canned crushed pineapple

1 cup heavy cream

3 tablespoons sugar

Fresh cherries

Fresh strawberries

Chopped pecans

Makes 6-8 servings

Dissolve gelatin in boiling water. Stir in pineapple juice and salt. Chill. When mixture is cold and slghtly thickened, whip with a rotary or electric beater until consistency of whipped cream.

Beat cream and sugar until stiff. Fold whipped cream and pineapple into whipped gelatin.

Pile mixture lightly in stemmed dessert glasses and chill. Serve garnished with cherries, strawberries and chopped pecans.

BRANDIED BING CHERRY SAUCE

¾ cup red currant jelly

1 can (1-pound, 13-ounces),
Bing cherries, drained

2 tablespoons Brandy

Makes about 2 cups

Melt currant jelly in a small skillet. Add cherries and Brandy. Heat slowly until mixture boils, stirring often. Serve warm.

This sauce is something special over ice cream, cup custard or angel food cake. E.B.

COFFEES AROUND THE WORLD

CAFE BRULOT DIABOLIQUE

CAFE CAPPUCCINO

CAFE AU LAIT

CAFE MOCHA JAVA

CAFE ESPRESSO

VIENNESE COFFEE

TURKISH COFFEE

DEMITASSE

IRISH COFFEE

CAFE BRULOT DIABOLIQUE

4 jiggers Cognac Brandy

6 pieces lump sugar

*Peel of 1 lemon or orange,
cut in a spiral*

1 1-inch piece stick cinnamon

8 whole cloves

4 cups Demitasse Coffee*

Makes 4 servings

Combine Cognac, sugar, peel and spices in a chafing dish. Stir until sugar dissolves.

Heat slightly to warm Cognac, then ignite and stir a minute or two. Slowly pour in coffee and continue to stir.

Strain into Brûlot or demitasse cups.

This coffee treat was first made famous in New Orleans and can be served with a flare at home. Be sure to lower the light for the full effect. E.B.

CAFE CAPPUCCINO

2 parts steaming Café Espresso*

1 part steaming milk

Whipped cream

*Cinnamon OR
Nutmeg*

Makes 1 serving

Pour coffee and milk simultaneously into tall cups. Top with whipped cream and a sprinkling of cinnamon or nutmeg.

This coffee is a real favorite in Continental coffee houses. It is often served with a touch of grated orange peel over the whipped cream. E.B.

CAFE AU LAIT

*1½ cups strong hot freshly
brewed coffee*

1½ cups hot rich milk

Makes 4 servings

Using two pots, pour simultaneously into coffee cups. Serve at the table.

Café au Lait is the breakfast drink of France. Every visitor enjoys a Continental breakfast on his first morning in France–fruit, Café au Lait and flaky croissants. E.B.

CAFE MOCHA JAVA

4½ cups hot coffee

4½ cups hot cocoa

Whipped cream

Makes 12 servings

Combine coffee and cocoa in a chafing dish. Heat, but do not boil.

Ladle into coffee cups or mugs and top with whipped cream.

Coffee and chocolate combine to make a happy flavor marriage. E.B.

CAFE ESPRESSO

8 level tablespoons (4 approved coffee measures) French- or Italian-roast pulverized coffee

1½ cups water

Lemon peel

Sugar

Makes 4 servings

A drip pot may be used, but a macchinetta is best. This coffee-making device consists of 2 cylinders, one with a spout, and a coffee sieve between them.

Measure coffee into sieve. Put together with cylinder having spout on top and with measured water in lower cylinder.

Place on heat and wait for small opening in lower cylinder to steam. Then remove from heat and turn macchinetta upside down until all the brew has dripped through.

Serve in demitasse cups or 4-ounce glasses with a twist of lemon and sugar, but never cream.

VIENNESE COFFEE

3 cups extra-strength coffee

Sugar to taste

Whipped cream

Makes 4 servings

Pour freshly brewed coffee into cups and add sugar. Float a generous spoonful of whipped cream on top.

The Viennese enjoy many versions of their world-renowned coffee. They may drink it spiced, with hot milk added, or plain, but always with a drift of Schlagobers–which is Viennese for whipped cream. E.B.

TURKISH COFFEE

1½ cups water

Measure water into a heavy saucepan. Add sugar and bring to a boil.

4 teaspoons sugar

4 tablespoons finely pulverized coffee

Stir in coffee, bring to a boil again. Reduce heat and allow to froth 3 times.

Remove from heat and add a few drops of cold water. Spoon some of the foam into each demitasse cup and pour in the coffee.

In the Near East coffee is served in tiny cups, about the size of an eggshell. Each guest is sure to get his share of the creamy foam formed by the coffee. In Arabic this is called "the face of the coffee," and you lose face if you serve coffee without it! E.B.

Makes 4 servings

DEMITASSE

4 cups water

Measure water into saucepan and heat to boiling. Preheat coffee pot by rinsing with very hot water. Measure coffee into cone holding filter paper or filter-section of coffeepot.

16 level tablespoons (8 approved coffee measures) Colombian drip-grind coffee

4 cups water

Place coffeepot into a pan of simmering water to keep coffee hot while dripping.

Lemon peel

Pour freshly boiling water into upper container of coffeepot; cover.

Sugar

Makes 8 servings

Pour into demitasse cups and serve with a twist of lemon. Pass the sugar.

IRISH COFFEE

2 teaspoons superfine sugar

Strong black coffee

1 ounce Irish Whiskey

Softly whipped cream

Makes 1 serving

Warm a stemmed glass. Place sugar in bottom of glass and fill ⅔ full with coffee and mix well.

Add Irish whiskey and float softly whipped cream on top. Serve at once.

Legend has it that Irish Coffee originated at Shannon Airport, leaped halfway around the world to San Francisco and from there to the rest of the country. E.B.

Saboyon Sauce, 305
Sacher Torte, 312
Saffron Rice, 293
St. George Salad, 120
Salad Dressing, 49
Salade Niçoise, 125
Salads, 113–27
Salamugundi Salad, 49
Salmon
    Coulibiac de, 236
    Parisienne, 243
Samosas, 68
Saratoga Salad, 120
Sauce Aigre-Doux, 140
Sauce Bordelaise, 141
Sauce Brazilian, 304
Sauce Bretonne, 142
Sauce, Chambertin, 234
Sauce Chasseur, 140, 142, 215
Sauce au Chocolat, 323
Sauce aux Cornichons, 141
Sauce Crème, 139
Sauce Espagnole, 136
Sauce Italienne, 143
Sauce Madeira, 239
Sauce Marseillaise, 148
Sauce au Porto, 145
Sauce Remick, 146
Sauce Smitane, 175
Sauce with Tiny Sour Gherkins, 141
Sauces, 135–49
Saucisson en Brioche with Hot Potato Salad, 205
Sauerkraut à l'Alsacienne, 205
Sauerkraut Garnished with Smoked Pork, 204
Sauté of Venison, 199
Sautéed Young Rabbit, 198
Savory Egg Soup, 80
Scallops Ventimille, 253
Scampi, Sauce Plaza, 145
Schwarzwaelder Kirschtorte, 301
Scotch Lamb Broth, 101
Scrambled Eggs Georgette, 153
Sea Bass Persian, 244
Seafood à la King with Wheatcakes, 262
Seafood Pot Pies, 266
Serena Salad, 120
Sesame Noodles, 120
Sevillane Salad, 120
Shakespearean Buffet, 48–50
Shashlik Caucasian Flambé, 188
Shellfish and seafood entrées, 246–69
Shrimp
    Avocado-Shrimp Salad, 124
    Butter, 91
    Créole, 250
    Curried, 249
    Fra Diavolo, Grilled, 248
    How to Cook, 248
    Jambalaya, 250

au Pernod, Casserolette of, 252
Remoulade, 71
Sauce Plaza, 145
and Scallops Poulette, 252
au Xeres, Casserolette of, 249
Soft-Shell Crabs Sauce Meunière, 258
Sole
    Marguery, Fillet of, 237
    Mousse of, 241
    Paupiettes of Dover, 241
    Sauté Meunière, Fillet of, 235
    Veronique, English, 238
Sorrel
    Cream of, with Oatmeal, 95
    Soup, 94
Soups, 97–112
Sour Cream
    Blinis with Caviar and, 60
    Mushrooms and, 65
Spaghetti Adolf, 292
Spaghetti Bolognaise, 295
Spaghetti al Pesto, 290
Spanish Eggs, 154
Spinach
    Florentine, Cream of, 82
    Ring, 281
    Salad, Palm Court, 127
    Salad Dressing, 127
    Salad Plaza, 125
Sponge Cake, 300
Spring Salad, 120
Squab, Grilled, 202
Steamed Dumpling, 180
Strawberry Chiffon Pie, 325
Strawberry Sauce, 324
Strawberry Tart, 310
Striped Bass
    Créole, French Baked, 240
    en Gelée, Cold, 232
    Poached, 245
    Printanière, 233
Stroganoff Sauce, 147
Stuffed Apple Salad, 120
Stuffed Baked Lobster, 256
Stuffed Pear Salad, 120
Stuffed Peppers, Arabian Style, 273
Stuffed Smelts, 235
Stuffings, 285–88
Supreme of Chicken Eugénie under Glass, 214
Supreme of Chicken Plaza, 220
Supreme of Halibut in White Wine Sauce, 233
Supreme de Volaille aux Champignons, 220
Sweet and Sour Sauce, 140
Sweetbreads, Bouchées of, Financière, 164
Sweetbreads Parisienne, 184

Terrapin Maryland, 268
Terrine Foie Gras, 76

Therese Salad, 120
Thin Custard, 157
Three-Decker Hamburger à la Plaza, 176
Timbales of Sweet Potatoes, 276
Tomato Sauce à la Plaza, 144
Tomato Surprise Salad, 120
Tomatoes
    Baked Stuffed, Bressane, with Bacon, Sauce Chasseur, 214
    with Cheese Salad, 120
    Grilled, 279
    Stevens Salad, 120
Touraine Salad, 120
Tournedos Richelieu, 171
Trianon Salad, 120
Trifle, 311
Turbot, Mousse of, 238
Turkey, Filled with Wheat Pilaff and Apples, Roast Maryland Baby, 229
Turkish Coffee, 334
Turquoise Salad, 120
Turtle Soup Amontillado, 90

Valenciennes Salad, 121
Vanilla Sauce, 312
Vanilla Sugar, 320
Veal
    Chops, Côte de "Plume de Veau" Plaza, La, 178
    Cutlet à la Stresa, Milk-Fed, 181
    entrées, 177–84
    Fricassee l'Ancienne, 183
    Goulash Austrian, 180
    Hungarian Style, Breast of, 179
    Kidney Flambé, 179
    au Madère, Noisette of Milk-Fed, 178
    Marengo, 182
Vegetable Salad, 123
Vegetables, 270–84
Velouté Joinville, 90
Velouté Sauce, 147
Venison
    Poivrade, Roast Saddle of, 198
    Sauté, 199
Venitienne Salad, 121
Vera Salad, 121
Victoria Salad, 121
Viennese Coffee, 333
Viennoise Salad, 301
Village Custard, 301
Vol-au-Vent of Seafood, 265

Watercress and Potato Soup, 88
Wedding Cake, 298
Wheat Pilaff, 292
Wheat Soup, Cream of, 89
White Stock, 112
Whitebait and Oyster Crabs, 259
Wild Rice, 291